WOMEN
AND THE PRESS
THE STRUGGLE
FOR EQUALITY

Patricia Bradley

Foreword by Gail Collins

MEDILL SCHOOL OF JOURNALISM

Northwestern University Press
Evanston, Illinois

Northwestern University Press
www.nupress.northwestern.edu

Copyright © 2005 by Patricia Bradley.
Published 2005 by Northwestern University Press.
All rights reserved.

Printed in the United States of America

10   9   8   7   6   5   4   3   2   1

ISBN 0-8101-2313-4

Library of Congress Cataloging-in-Publication Data

Bradley, Patricia. 1941–
    Women and the press : the struggle for equality / Patricia Bradley.
        p. cm. — (Medill school of journalism, visions of the American press)
    Includes bibliographical references and index.
    ISBN 0-8101-2313-4 (pbk. : alk. paper)
1. Women in journalism—United States—History. I. Title. II. Visions of the American press.
    PN4888.W66B73 2005
    071'.3'082—dc22

                           2005018736

To Laurien D. Ward
Help, hand, and heart

CONTENTS

FOREWORD

Gail Collins

The struggle for gender equality, so ably recounted by Patricia Bradley in this analysis of women in journalism, has deep roots in the public narrative of American history. There have always been American women who weren't afraid to speak their minds on public matters. Back in the 1670s, when frontier farmers were chafing against the rule of the Virginia colony, it was a woman, Sarah Drummond, who rallied the rebels. Picking up a twig she snapped it and said, "I fear the power of England no more than a broken straw." In New England, Anne Hutchinson led theological discussions that put the traditional ministers to shame. "She preaches better gospell than any of your black-coates," a Boston woman bragged to a male newcomer. And by the early 1800s, Frances ("Fanny") Wright, the first woman to speak to public gatherings of both men and women, drew huge crowds for her lectures on abolition.

The results were not entirely ideal.

Drummond helped start Bacon's Rebellion, which failed and as a result her husband was hung as a traitor. Anne Hutchinson was banished from Massachusetts and wound up being killed in an Indian raid in Long Island. Fanny Wright failed to realize that her audiences regarded her as more a curiosity than a moral leader. After some of her followers wrote more about their sex lives than was advisable, she was denounced as "the Great Red Harlot" and run out of the country.

It's a wonder that following generations ever opened their mouths at all. But nineteenth-century opinionated women found new, safer methods of getting their messages across. Most of them avoided the podium and took to the pen. They became novelists or short story writers for popular magazines, and they became extremely skilled at pushing the cultural party line (woman's place is in the home) while nonetheless sending their heroines off to become world-famous singers or writers or—my own personal favorite—an internationally acclaimed philosopher. Their cover was always a family emergency, in which the husband or father dies or abandons the heroine, leaving her with children or siblings to support. It was a version of the same all-purpose explanation used by Sarah Josepha Hale, the powerful editor of *Godey's Lady's Book,* who preached the importance of keeping women away from the evil outside world while she personally ran one of the most important periodicals in the country. (Mrs. Hale, a widow, said she needed to support her orphaned children—an effort that apparently required continued employment until her youngest child was fifty-five.)

It was a creative, if obviously hypocritical, way to gain entry into the public sphere. We might prefer a story line in which American women simply demanded to be given an equal voice in the affairs of the world and kept talking and writing until the male half of society recognized their rights. But as oppressed groups go, women tended to be conservative, in need of a bridge that would let them keep one foot in traditional society while the other was edging toward something more complete and fulfilling.

In the pre–Civil War era, Americans had a particularly repressive view of the appropriate behavior for respectable women. Victorians, unlike their predecessors who felt women were vaguely depraved and definitely lustful, saw women as innately good (and possibly frigid). They put them in charge of the household morality, while their husbands, who had to labor in the evil world of commerce, counted on their wives to keep the heart of the family beating true and clean. The True Woman of the nineteenth century was perhaps not too bright, but she was inherently, instinctively virtuous. She stayed at home, fearful of the contamination of the outside world, and radiated goodness that ennobled her family.

Harriet Beecher Stowe certainly thought of herself as a True Woman, although she wouldn't have agreed that women have inferior intellects. Everyone had always taken her seriously. She was a member of one of the most prominent families in the country, populated with thinkers, writers, and ministers. When she decided she wanted to write a novel about slavery, her relatives were so sure the project was important that two sisters moved into her house to help with the chores and copy her manuscript. And, of course, *Uncle Tom's Cabin* was worth the effort. We all know that it helped turn popular opinion in the North against slavery, but it was most influential in the way it gave middle-class Northern women one of their first bridges into the world of political debate. Stowe, a middle-class woman to the bone, spoke to her female readers about an apolitical view of slavery. The issue was not about equal rights or the mechanics of abolition; it was about slavery as a threat to the family, something that separated mothers from children and husbands from

wives and put innocent young women at the mercy of lascivious slave owners. If an evil like that was abroad in the
land, obviously it was the business of the True Woman to
make it right, even if that required going door to door col-
lecting signatures on petitions to Congress or perhaps even
speaking out at antislavery rallies.

Once that great leap was made, there was no turning
back. Before *Uncle Tom's Cabin,* the history of American
women in the public world was a story of individual rebels
who made their marks but failed to have a lasting impact on
the lives of the rest of their sex. But grabbing onto that
morality banner, women marched into the battles for abolition and suffrage and eventually took part in anything that
protected mothers and children—from clean milk to temperance. "They've taken the notion to speak for themselves,"
wrote the clever Maria Chapman slyly. "And are wielding
the tongue and the pen/They've mounted the rostrum, the
termagant elves! And—oh horrid!—are talking to men!"
(Chapman, who became a leader of the antislavery movement in Massachusetts, had a genius for fund-raising and was
an aggressive behind-the-scenes organizer on behalf of
William Lloyd Garrison. She must have been very good at
her work since Lewis Tappan, Garrison's chief opponent in
the abolition movement, called her "a talented woman with
the disposition of a fiend.")

Big as the breakthrough was, this vision of women's
public role had several defects, not the least of which was the
fact that once slavery had been abolished, public women
tended to focus their sights on remaking all of American
society in the image of white middle-class native-born ma-

trons. Enthusiasm for suffrage was firmly linked to women's expectation that if they got the chance to vote, they could vote to make liquor illegal. "Purity" campaigners sometimes fought against the availability of birth control information under the delusion that it was connected to prostitution (an evil that many female crusaders preferred to believe happened mainly when innocent young women were kidnapped by male "white slavers"). There was also a sense that women only had the right to be outspoken on public matters when the questions at hand involved families. Even the great Eleanor Roosevelt felt compelled to present herself not as the extraordinary political organizer she really was but rather as a simple wife who was off visiting coal mines or speaking at New Deal rallies because she was duty-bound to make the trips on behalf of her crippled husband.

Americans who were born after the social revolutions of the late 1960s and early 1970s often don't realize how long that era continued. By 1960, the world might have moved into the jet age, but women's place was still pretty much confined to the home. Although millions of women worked, it was often in part-time clerical or retail jobs. In the professions, they were almost entirely restricted to fields like teaching and nursing, which had been regarded as uniquely female for a century or more (and which required the services of armies of well-educated, motivated, and poorly paid recruits). Only 5 percent of working women were in management, and it was perfectly legal to pay them less money than men in the same position. Newspapers facilitated the process by dividing their classified ads into "Help Wanted—Men" and "Help Wanted—Women."

The media weren't any different. Women had been doing amazing things in newspapers and magazines since the late nineteenth century—people like Dorothy Thompson, the famous foreign correspondent of the pre–World War II era, and Nellie Bly, who became an international sensation in 1888 when she went around the world in eighty days carrying only one small bag crammed with underwear, writing equipment, and a large jar of cold cream. But they were unique—exceptions who didn't open up a path for large numbers of other talented women to follow their lead.

In 1960, newsmagazines were still relegating almost all women to jobs as "researchers," who sat in the office library checking facts while men did the reporting and got the by-lines. On television, the number of on-air female reporters could be counted on a single hand. In newspapers, women were wildly outnumbered by men and were mainly relegated to sections like Home or Style.

All this changed in just a few decades. I can remember doing my first reporting internship at a paper in Milwaukee where women were barred from working on the copy desk because they were considered bad luck. At the *New York Times,* where I work now, it was 1972 when fifty women signed a letter pointing out that there were no women among the top editors at the paper, no women photographers, no women reviewers, and no women national correspondents. Of the thirty-three foreign correspondents, only three were women.

Those of us who were lucky enough to be around at the time actually got to witness the shattering of presumptions about women's role that had been dominating western society for millennia. Now, it's natural to expect women to

work on every conceivable level of the business—following the troops in Iraq, covering the president on the campaign trail, or deciding what goes on the front page the next day. The *Times* currently has women in jobs that include managing editor, editorial page editor, and CEO of the whole shebang. But we got those jobs by standing on the shoulders of the people who came before. We arrived about five minutes after a generation of newswomen that risked and sometimes ruined their careers to get papers to treat female journalists just like they did the boys. It's a familiar story—and an important part of the larger chronicle that Patricia Bradley's *Women and the Press* examines so insightfully. But the wonder is that it's so close you can still touch it.

PREFACE

This book provides an overview of women in journalism history against the background of U.S. social history in general and U.S. women's history in particular. It is not a "great man" version of American women's journalism as much as it is an exploration of how American women journalists have operated within a professional culture that has limited their role and in a national culture that has used mass media to uphold standards of difference.

From the beginnings of commercial media in the United States, women have had to walk a delicate balance, seeking to find ways to make a living within the narrow confines of what was available to them, advancing their own careers beyond those limitations, and seeking to be responsible to other women. The history of women in any profession can be told in terms of the culture in which it operates. But what makes the history of women in journalism particularly interesting is the constant interaction of women in journalism within the enclosures of culture and craft. Throughout women's connections to commercial media, women journalists have had to negotiate their own needs to maintain hard-sought jobs with decisions on how much to accommodate to the messages of a craft that has discounted their work as much as it has the work of women in general.

These kinds of individual negotiations have had to be accomplished against the backdrop of national understandings of women. From the revolutionary era, when some voices proclaimed that equal rights for men meant equal rights for all, the concept of equal rights for women has been extraordinarily difficult to ensure. This was partly because it was never clear how to delegate rights for a gender whose definitions were always under discussion. Are women a bundle of separate sensibilities operating on a higher moral plane that make women most valuable in traditional roles (that nonetheless have needed supervision by a skein of expectations and their legal ramifications)? Are women to be located, along with men, somewhere on a continuum of "human being"? In which case, is childbearing an accident of gender or essential to understanding? If women are to be different, are they different enough to warrant separate rules and regulations? On the most practical level, should allowances be made for women's differences and related responsibilities, such as child raising?

The questions have been the subject of discussion in all the varying "waves" of feminism, and in each period of feminist development, feminists have not united under a single philosophy. Perhaps as many suffragists as not campaigned for the right to vote in the belief that women were morally superior to men and were better equipped than men to vote for clean government. Political strategists today consider there is a "gender gap," one in which women give more credence to issues of home and heart than male voters. The existence of a gender gap is problematical, but the ease with which it was popularly accepted as a matter of gender over the more complicating issues of needs and experience indicates that the nation is far from coming to conclusions on questions of essential difference.

Although questions of gender difference are influenced by philosophy, religion, immigrant and ethnic traditions, it is part of this work to address how gender differences were (and are) upheld by media interests, largely for their aligned purposes. In the early national period, for example, the political press found women in the home most useful in promoting a conservative political ideology. In midcentury, the availability of mass goods and the tweak of advertising redefined women in the home to be in terms of consumers. Women found entry into the mass magazines and mass newspapers that sought advertisers for the new rush of industry-made goods by providing the "women's angle," thought to attract female readers. But it was still the job of the "women's angle" to maintain domesticity as the major definition for women, not only to maintain women's role as consumers but, increasingly, to maintain the hegemony of a Protestant home when that was seen to be under siege. The importance of women in defined roles for various purposes may make the definitions suspect, although no less powerful when distributed by media as another major arm of influence.

Women in the newsroom had to face the realities of a profession that did not want them there in the first place, craft traditions that served to encourage stereotypes, and an acceptance of themselves as workers in a culture that said they should be at home. Women came to respond in varying ways, from being one of the "pals" in the newsroom to forging a separate female culture within the newsrooms. But on top of these personal resolutions were decisions to be made about what responsibilities media workers have to the members of the public they ostensibly serve—or, indeed, *if* they have these responsibilities. What is the responsibility of women in journalism to women outside the newsroom? What craft traditions need to be rejected? What are the lines to be drawn and at what point should a journalist quit over them? Should she quit at all? Is it better to work from within, from some platform, than from without, without any?

Beginning with their ability to make some kind of living in magazine writing in the early part of the nineteenth century, women in journalism have had a full agenda: seeking economic parity, establishing individual worth, and fulfilling a responsibility to women at large. For some women, achievement was enough. The successful woman needed only to offer her own achievement to inspire others. Other women, however, found ways to work against the grain, even in positions that would not seem to allow for such opportunity. Modern readers of the sentimental fiction of the nineteenth century, for example, may find oppositional messages. The society writers brought in to build newspaper circulation put suffrage on the news agenda. Women advice columnists sometimes gave countercultural advice under the noses of bosses. Women magazine editors addressed important subjects. Women's sections expanded their scope. Female stunt reporters broke out of the frame of the endangered females to representations of power and ability. Women reporters interpreted the "woman's angle" to mean everything, including war, in whose foxholes angles, like atheism, tended to disappear.

Wherever I have been able, I have studded the following pages with names of women, but they are women who are now mostly forgotten and must represent many thousands more. Although individual stories of women reporters are interesting and compelling, I have chosen to position this story of women in journalism in its systemic concerns—women between the poles of commercial culture, which did not want woman to change, and an outsider culture, which did. One of the unrecognized aspects of organized feminism in the nineteenth century was its interactions with the press. While feminism has always had its own reform press, organized feminism of the First and Second Waves were highly cognizant of using the mass press to spread its messages: notably by mounting events that would draw press attention and developing a corps of professional writers. The women in journalism of both the First and Second Waves included women activists who worked for women's rights primarily in the context of the mass press. For women in journalism who did not come from an activist perspective, the successes of these early public relations activities (when the field was still developing) put pressure on women in journalism to emerge from corners of safety to public positions. Nor were suffrage activists shy about putting direct pressure on women reporters.

Women, of course, were active in many important reforms in the nineteenth century, and most of these movements had associated publications that women edited and wrote. Readers will want to explore the full stories of Ida B. Wells-Barnett, Margaret Sanger, Dorothy Day, Frances Willard, and others whose careers involved important reform publications.

For this work, I have drawn on the scholarship of the

burgeoning field of women in journalism history, as well as on the many biographies and autobiographies of women practitioners in journalism. Some standard works—Frank Luther Mott's five-volume *A History of American Magazines,* for one—continue to be irreplaceable. However, as we know, the revolution in historical research has come by way of the Internet. Some institutions that specialize in women's history have made at least part of their collections available online. Some collections exist only as Internet sources. The Gerretson Collection allows access to previously difficult-to-find suffrage and antisuffrage publications. The Woman and Social Movements Web site provides access to important feminist documents. The Washington Press Club Foundation has many of its oral histories of women journalists online. The American Periodical Series, with its collection of magazines from colonial times to the twentieth century, can now be accessed (and searched!) online. Equally useful are the online Historic Newspapers and *Harper's Weekly* and *The Nation* online archives. These online sources are expanding, daily it seems, offering opportunity for all to research, explore, and weigh in on the discussion in a democratization the field of history has never experienced.

Primarily, however, this work relies on the research of many scholars in the field. I encourage readers to examine the bibliography for an understanding of the interest and energy the subject of women in journalism has engendered in recent years. My thanks to all those scholars, many of them associated with the professional organizations the Association for Education in Journalism and Mass Communication and the American Journalism Historians Association, for, quite literally, making this work possible.

Finally, may I thank David Abrahamson and the Medill School of Journalism of Northwestern University for including me in this, their launch of their new imprint. Our appreciation for the tools offered by technology is not diminished to say that books, in all their varieties, have yet to be improved upon.

PATRICIA BRADLEY

ONE

"ARE NOT WOMEN BORN AS FREE AS MEN?"

In 1773, at a time of bold statements, the Daughters of Liberty declared: "Woman is born a free and independent Being; that it is her undoubted Right and Constitutional Privilege firmly to reject all attempts to abridge that Liberty." Six years later, as the male members of the revolutionary circle prepared to elucidate the rights and responsibilities of the citizens of the new nation, Abigail Adams wrote a famous letter to her husband, John. "Remember the Ladies," she said. "If particular care and attention are not paid to the ladies we are determined to foment a rebellion, and will not hold ourselves bound to obey any law in which we have no voice or representation." But John Adams "could not but laugh." Was it not enough that children, apprentices, Indians, and Negroes had been influenced by the struggle? Now, another discontented group "more numerous and powerful than all the rest," added its voice.

John Adams and his circle thought slightingly about women's political role in the new nation. The rhetoric of natural rights that fueled liberation for men came to be reinterpreted to mean obligation and duty for women. As Sara Evans writes, "The very language of the Revolution reinforced the view that political activities and aims were male." A character in a Charles Brockden Brown novel put it more strongly. The framers, said his Mrs. Carter, "thought as little of comprehending us in their code of liberty as if we were pigs or sheep."

However, the crux of revolution had given women, as men, the impulse to freedom, the logical step in a society where their contribution had made a new nation a possibility. In the preindustrial world of the colonial United States, women were needed on the farms and at the front counters and in the back shops of the businesses of the time, sometimes as partners with their husbands, often as widows, and occasionally as independent businesswomen. Between 1740 and 1775, more than 300 women retailers existed in New York and Philadelphia, not counting tavern keepers, boarding house proprietors, midwives, wet nurses, and schoolteachers. To take as example the artisan occupation of printing and publishing, the daughters in printing families were often employed in the back shop as compositors, and they sometimes married the male apprentices and helped establish a new branch of the family business. Women also conducted printing establishments on their own: Cornelia Bradford married the printer Andrew Bradford in the 1740s, continued to run the newspaper *American Weekly Mercury* after his death, and became the largest landowner in Philadelphia. Mary Katherine Goddard was publisher of the *Maryland Journal* and was the colony's official printer, bookseller, and postmistress. In Charleston, publisher Elizabeth Timothy was so well regarded that Benjamin Franklin loaned her money.

Moreover, colonial society was one in flux, with ambitious young men and their families moving up the economic scale when times were good. Wives of successful artisan husbands left the counters behind and into the new front rooms took with them an understanding of the wider world. White women were likely to have some degree of education, enough to read and write, if not well. Deborah Read, Benjamin Franklin's wife, laboriously maintained a correspondence with her husband during his lengthy absences, keeping him up to date on his various business interests. Books were imported from England and magazines were an increasing part of late colonial life. Elite homes produced educated women whose métier was the written word: playwright and historian Mercy Otis Warren; diarist Elizabeth Drinker; essayists Elizabeth Magawley and Judith Sargent Murray; versifier and proprietor of an early literary salon, Elizabeth Graeme; as well as prolific correspondents like Abigail Adams, who helped record the age. The African American poet Phillis Wheatley occupies a special place, awkwardly and suspiciously regarded by the Patriots for her calls for liberty for all, including black Americans, and her British evangelical associations.

Still, it was clearly not a golden period. Across classes, both law and custom were different for men than for women. The role of women in the commercial world was not necessarily an opening up of opportunities to women as much as an extension of the domestic world of responsibilities. Women "scolds" were dunked. Unmarried women who gave birth were fined and beaten. Education for young girls, at best, was at a local "dame's school." Although women could sometimes outwit it, coverture prevented married women from controlling property. Widows could lose all at the death of a husband. Most disturbing was that public attitudes toward women were narrowly conceived and often distinctly hostile. Philadelphia's Elizabeth Magawley challenged a particularly vituperative essay that said of women, "The best of the sex are no better than Plagues." "As in your sex," Magawley wrote in the *American Weekly Mercury*, "there are several Classes of Men of Sense, Rakes, Fops, Coxcombs and down-right Fools, so I hope, without straining your Complaisance, you will allow there are some Women of Sense comparatively."

Thanks to a world of letter writers, evidence exists that many marriages were mutually respecting, companionate, and loving. But the public prints of the time indicate an undertow of attitudes that sought, from the 1730s on, to characterize women by rigid standards. Prescriptions of what it meant to be a good wife abounded, as in the poem submitted to the *American Weekly Mercury*, "She as a Wife must please, and she alone. O! Give me such a Wife or give none." Wives should obey their husbands and avoid "managing your Husband." Women were acknowledged when they were "fruitful Dames," helping to populate the colonies. Most of all, women were unremittingly counseled to be "virtuous" in ways that called for modesty, amiability, and the happiness of their husbands as their own.

THE CALL TO DOMESTICITY

As the revolutionary era began, public advice to women increased exponentially. The Patriot boycott against tea and imported goods often seemed less a political tool than an opportunity to upbraid women for paying too much attention to fashion. Female attention to "trifles," such as novel reading and card playing, was derided. The call for education for women—which had existed in the earlier period as a tool helpful to the family business and for the early education for children—opened the door to comments on women's lack of mental abilities. Women should "avoid all abstract learning, all difficult researches" as beyond their abilities. One newspaper contributor begged that a good wife should have "No Learning; No Learning." The *Pennsylvania Magazine* reprinted the story of married discontent amplified by "grave conversations with her, in which she always got the better," which served to "establish her empire over me." When female intelligence was apprehended, it came with the caveat of a "masculine mind." As a Boston minister described it, "Women of masculine minds have generally masculine manners, and a robustness of person ill calculated to inspire tender passion." The essayist "Sophia" voiced a complaint that would echo down the years: An intelligent woman "is represented as disgustingly slovenly in her person, indecent in her habits, imperious to her husband, and negligent of her children." The advice rolled on, so frequent in the new magazines that magazine historian Frank Luther Mott notes that in the 1770s, "Counsel upon Female Virtues" and "Advice to the Fair" were "sickeningly frequent titles."

Given this drumbeat, it was remarkable that any of the revolutionary cabal gave attention to equal rights as they pertained to women. Early on, in his 1764 pamphlet, James Otis raised the question of the role of women in the original compact of natural rights. "Are not women born as free as men?" Benjamin Rush thought seriously about women's education.

But it was Thomas Paine whose benchmark essay—among many articles he included on the married state in his year of editorship of the *Pennsylvania Magazine*—addressed not only women's global subjugation but, unusual for the time, female anonymity. Writing in a female voice, he asked, as if addressing the male sex: "While your ambitious vanity is unceasingly laboring to cover the earth with statues, with monuments, and with inscriptions. Permit our names to be some time pronounced beyond the narrow circle in which we live." Not incidentally, all three men also took antislavery stances.

In the Patriot context of defining women's role, it was not out of place for the colonies' most radical printers, Benjamin Edes and John Gill, publishers of the firebrand *Boston Gazette,* to publish in 1772 the British cookbook, *Frugal Housewife, or Complete Women Cook.* When General George Washington—a master of nuance and symbol in the practice of leadership—refused a donation of money from the Daughters of Liberty, insisting on shirts instead, he was representing a revolutionary society that urged women to make their contributions in terms of their domestic capacity.

It was a peculiar position for the revolutionary leadership—calling for contributions from women whose perceived characteristics were so often derided. Nonetheless, it was women's contribution as spinners and weavers that was essential to the success of the Patriot call for nonimportation, the first colonywide agreement to boycott Great Britain's manufactured goods in favor of American "home-spun." It was, perhaps, that dependence on female competency that made the revolutionary leaders less able later to reward the contributions. Given the tensions of the time, Esther Reed, the founder of what would become the Daughters of Liberty, couched her call for women's participation in terms of renunciation, as if colonial women routinely enjoyed the pleasures of the French court: In the 1780 "The Sentiment of an American Woman," she asked, "Who Amongst us, will not renounce with the highest pleasure, those vain ornaments?" It is significant that the dramatic call from the Daughters of Liberty already noted found no Patriot publisher, but appeared in the Tory *Boston Post-Boy*.

The graphic images of women in revolutionary rhetoric reflected an almost bipolar attitude toward women. Benjamin Franklin's grisly 1766 design of a bloody and dismembered colonial America—arms and legs chopped off and left about—may have been less about the Stamp Act and more a metaphor for other anxieties. The companion piece had Lord Bute among the cluster of male images shoving Britannia toward yet another male representation, Spain. The Boston Tea Party prompted Paul Revere to republish the English pro-Patriot cartoon in which the colonies are portrayed as a vulnerable Indian woman, bare breasted and held down while tea is poured down her throat and a lascivious Lord Sandwich peers up her robes. Its rape image overtones are clear. But by 1787, the frontispiece of *Columbia* magazine portrayed the new nation as a slim female figure, as the goddess of wisdom being approached by her younger version with two children, the more forward figure a boy. Amid debates about education for women, much less whether women should educate boys, wisdom has been elevated into a female figure—but clearly an ethereal one.

As Patriots built propaganda on the notion that Great Britain put its American colonies on the same level as America put its slaves, the image of the raped woman suggests that

Patriots saw the same metaphor applying to women. Both metaphors were constructed on an understanding, but not a rejection, of the status of slaves and women. They were not images that suggested American women were powerful, protected, or esteemed.

What can account for this effort to constrain the women who had labored beside men to build a colonial society, while the opposite was argued for the men of the time? Clearly, colonial society was undergoing change in some regard because of factors over which colonists themselves had little control. Demographic changes resulted in a surplus of unmarried women on the eve of the revolution, while the economic dislocation of the times had particular impact on widows and the families of artisans. Petitions for divorces were up in Massachusetts, and premarital pregnancies rose as high as 30 percent before and after the revolution.

Amid these changes came an increased attention to female sexuality by way of the British Whig piety campaigns, aimed at illustrating the debaucheries of royal life. Colonial newspapers provided their readers with unending serials of royal affairs fomented by female royals. As lively reading as was the trial of Princess Carolina and her Danish lover (who was to be bloodily drawn and quartered for his indiscretions), readers could only conclude sexuality had the power to topple governments. Evangelicals preached its dangers, as did revolutionaries, by way of their propaganda.

THE SEXUAL FEAR

In a private letter in 1745, Benjamin Franklin advised his correspondent to take an older woman for a lover because "in the dark all cats are gray," and "They are so *grateful!*" This was surely no account of female empowerment, but 30 years later sexual attitudes had more complicating layers. The "captivity narratives" of white women abducted by Native Americans had already placed in the culture ideas of power by kidnap and its intimations of rape. But it was the sexuality of black men that prompted the deepest fears. The revolutionary press achieved much of its strength by playing on the fears of white colonists vis-à-vis slavery, particularly when it seemed that the growing British antislavery movement might lead to the freeing of American slaves. The Patriot propaganda campaign was not shy about playing on black crime and black sexuality alongside the accompanying fears that black men desired white women. Hovering just below that surface was the even more disturbing notion that white women might desire them back—fears certainly in the South but also in the North. Boston, the hotbed of revolutionary fervor, long had exerted controls on black activity and severely punished those blacks who broke the laws. There could be no better evidence of the nexus of sexuality and black crime than the 1763 execution of a 16-year-old slave for the rape of a white girl. Four years later, slave sexuality was again in Bostonian public consciousness when a Worcester slave, Arthur, was executed for the rape of a white woman, not the usual punishment in Massachusetts when rapists were white. It is noteworthy that the next two accused rapists in Massachusetts after Arthur were Irish Catholics, who shared a status that was little higher than black bondsmen and who also shared their executionary fate.

Comic verse and plays further set racial tensions in place. White females who consorted at black celebrations were "trulls" (prostitutes). Female black colonists were portrayed comically or as sexual aggressors. The practice of southern gentlemen to have black mistresses was not a point of discussion. Although the history of race and feminism is often located in the post–Civil War era, emphasis on black sexuality in the revolutionary period was a predictor that in the United States women and the history of race were to be intertwined. We might consider that the imperative of the home had to do with the enclosure of white women under the guise of protection wherein questions of sexual potency would not occur.

THE RIGHTS OF WOMEN

Women were not to benefit economically from the American Revolution, any more than were blacks, Native Americans, and propertyless men. Instead, advice continued on how to be virtuous. As women had been expected to make contributions by way of domestic endeavors in the revolution, their contribution to the new nation was to be in an enlargement of the domestic role. Rosemarie Zagarri views the separation of men and women into commercial and domestic spheres a result of the application of two strands of revolutionary philosophy. For men, she writes, equality was based on the Lockean idea of the social contract: Men give up certain liberties to benefit from governance but retain the option to rescind their permission if the contract is breached. But the second strand of revolutionary philosophy, that of the Scottish Empiricists, saw equality in terms of responsibilities, and that was the strand that was applied to women. Men's rights involved liberties that allowed choices,

Zagarri writes, "while women's rights consisted of benefits that imposed duties." What was to have lasting importance, however, was that the application of equality, even though in different forms, was to put women at the table of discussion. By applying one strand of revolutionary thought to women, even as a rhetorical construct, it nonetheless established that a subsequent discussion on equal rights would occur. "Rather than an unquestioned given," Zagarri writes, "women's exclusion from politics now had to be rationalized and justified."

But first was the focus on education, a subject already broached in prewar times. Linda Kerber has described the construction for white, middle-class women of the "republican motherhood" role as a heightening of domestic duties to a level at which the duties came to embody female citizenship. A republican mother was not only expected to maintain the household economy, but to be acquainted with public affairs; read history instead of novels (or play cards, or be involved in other trifles); be both rational and religious; and serve as a teacher, moral and otherwise, to her children. Republican motherhood expanded ideas of female virtue from the promotion of simple domestic tranquility to notions that elevated women's role as the moral center of the home. Increasingly in the nineteenth century, these ideas were to undergird many of the century's reforms, including antislavery, temperance, civic improvement, children's protection, and the promotion of suffrage for women as a means to improve all of society. It was a philosophy that cultivated the idea that women's nature was essentially different, one that has been a point of contention of feminist discussion to the modern day.

In the early republic, an expanded role of women in the home was also a strategy by which women could argue for the necessity of female education, not just to help women be better companions or as an artisan strategy for survival and improvement, but to prepare sons for civic leadership in the new nation. On a practical level, the emphasis on female education also had some application in a society in which women had few choices outside of making good marriages, and a man had to choose carefully if a wife was now responsible for the success of his heirs. In 1785, for example, "Humanus" suggested that females needed public schools so wives could be better companions, the choice of men of "sense and virtue." Clearly, this was an argument that served to make education for women a kind of value-added ingredient to the marriage package rather than a logical requirement of a nation that promised equal rights. But it was a small platform that was used as a place from which to begin the larger argument.

Most connected to the argument for female education is Judith Sargent Murray, who expanded on the theme in Isaiah Thomas's *Massachusetts Magazine.* In her two-part essay in 1789, notably titled "On Equality of the Sexes," Murray ("Constantia") agreed with the stereotypes that women's minds were often filled with trifles—presumably a rhetorical strategy that sought to find a starting place of agreement. However, educated women would lose unattractive traits and find better partners and thus embark upon happier marriage, "now the reverse." Would domestic chores suffer? No, routine as they were, the mind would be left free for reflection. More importantly, education for women was right because women were equal in that "our souls are by nature equal to

yours: the same breath of God animates, enlivens and invig-
orates us." But, finally, Murray promises an exchange: "Shield
us then, we beseech you, from external evils, and in return
we will transact your domestick affairs."

Later, Murray published a collection of essays under the
title *The Gleaner* as a moneymaking project for support of
herself and her child. Although it was clear the essays were
composed by "Constantia" (whose name is on the title page),
Murray constructs a male "Mr. Vigillius" for the narrator, and
it is in this male voice that Murray calls for female education
on the pragmatic basis that it will help young women find
husbands (while disguising the "avidity" of the husband
hunt). But Mr. Vigillius also argues that the female mind is as
competent as that of the male mind and needed only the opportunity for education. What is interesting in Murray's use
of voice—both female and male pseudonyms—is its definition of what is appropriate for gender-defined authorship.
Her own arguments for female education (and other topics)
are seemingly given strength by the male voice, but at the
same time, because there was no secret that Murray is Mr.
Vigillius, there can be no doubt that a male voice is a construction of society, not of a gender.

In the voice of Mr. Vigillius, *The Gleaner* also reflects
Murray's admiration of Mary Wollstonecraft's *Vindication of
the Rights of Women*. Excerpts from it appeared in 1792 in
Philadelphia's *Lady's Magazine*. By 1795, three American editions had been published; two scholars find it was held in 18
percent of private libraries in America, compared with just 12
percent for Paine's *Rights of Man*.

While Judith Murray Sargent proposed education for
women as a domestic social contract, at least in her Constan-

tia voice, Wollstonecraft demanded equality as an inborn, natural right, outside of pragmatic implications. Wollstonecraft claimed men and women shared rights equally and unequivocally, and, although *some* men had been denied equal rights, all women had been denied equal rights on the basis of their gender. How could men assume that rights belonged to men alone, when men had put in place a system of power that kept half of the population subjugated? She called for a "revolution in female manners," better education, and the opening up of professional opportunity. And, finally, she came to the subject of political rights for women: "I might excite laughter," she wrote, "for I really think that women ought to have representatives."

Wollstonecraft's work was the culmination of 200 years of women's intellectual writing in Great Britain that challenged notions of female inequality. Nonetheless, the rhetoric of equal rights was in the ether of the new nation, discussions of who should participate in democracy were heated, and political parties were formed along lines of fitness to govern. Moreover, Wollstonecraft's ideas coincided with the expansion of the public sphere into the most private recesses of the home.

THE ROLE OF MAGAZINES

Magazines had been published sporadically in the colonial days, but the need of printers to find business, the lack of copyright laws, and a populace that was seeking to understand who would share in the citizenship in the new nation helped encourage their spread. As early as 1784, the printer/publisher of Boston's *The Gentleman and Lady's Town and Country Magazine* was finding benefit in an overt attraction to women readers by way of fiction and advice. Moreover, the Federalists, the nation's new power elite, saw that magazines could help spread a national culture based on a philosophy of republican motherhood that could limit the feared rise of popular democracy. By the emphasis on the home as the incubator for elite male leadership, educated women in the home were seen to help maintain a hierarchal society. In their elevated roles, women were courted as readers. In 1787, the Federalists' Noah Webster was assuring readers of his new publication, "*Fair* [women] readers may be assured that no inconsiderable pains will be taken to furnish entertainment." Thomas's Federalist *Massachusetts Magazine* promised, "The fair sex merits our highest attention." Indeed, "women were 'the daughter of the sky.'" By early in the next century, magazines for women alone had been established, and during the nineteenth century—on a foundation of republican motherhood—the role of women in the home would be elevated, celebrated, and perennially affirmed.

Not surprisingly, it was not a Federalist publication that was home to the first appearance of Wollstonecraft's *Vindication*. The initial excerpt from one of the major documents in the modern history of western women appeared in the Philadelphia *Lady's Magazine,* established in 1792 by a young printer with the advice of a group of female advisers. Although the names of the advisers are unknown, it was these women who probably provided the access to Wollstonecraft's work in its British publication, the capital to hire the engravers for the elaborate frontispiece, and, perhaps, authorship of the mission statement, which delineated the magazine's purpose as one to showcase the work of "the female patronesses of literature."

The *Lady's Magazine* was short-lived, ending as a result of the yellow fever epidemic in Philadelphia the following year, but the subject had been placed on the public agenda in ways that had not occurred in the revolutionary period, and it would stay in the public sphere in many permutations.

While the Federalist press did not publish *Vindication,* it was quick to diffuse revelations of Wollstonecroft's living arrangements (she had lived with a man without marriage) when William Godwin was pleased to publish the details in his 1798 memoir of her. Still, the resulting scandal did not quash the focus on women and the demands for education. In the 1795 satire, "Philander" noticed that his wife possessed charm and beauty but "her mind is a perfect blank." "Juvenis" had the best of both worlds: "I would describe—but description fails—the exalted pleasure that I find in her refined conversation." Here was proof, the writer argued, for the value of a well-informed wife. In the same year, another magazine contributor put forward the confusing nature of the "matrimonial creed": "The man is superior to the woman, and the woman is inferior to the man; yet both are equal, and the woman shall govern the man."

In 1802, one of the new women's magazines took up the subject of equal education in classic terms of republican motherhood. "Plan for Emancipation of the Fair Sex" argued the importance of education if women were to achieve their role in the home. "Young women entrusted to the tution [*sic*] of female philosophers in this [proposed] university, may, when they become mothers, instruct their children in the rudiments of knowledge, preparatory to their being sent to college; and thus a gradual increase of wisdom, and consequently of happiness, will be diffused throughout the community."

Occasionally, the argument for complete equality was heard. In 1812, a writer to the *New-York Weekly Museum* noted, "With respect to myself, I am of opinion that women are entitled to equal rights with ourself. In common with us, they possess the qualities of honour, reason, wit, courage, perseverance, and patience; and their importance, which unites us, is equal to our own." Some months later, however, a writer for the same magazine urged young women to remember their roles: "Remember that the duties of woman are comprised in her tendencies to her relatives, as daughter, a wife, and a mother." Her reward is in the influence of a virtuous woman over the "mind of a man." These were as clear as arguments could be for two continuing strains of the discussion that would remain in the culture long after the Federalists lost power.

Perhaps the most radical American response to the discussion on equality was made by Charles Brockden Brown, considered America's first novelist and editor of an early literary magazine. Writing in 1798, with no mention of Wollstonecraft, he put a female character in his novel *Alcuin* who could have been her American version. She called for absolute equality on no other basis than the view that women shared as many abilities as men. Education was necessary; all professions and trades should be open; legal protections should be equal. Women should not be at the mercy of husbands, forced to grovel for household needs. Poor women were to be remembered. And more than two centuries before scholars were discussing "hegemony," the idea that victims can participate in their own victimization, Brown's Mrs. Carter asserted: "All despotism subsists by virtue of the errors and stupidnes [*sic*] of its slaves." The novel did not get much attention; at Brown's early death it was not mentioned in his obituaries. But he had taken the precaution of publishing parts in his magazine.

Mrs. Carter's views were strong words in the early republic, particularly when education for women was not a consideration for political leaders. Education for women, said Thomas Jefferson, was not something he much thought about, but when he did, he considered some ornamental education useful if it could be accompanied by less novel reading.

Novel writing, however, and its handmaiden, writing for the new magazines aimed at women, provided one of the few areas in which women could earn a living. Thus, laden with a cornucopia of ideas based on male versions of what women should be, women's versions of the same, notions of equality and inequality, the meanings of nationhood, and the place for women in the nation—all leavened by the need to make a living in an era that wanted romance—women moved into a new marketplace.

TWO

THE RISE OF THE
PROFESSIONAL WRITER

The great irony of the call for republican motherhood, with its Enlightenment requirements for soberness, place, and duty, was that it arrived at a time when the Romantic revolution was pulling the other way. Direction was to be taken more from the "common sense" of people—that is, the commonalities of shared feeling—and less from classical notions of virtuous citizenship. Magazines that had been prompted by the Federalist vision of women's place in the home found that readers were less interested in rational explications of duty and more in an exploration, already under way in sentimental novels, of the seamy underlife of the emotional world.

Sentimental writing was ceaselessly derided in the conservative press, not only for the emphasis on emotion rather than rationality, but also for the foolishness with which the concept of the home, as they conceived it, came to be equated. Indeed, instead of maintaining the hierarchical order expected from the female commitment to home by way of sensible, companionate marriages, the sentimental fic tion, without ever moving from the domestic circle, threatened the opposite. Home and hearth became the fount of untrammeled feelings, not order, and, to a generation raised on the fear of "mobocracy," disorder was to be rejected.

Early in the life of the new nation, it was clear the founders had lost the battle over novel reading. Susanna Rowson included among her many achievements the authorship of the nation's first and most persistent best seller, *Charlotte Temple.* It was only replaced in popularity by *Uncle Tom's Cabin* a half century later. Charlotte was far from a republican mother; she may have been the classic antiheroine, getting impregnated by a British officer who refused to marry her. She and the child died pitiful deaths from simple poverty. So affected were readers they came to believe that a real-life Charlotte Temple had been buried in Trinity Churchyard in New York. By midcentury the book was still being read, and the churchyard had become a place of pilgrimage that was, as a newspaper put it, "the spot where repose the ashes of that poor girl, over whose story more tears have been wept than have yet fallen for all the dead of the great battles that Europe is witnessing."

Rowson herself was a woman to be admired. She survived the revolution as a child of a Tory family, established a seminary for young women as the discussion for female education got under way, performed as an actress (and maintained her respectability), and wrote successful plays as well as the most successful novel of the early national period. In short, she took advantage of opportunities that had been made available by the changing times, as did hundreds of other women who were launching schools and seeking to write popular novels and contribute to the new magazines.

Like Rowson, they could not remake the standards of the time and make a living. Professional writers to the present must select their battles and often fight them in subterranean ways. Bridging the changing times, *Charlotte Temple* was surely a warning tale about impetuous behavior, but scholars of cultural studies today might read it differently, seeing less blame on Charlotte and more a critique of a society that made no provisions for women caught up by male-sanctioned behavior.

The works of the female writers in the first half of the nineteenth century have helped anchor interpretations of an understanding of the period as "the cult of true woman-hood." The formulaic plots reflected what Barbara Welter called the four cardinal virtues of women at the time—piety, purity, submissiveness, and domesticity. Knowledge of public affairs and the necessity of education disappeared into what was increasingly the emotional vortex of home, a world in itself, swirling in a sea of emotionality.

What is to be considered is how the nation's first female professional writers—that is, the women who wrote to make a living—intersected with the commercial demands of the time. The tension between the need to make a living as a female writer and the demands of a commercial culture that took up the Romantic notions of the day and shaped them along particular lines vis-à-vis women was played out in the pre–Civil War United States as much as in any other time. While sentimental fiction allowed women a paid entrance into a commercial world, the fiction women wrote was not necessarily based on ideas they believed in, or even necessarily shared with their readers. Current cultural studies discussion of how a commercial press can still represent alternative messages may be related to the beginnings of women in professional writing. Deliberately or otherwise, and whether in a historical context or our own, a commercial press can allow room for other voices and even provide opportunities for alternative interpretations of the overt message. Formulaic writing, for example, allows a willing suspension of disbelief, because the formula is known before the reader starts. But it is not at all so clear that formulaic writing is prescriptive, or even if it were, that the prescription would be followed, as Janice Radway found in her study of present-day readers of romance novels. The very existence of a demarcation line can provide a clear announcement that another side exists. Boundaries, like prison walls, promote what is unseen. Readers may have recognized that the pillars of piety, purity, and submissiveness were the nation's ordering devices, not its commandments.

In her examination of midcentury bestselling novels by women, Joanne Dobson finds "'the hidden hand' of subversion." The books of the 1850s, as formulaic as those written in the first part of the nineteenth century, emphasized self-sacrifice as a common theme, leading Dobson to doubt "an entire generation of women writers wholeheartedly subscribed to such a limiting ethic." Her reading of three of the most popular women's novels of the midcentury (Susan Warner's *The Wide, Wide World,* Emma D. E. N. Southworth's *The Hidden Hand,* and A. D. T. Whitney's *Hitherto: A Story of Yesterdays*) finds that the authors subvert conventional sentimental narratives to provide double meanings. "In each novel, the protagonist's struggles speak to the reader on more than one level, allowing a complex reading experience that both affirms and indicts the conventional female life." One conclusion might be that whatever the overt message, the subversive nature of the novels helped account for their best-selling status. Readers of *Charlotte Temple* may have had many levels of enjoyment, not least of which was the opportunity to think about illicit sex, even if it had to be wrapped in a parable of denunciation.

THE SENTIMENTAL WRITERS

The prewar period produced hundreds of female writers and some literary stars: Louise May Alcott, Sarah Josepha Hale, Lydia Maria Child, Harriet Beecher Stowe, Catherine Beecher, Lydia H. Sigourney, Elizabeth Oakes Smith, Sara Jane Lippincott ("Grace Greenwood"), Catharine Sedge-wick, Caroline M. Kirkland, Sara Willis Parton ("Fanny Fern"), and Susan Warner. So many existed that, famously, Nathaniel Hawthorne described them as "damned scribbling women." His full comment reveals he was not condemning women writing or their talent, but a market that turned them into, indeed, scribbling women for the magazine publishers, who would brook no other kind of writing than the sentimental.

Women writers of the pre–Civil War era are seldom included in the canon—that is, the collection of literary works that are considered the best examples of the time. The canon includes Ralph Waldo Emerson, Herman Melville, Henry David Thoreau, Edgar Allan Poe, James Fenimore Cooper, and Nathaniel Hawthorne, and, occasionally, Margaret Fuller. Defining women writers as only sentimental writers led to conundrum. Because women writers were expected to write only in the sentimental fashion, women were not seen to have the ability to write about other affairs; or, when they did, they were considered to be aberrant (Margaret Fuller's fate). Meantime, what was written about in the sentimental fashion was not seen to carry important ideas outside the re-inforcement of the period's ideas of women, family, and affective feeling.

At its most typical, sentimental writing was conscious writing, described by Susanna Rowson in the 1790s: "[R]emember to mix a sufficient quantity of sighs, tears, swooning hysterics and all the moving expressions of heart-rending weeping. Be sure you contrive a duel; and, if conven-ient, a suicide might not be amiss." Rowson's ability to ridicule her own kind of writing suggests that such writing was not so much naturally occurring as her own understand-ing that this was the kind of material that the market de-manded. But also clear is a sense of embarrassment, as if she was trying to distance herself from a style that was—she knew—ridiculed.

This denigration of female sentimental writing turned out to be a constraining influence on male writers as well as women writers. Although some male writers participated in sentimental writing only for money, the writers who wanted canonical remembrance were forced to develop other lines of Romanticism, primarily the Gothic, for their story telling. It is telling to note that the masculine fear of sentimental writ-ing in the United States was so great that it could not pro-duce a male writer such as Charles Dickens, whose work centered on home, but it produced Herman Melville, whose work notably did not. However, male writers, even if so in-clined, found significant barriers to sentimental writing that made the genre difficult to wrench from female hands as it became connected to the domestic sphere almost exclusively. Sentimental writing of the 1790s had to do with sexuality in the form of love and romance, but not in ways that were particularly connected to domesticity. Considering the average age of Americans at the time, the interest in sexuality was not surprising. However, the sentimental writing of the new century, moving from the privacy of the novel to the pages of magazines for the home, had less sexual energy and more acceptance of fate, duty, and even suffering. Early in the new century, the Federalist *Port Folio* thought it important to devote its front page to the reprinting of an essay of advice— indeed, "it ought to be engraven in letters of gold, in every seminary of female education." The world was far from perfect, said the advice giver, and women should accept it the way it was: "In sacrificing your own will, do not hope to influence that of your husband, for men are by nature more obstinate, and in their education, less accustomed to restraint than women. They are naturally tyrannical, attached to pleasure and liberty, and no reasonable woman will expect them to renounce this inclination.... They are the masters, there is nothing left for us but to obey, and to suffer (if so ordained) with good grace." Such messages, if not engraved in gold, stood ready to be carried into the new commercial magazines of the coming era.

THE RISE OF COMMERCIAL MAGAZINES

The rise of the female professional writer was made possible by the rise of commercial magazines that aimed to include women in their audience and sought female contributors to appeal to that audience. The *New-York Mirror* focused on sen-

timental verse, but as it sought a more general presence in arts
and the popular culture of the day, some female contributors
of prose pieces survived, including Hale, Emma Embury, and
Harriet Muzzey. Specialized magazines also came upon the
scene. Caroline H. Gilman was a popular writer who was
founder and editor of the South Carolina magazine *The
Southern Rose,* eventually an apologist for slavery. Not surprisingly, women writers also found employment in the specialty magazines aimed at children. Notably, Louisa May
Alcott, already a writer for juveniles, was invited to be editor
of *Robert Merry's Museum* in the 1860s. Upon the strength of
the annual $500 salary, Alcott was able to set up housekeep-
ing for herself and work on another invited project, *Little
Women.* Other woman writers such as Eliza L. Follen tried to
be entrepreneurs by founding their own magazines aimed at
children, although men dominated in the juvenile field as in
magazines aimed at women.

As in other areas of national life of the time, the publishing business attracted entrepreneurs whose interest in
magazine publication was purely commercial and who subjected magazine publication to the same market standards as
any other business. It was in these magazines that professional
women writers made their mark.

The men who established *Graham's, Peterson's, Arthur's,
Sartain's,* and *Godey's Lady's Book*—following the custom of
naming their publications after themselves—were not intellectual, reform, or political leaders of the day but generally
young men from hardscrabble backgrounds looking for a
successful business niche. In that pursuit the magazines pulled
together the threads of the new culture, melding the high-
flown duty of republican mother with the sentimental style

of *Charlotte Temple* (still doing brisk business) alongside the crowd-pleasing illustrations made possible by technology and, in *Godey's* case, the availability of young women to hand paint each print individually. The publications they founded sought subscribers more than glory. The aim was to reach audiences as large as could be gathered. Louis Godey, a great promoter of his magazine and early to adopt copyright protections for *Godey's* material, described his magazine in terms of reach, not literary influence. In 1837, Godey predicted of circulation, "If we can judge the future by the past, it will reach by next year the astonishing number of 25,000." The magazine actually reached a circulation of 150,000, certainly astonishing for the day, and left Godey a millionaire.

The new entrepreneurs, whatever their private politics, recognized that the corps of women writers who had developed in the era of the sentimental novel were a workforce ready to be tapped. Utilizing writing women already skilled in meeting the needs of audiences, the magazines were filled with content that turned on the sentimental conventions that had been honed in the sentimental novels. Some of the passion would be lost in domestic transformation, but content that turned on domesticity would be found increasingly appropriate for advertisers for the home. And the women writers found that producing such content allowed them to make a living in one of the few ways available to them.

Indeed, to be a successful woman writer was not only to be in possession of one of the few professions by which women could make a living, but also to achieve enough fame to be courted by magazine entrepreneurs as an "editress" whose name would be associated with particular magazines. Lydia H. Sigourney provided an example of the benefits of

the successful female sentimental writer. She was om-
nipresent in the period, author of several thousand works
appearing in 300 publications and serving as editor of several
major magazines of the period. She is the premiere example
in the period of the successful woman writer in the sentimental and moral mode. Depiction of death, particularly of
children (three of her own died at an early age) was a main-
stay, and one collection of her poetry is entirely devoted to
the subject. As one scholar noted, "Her poems often end with
the spirit floating skyward." Whatever her subject, however,
and many of them were what she called "effusions," sentimental writings were encased by the routine of homemaking
and moral preachment.

Whatever she said, Sigourney herself was not to be
constrained by routines of homemaking. She published her
early work anonymously for little or no money in order to
acquiesce to her husband's desires, but she eventually eschewed anonymity on a rationale that her pen could help
with family finances. Her resulting fame provoked her husband's charge that she evinced a "lust of praise" even as she
was writing that a woman should be "like the sun behind a
cloud." The observation was not without merit. Despite a
body of work that promulgated notions of women's innate
modesty, Sigourney assertively courted and enjoyed the fame
amid disclaimers of her own ambition.

Ann Stephens similarly found fame as a writer of sentimental novels, short stories, and poems and as an editor of
major journals. She founded two journals of her own but
found success as editor of various magazines including
Ladies' Magazine, Peterson's, and *Frank Leslie,* all the while
publishing sentimental stories herself. She reached certain

fame with the publication of a historical Indian romance, *Malaeska,* a dime-novel best seller. Like Sigourney, Stephens evinced every indication of seeking and enjoying achievement while her characters, like Sigourney's, shunned success and lived to serve others. "Women," she wrote in one of her works, "were born to look inward with their hearts and cling to others for their support. Men were made to give this support. You cannot change places and be happy!" Stephens, herself, however, clung to no one.

Seeking to extend the realm of the sentimental writer, Sara Jane Clarke Lippincott, using the pseudonym "Grace Greenwood" to such an extent that it really functioned as her name, was a sentimental writer who also addressed issues outside the female sphere. Her essays, poems, and stories appeared in major newspapers and periodicals of the day, but in addition to writing about the usual subject matter of the sentimental writer, she increasingly expressed views on contemporary issues, including slavery and women's rights. However, it was precisely her "sentimental propriety" that made her an acceptable voice on issues outside the usual agenda. At the same time, her sentimental use of language made her the object of criticism—making clear the conundrum of trying to use the acceptable forms of the day to comment on issues considered outside of the purview of the sentimental writer. We may assume that Greenwood herself was not unaware of the dichotomy. In 1850, in an article in the *Saturday Evening Post,* she defended woman's right to a literary profession: "Woman can best judge of woman, her wants, capacities, aspirations, and powers. . . . Thank Heaven, woman herself is awaking to a perception of the causes which have hitherto impeded her free and perfect development. She is beginning to feel, to cast off the bonds which oppress her. There surely is great truth in this question of 'Women's Rights.'"

She took her liberty seriously enough to publish an antislavery essay in the major antislavery publication, *National Era,* which led to her dismissal by Godey from her assistant editor position at *Godey's Lady's Book.* He later recanted, but by that time, Greenwood—another woman who needed to support her family—was at the *National Era,* from whose platform she upbraided him publicly, turning the issue into a cause célèbre that extended her reputation.

Clearly, the Greenwood episode was cautionary for the new *Godey's* literary editor, Sarah Josepha Hale. As a widow with five children to support, Hale came to Louis Godey's attention after a career in Boston as a novelist and magazine editor. *Godey's* made her the offer to become the "editress" of the magazine that came to represent the era. Hale was a kind of Queen Victoria of the magazines of the time, holding the position from 1837 until 1877, when she was 89, at which time the magazine passed into the hands of another woman, S. Annie Frost.

Hale tends to be remembered in less than heroic roles as the composer of "Mary Had a Little Lamb" and sentimental verse, the promoter of Thanksgiving, and a willing expediter of Louis Godey's vision. However, Hale began her career not as a sentimental writer but as a writer of a gothic novel, *Northwood: A Tale of New England.* Although Hale's name would later become inextricably associated with the promotion of the role of women in the domestic circle, this initial work "portrays ideal men and women as practically identical—rational, industrious, and frugal." Moreover, she conceived *Lady's Magazine* as a way to promote female education. When her magazine was combined with its more successful Philadelphia rival, what would be *Godey's Lady's Book,* Hale helped define a separate cultural space for women, promoted by an intimate, conversational writing style that would come to be typical for women's magazines into the present day. Defining that space broadly made her even more a proponent for women's causes. In 1837, the first year of her association, Hale wrote an extensive essay supporting New York's proposal for the reform of marriage legislation. "The custom of wresting from a woman whatever she possesses, whether by inheritance, donation or her own industry, and conferring it all upon the man she marries" was, she wrote, "barbarous." The law as it stood "virtually degrees the woman to the condition of a slave," a status that "impairs her influence, not only with the husband but her children." And although she certainly could provide examples of victimized women, her article turned on the role of women to join with men as equal partners in marriage.

Biographies make no mention of it, but it is likely that Hale as an educated woman had some understanding of Wollstonecraft beyond the scandal of Godwin's revelations. Nearly 30 years after Wollstonecraft's appearance in the early press, her ideas were still abroad, rather directly in an 1830 article, "Mary Woolstonecraft" [*sic*], written for the *Saturday Evening Post* and republished in its sister publication, *The Casket: Flowers of Literature, Wit and Sentiment.* But Hale's reform platforms were constrained by Louis Godey's understandings of his readership. Still, for the time, Hale's reform activities were considerable. She continued to agitate for female education, promoted women as teachers, doctors, and seminarians, and played a role in the civic leadership of Philadelphia. Moreover, she compiled a biographical collection of "distinguished women" published as *Woman's Record* in 1853 (although Stowe was not included because of her radical abolitionist sympathies, and Fuller was held up as an example of someone who was too clever for her own good).

Yet *Godey's* circulation in the South limited an outspoken political position. Hale, who herself opposed slavery, adopted a view that blamed abolitionists for being too partisan. Thus, even Hale's support of the American Colonization Society's notion that former slaves could be "resettled" in Liberia was argued as a religious concern and thus within the female sphere of responsibility. As the Civil War threatened the Southern circulation, all mention of current issues disappeared and the Civil War's bloody passage into American history crossed the pages of *Godey's* not at all.

As the foremost women's editor of the time, Hale had the opportunity to hire women writers, and in the magazine's prewar days, all of the popular women writers of the time appeared in *Godey's:* Miss Leslie, Ann Stephens, E. F. Ellet, Caroline Lee Heinz, Frances S. Osgood, Sela Smith, Hannah Golden, Grace Greenwood, Catharine M. Sedgewick, Caroline M. Kirkland, Lydia Sigourney, and Harriet Beecher Stowe, before *Uncle Tom's Cabin* made her persona non grata at *Godey's. Godey's* recognized the number of female writers in self-promotional ways as early as 1840, providing the names of eighteen female authors it had been proud to publish.

Although the sentimental and rambling fiction of the first part of the century was connected to women, the most often published and best-paid "magazinist" of the time was the male writer Nathaniel P. Willis, who wrote "dandified" romantic travel tales for New York's *The Mirror* in the 1840s. As one writer described him, "If it demanded prose embroidery and short-story tatting he could produce it in more elegant designs than could even Fanny Fern or Grace Greenwood." *Graham's* and *Sartain's,* also in Philadelphia, were soon imitating *Godey's* and offering a similar brand of sentimental fiction.

Even the literary stars, as well as the corps of lesser lights, found it necessary to write in the sentimental mode if they wanted to be published. Caroline Kirkland, another of the several women who sought to support her family by her pen, wrote to her daughter that she had submitted to *Graham's* "a very sentimental love story—or as near that as I can persuade myself to come." Later, as editor of the *Union Magazine,* she wrote even more strongly: "Nine-tenths of the magazine stories, so popular among us, have nothing to do with life, and fiction which has no relation to what has been, or what is to be, must be both vapid and valueless."

For writers, one problem was that editors demanded the plot of a novel in the space of a magazine. But authors who submitted novel-length manuscripts to accommodate the complications of the plot found their stories abruptly ended, leading one writer, Seba Smith, to declare in her headlong rush through incident, "But we must not stop for details. . . . We must not dwell on particulars. . . . We must pass over the details." Such writers had to develop a code for readers, expecting them to understand the stock figures and situations. Week after week, readers of the magazines were subjected to representations of women in unrelenting patterns of "pining," "abnegation," and "orphans and widows." The existence of these caricatures should not be equated with readers' acceptance of the figures as anything more than conventions. Writers of sentimental fiction and their readers appeared to share an understanding of the role of stock characters to speed the story along, but that did not equate to a belief on either side that the stock characters were to be understood outside of their place on the chess board of the story.

What the careers of many of the professional women's magazine writers suggest is how much of their lives were devoted to the promulgation of careers along the lines that were open to them. Despite what they said publicly, the women were not shy about changing and improving their positions, nor making time and room for their own entrepreneurial efforts. Whether, like Kirkland, participating in the marketplace with their eyes wide open, or like Sigourney, seemingly oblivious to how her own career path did not intersect with the philosophies she promoted, they adjusted their own abilities to the realities of the time.

By the post–Civil War era, sentimental fiction became increasingly out of favor for magazines whose readers included men. Sentimental fiction became the purview of magazines with high female readership such as *Leslie's Popular Monthly,* established in 1877, a "story" magazine that appealed to working and immigrant readers. *Leslie's* made impressive strides thanks to its sentimental contents—a circulation of 100,000 nationally in the 1880s, dropping only in the 1890s when women wanted a new kind of sentimental fiction that took women out of the home and into the workplace. Readers demanded more resilient heroines. The continuing supply of women writers was happy to comply.

RISE OF NONFICTION

Early women professional writers who wanted to make a living were confined to the form that was commercial. By mid-century, with the advent of cheap city newspapers, women writers found other opportunities that still fit within the realm of approved writing for women but provided new ways of making a living—nonfiction writing on domestic topics. The group was composed of such notables as Harriet Beecher Stowe, Catherine Beecher, and Lydia Child, all of whom produced domestic advice books. Less well known today but celebrities in their time were the professional women who wrote on domestic topics in newspaper columns: June Croly ("Jennie June," later discussed) and Sara Willis Parton ("Fanny Fern").

As author of the popular 1854 novel *Ruth Hall,* Parton was one of the professional women fiction writers of the period. But according to Carolyn Kitch, Parton's contribution to the discussion of feminist issues in the mass press came by way of her newspaper columns written between 1851 and 1872 under a name she legally adopted in 1852, "Fanny Fern." Her columns addressed many of the issues that were being raised by reformers, but her strength, Kitch notes, was in the fact that her audience was broader than what was reached by the women's rights activists of the period. "Fern was probably the first American journalist to regularly champion women's rights in a consumer medium with a large readership that cut across the divisions of gender and class."

Like other writers, Parton had to support family members after the death of her husband, taking in sewing from Boston boarding houses. A second marriage to an abusive husband failed, and she was divorced at a time when the word was hardly breathed (which was one reason she changed her name). She turned to writing, encouraged, perhaps, by the example of her school friend, Harriet Beecher Stowe, and the success of her brother, N. P. Willis, then a magazine editor (who turned down her first literary efforts). Nonetheless, she found acceptance in several Boston publications. Two years later, she published a book of her columns that sold 100,000 copies and led to an offer to write for the *New York Ledger* at $100 a column. She had a large audience, a new husband, and money in the bank, and she turned her staccato, humorous, and informal style to challenging the accepted standards for women's role in the domestic circle. She urged women to get out of the house, to seek physical and mental stimulation, to read and write, to work, to free themselves of restrictive clothing. In the 1860s, she was arguing for women's suffrage and married women's property rights. She called attention to urban poverty, child abuse, and the problems of poor working women long before Progressives had identified them. Altogether, she called for the "coming woman," as she put it, "a bright-eyed, full-chested, broad-shouldered, large-souled, intellectual being; able to walk, able to eat, able to fulfill her maternal destiny [or equally able] to go to her grave happy, self-poised and serene, though unwedded."

One woman of the period became a newspaper editor in a major city. That was Cornelia W. Walter, whose Boston antecedents went back to Increase Mather and who took over the *Boston Transcript* in 1842 at the death of her brother. Accounts of her managerial skills were legion as she became "the brilliant lady editor of the *Transcript.*" The *Transcript* was no ladies' magazine—it was quite willing to cover murders. During her editorship she wrote for at least two magazines, including an essay for *Sargent's* that called for recognition that woman is "naturally intellectual." But her place on the journalistic stage was short-lived when she left daily journalism in 1847 for marriage to William B. Richards and, as a well-to-do matron, sat for the American artist Thomas Ball for a portrait that is now in the hands of the Museum of Fine Arts in Boston. This was not the usual trajectory for a woman in journalism and was an early indicator of the difficulty of accommodating class as well as gender issues in the American newsroom, even as the boss.

THE INTELLECTUAL WRITER

Margaret Fuller is regarded as one of the nation's early female intellectuals, the closest American equivalent to the British intellectuals Mary Wollstonecraft and Harriet Martineau. As a literary woman without means, Fuller nonetheless refused to write in the acceptable sentimental tradition. But her career path was far from straightforward as she combined other areas of acceptable women's behavior in ways that allowed her to remain true to her intellectual ambitions. Before she became recognized as a writer and editor of the Transcendentalist magazine *The Dial,* Fuller drew upon the permissions given to women to be teachers and to operate in social circles of other women by setting up a series of paid lectures among the Boston Unitarian female circle, themselves constrained from learning in more formal settings. These lectures became the basis for a series of essays that eventually became the book *Woman in the 19th Century*. It sold briskly and made her a celebrity.

Her connections to the wives and daughters of the Boston literati by way of the learning circles had other commercial benefits. Thanks to Mary Greeley, the wife of the New York editor, Horace Greeley, who adopted many of the new ideas of the time, Fuller was hired by Greeley's *New York Tribune* for work that was definitely outside the sentimental traditions. Her columns reviewed literary works and books about social reforms, and these latter articles provided her a platform to air views on women's rights, abolition, hygiene, and prejudices against the Irish and the poor. In addition, she wrote a series of articles on city institutions, including articles about visits to New York's prison, Sing Sing, and to the city's insane asylums—remarkable eyewitness accounts for a woman of the time to undertake. "They crouched in corners," she wrote of the inmates of the city's insane asylum on Blackwell Island. "They had no eye for the stranger, no heart for hope, no habitual expectation of life." Unlike the social reform writers of the time or later the sensational stunt writers, Fuller's observations were less about the lash than about public attitudes toward such institutions.

Why Fuller was permitted such a wide range of operation when most women were confined to sentimental writing had to do with Fuller's perceived identity as something outside the norm. Fuller was soon publicly constructed by an array of personality characteristics that aimed at making her different. When her literary criticism took on revered writers such as Henry Longfellow, she was called waspish. Such work, according to one biographer, "roused the witch-hunting instincts of men who were ready to see in any negative comment . . . evidence of that kind of spitefulness they expected from a woman; who 'unsexed' herself by writing like men." Poe, one enemy, said humanity could be divided into three classes: "men, women, and Margaret Fuller."

Nonetheless, Greeley, no stranger to criticism himself, made her a European correspondent for the *Tribune,* where she covered the Italian political turmoil in 1847 and 1848 and, challenging her U.S. reputation as an intellectual and thus "unsexed," took a lover. That occurrence until fairly recently was explained by her biographers as a "discovery" of her feminine side that had been submerged by her previous intellectuality. As Mason Wade wrote: "The Latin concept of woman as mother and wife had appealed to her frustrated femininity and sunk into her consciousness, gradually displacing her notion of herself as a Feminist consecrated to a single life." In 1850, Fuller and her lover, Ossoli—their marriage status has been unclear—and their two-year-old child returned to the United States. The captain of their vessel died on the journey, and as the small ship approached Long Island guided by its inexperienced second captain, it struck a sand bar off Fire Island. Trapped on board, Fuller and her party could see figures on shore, but rescue attempts were confused. Fuller, Ossoli, and their child drowned in their attempt to make it to shore.

Fuller's legacy to the struggle for equality was double sided. On the one hand, she had proved that a woman could throw off the bondage of sentimental writing and be accepted in a mass media journal of the time for her intellectual abilities. But just as profound as that influence was her image of the "bluestocking," asexual woman. This was a useful cubbyhole in which to store her—serving to set her apart from male writers much as other writing women were set apart by their sentimental style in the assumption of the time that a female writer could not be both an intellectual woman and a sexually functioning one. They were images that had already been established by writers to colonial newspapers and became further embedded in the nation's collective memory by Wollstonecraft and Fuller. They emerged into First Wave images of suffragists as spinsterish and into the Second Wave, when young women activists who could not be so easily dismissed as asexual, in terms of stridency. But these kinds of images surely provided the counterpoint to the pious, dutiful women of sentimental fiction, and that had its own strength and was the greatest subversion of all.

◈

THREE

THE LEGACY OF REFORM

In 1857, Susan B. Anthony described a dinner at the "James Motts" amidst a group of reform activists. "We had a chat, spiritualism as usual being the principle [*sic*] topic. Mrs. Rose and Mr. Curtis believing the spirit inseparable from the body, of course, were on the unbelieving side, while Sarah Grimpke [*sic*] was all enthusiasm in the faith."

It may have been a fairly average dinner-table conversation for reformers of the time, and it points up that reform for women was but one thread of a stew of pre–Civil War activity. In the prewar United States, activists, usually anchored in opposition to slavery as a shared bottom line, crossed into dozens of areas—vegetarianism, nontraditional spirituality, healing and health, and economic, labor, and moral reform. The Oneida Community, Brook Farm, Fourism, theosophy and many other experiments reflected Jacksonian energy and confidence that all problems could be solved. Men and women drawn to reform often moved in and out of each other's circles, and in the crosscurrents of the day, sometimes combined elements from several ideals. At the same time, the women's movement benefited from the energy of reform and from the discussion about women that many reform groups were conducting. In the utopian community of Brook Farm, for example, men as well as women were expected to share in household chores. Labor advocates and the fledgling union movement had to examine the place of women—not always as generously as the "Friend to the Fair Sex," who argued in a trade magazine that "When we consider that the number of women brought into the world equals the number of men, is it not right that all employments which are suitable to them should be kept free of intruders?"

From the beginning, women's rights leaders would be faced with the decisions of fixing lines of demarcation among the movements, beginning with their own decisions on where to put their energies. Second was to determine what level of loyalty should be given to their coreformers, since reforms represented various approaches and various political views and were greeted by various levels of distrust by the larger world.

The Scottish-born author and intellectual, Frances Wright, for example, established a utopian community for freed slaves. When it failed, she joined with Robert Owen in the publication of *Free Enquirer* and gave her attention to education, socialism, sexual freedom, dress reform, and married women's rights (at her divorce her husband had gained control over all her property, including her earnings from royalties and lectures). She was soon abhorred: "a procuress of atheism and infidelity." Warnings abounded that wives would be "seduced by her diabolical doctrines" and she was ridiculed in a famous cartoon. At the 1858 National Rights Convention, Ernestine Rose credited her as "the first woman in this country who spoke on the equality of the sexes." Her reward, Rose said, was to be "subjected to public odium, slander and persecution."

These were confusing times for the understanding of gender and its responsibilities. "Wrightism" became a code word for female licentiousness, the example of where redefinitions of gender could lead. Proponents of slavery held up the southern home as ideal and attacked abolitionism as an attempt to desexualize gender by permitting women to speak publicly and be in mixed-gender settings. Female temperance and "moral" reformers were similarly attacked as representing the first step in the desexualization of gender. However, moral reformers often upheld gender differences, arguing their case that women were morally superior, eventually one of the undergirding principles of some suffrage argument

Beginning in the 1830s as a crusade to offer alternatives to New York's prostitutes, the Female Moral Reform Society moved to attack the double standard of male/female sexual behavior. Despite public opinion that considered such matters better left alone, the society sought to "treat the guilty of both sexes alike, and exercise toward them the same feeling." "Why should a female be trodden underfoot and spurned from society," the society asked, "while common consent allows the male to habituate himself to this vice, and treat him as not guilty?" In its national campaign, readers of the society's national newspaper were invited to contribute specific examples of seduction for publication, accounts that included all the specifics and the offending male's initials. The campaign against the double standard led to a larger critique of women in society, including a call for an opening up of jobs so women were not economically dependent on men. And the society sought to bring attention to the unequal power arrangements that lay behind the domestic veil: "Instead of regarding his wife as help-mate for him and an equal sharer of his joys and sorrows he looks upon her as a useful article of furniture, which is valuable only for the benefit derived from it, but which may be thrown aside at pleasure." As Carroll Smith Rosenberg notes, there was a great undertow of anger among female moral reformers that was channeled into reform activities accompanied by a "compensatory sense of superior righteousness." However, Therese Lueck interprets moral reform in terms of establishing female culture within the male patriarchal system, which gave female culture a freedom to discuss subjects, such as adultery, that religious leaders avoided. This would turn out to be a long-lasting thread in American feminism, inculcated by the women's shelter magazines into the post–World War II era.

Yet at the time, given the variety of reform movements and the growth of female moral reform, it was hard to tease out what "women's rights" meant. Some areas seemed to conflate. For temperance advocates, temperance was as much a women's issue as a suffrage or legal rights issue, and many early leaders of women's rights, including Elizabeth Cady Stanton and Susan B. Anthony, first came in contact by their shared belief in the temperance cause. The women were introduced to each other by the temperance activist Amelia Bloomer, a neighbor of Stanton's in Seneca Falls, New York, who had founded a temperance newspaper. Even as a temperance organ, Bloomer's newspaper proclaimed it was "Published by a Committee of Ladies," leading some to assume it was the first newspaper to be entirely owned and operated by a woman. Under Stanton's influence, it was not long before the newspaper turned into a women's rights newspaper, the first ever, and Bloomer herself—although best remembered as a clothing reformer—was a speaker and organizer for women's rights by the time she moved to Iowa.

For other women, women's reform was part of a picture of reconfiguring relationships in the culture, beyond the legal protections of New York State's amendment to the Married Women's Property Act. Wright was called the "red harlot" for her call for freer sexual attitudes, liberal divorce laws, and birth control. In the post–Civil War period, Victoria Woodhull, the "notorious" woman who declared herself a candidate for U.S. president in 1872 on a wide-ranging platform, was also the subject of ridicule for her attitudes toward sexual freedom. Moral reformers were soon viewed as asexual and prurient and trying to change nature. And added to this was the relationship of African American women to women's rights. There was no easy place: Sojourner Truth was constructed by female abolitionists as a kind of indestructible folk figure, while middle-class African-Americans, such as Philadelphia's Forten family, adopted respectable domesticity to such an extent to suggest that African Americans would adhere to gendered roles as much as anyone else once the yoke of slavery had been removed.

As the organized women's movement took center stage, the early connection of women's rights to the various reform movements became problematical. Although most women involved in reform activities in general also had an interest in women's status, there was no consensus of goals. Temperance advocates were likely to see abuses of alcohol as the major key to the destruction of family life, but might be quite traditional outside that concern. And while the anti-slavery movement was the prime influence on the women's rights movement and provided the new movement with women leaders of national experience, women's suffrage was soon positioned in conflict with the demands of African Americans rather than as partners in an equal struggle.

In one important tactical way, all the various reform impulses as practiced by women helped women learn about the techniques of organizing. In his tour of the new United States, the French observer Alexis de Tocqueville noted that every hamlet seemed to have its own newspaper. He could also have included reform groups. Hundreds of publications across the nation spread the news of reform and served to maintain a loose confederation among reform movements. They were also often written and edited by women. The Female Moral Reform Society, for example, published the nationally distributed *Advocate,* perhaps the nation's most widely read evangelical paper with 16,500 subscribers. Its original male staff was replaced in the prewar era by women as editors, agents, and writers. Women also held major roles as editors and contributors to the substantive antislavery press. Even when those women—Lydia Maria Child, Harriet Beecher Stowe, or Grace Greenwood—did not move into women's rights, they provided examples of the role of a reform press in building a social movement.

Antislavery women were also part of a skein of family and friend relationships connected to the antislavery movement, which gave them a prominence that would be useful later in the initial organizing of the women's movement. Lucretia Mott was part of a large and well-known Quaker family circle devoted to abolition. Stanton was also prominent in the antislavery reform movement by her marriage to a traveling abolitionist as well as by her contributions to the *National Anti-Slavery Standard*. Both women were already prominent in their time, and their endorsement of a separate organization devoted to women's concerns was an imprimatur that was not easily ignored in the reform communities.

Finally, women in antislavery who moved to women's rights brought a variety of skills—platform speaking skills, important for a movement that was going to rely so heavily on conventions and speaking tours, and the more mundane proficiencies of bureaucratic organization, fund raising, and editorial skills.

Still, there were difficulties associated with constructing a women's movement using templates established by other reform movements. The women who came to women's rights from antislavery, temperance, morality, or the many "isms" of the day brought into feminism ideas that had been shaped by their starter groups, which did not always comport with feminism as it was developing. Antislavery, despite its many contributions to women's rights, also brought to the table rhetorical strategies that did not necessarily translate into women's concerns.

THE USES OF SENTIMENTALITY

As the Civil War approached, the antislavery argument found its strongest voice in the kind of writing associated with the sentimental style connected to the domestic circle. This was not simply a reflection of the sentimental writing of the age, but rather a long-held strategy of Quaker antislavery rhetoric that predated the American Revolution. First in Great

Britain and then in the American colonies, antislavery writers called on affective feeling to persuade and had cultivated familiar tropes to do so: the separation of a slave family that had the same values as a white family, the cruelty of the slave master, and the enslaved as pious. It was a style of persuasive writing that depended for its success on the evocation of an outpouring of feeling. Right feeling came to be the rationale for change: To be horrified by slavery, particularly as related to the destruction of the family, was the first step in conversion. Such a style was the entrée for women antislavery writers. Women writers could become writers for reform, since their traditional roles as mothers and wives provided them with a kind of professional know-how about domestic life. Moreover, women were expected to be feeling individuals, carrying sensibilities that were less distributed to the male of the species, even in antislavery circles.

One antislavery rhetorical strategy attacked the institution of slavery as robbing enslaved men and women of the rightful gender roles that operated in civilized society. It was a rhetoric that embraced difference between the sexes, and it held up slavery as a destroyer of those differences. Even as the radical antislavery wing challenged traditional gender roles by its use of women in the work of antislavery, the African American female constituency was encouraged to represent itself in terms of domestic gentility. William Lloyd Garrison, for example, invited members of Philadelphia's African American female literary society to submit to his newspaper's "Ladies' Department," a far cry from the fiery rhetoric of the front page. There seemed no middle ground for African American women: either the folk motif of Sojourner Truth or the respectable confinement of the literary society.

There were disadvantages in the antislavery rhetoric that was so quick to sentimentalize the domestic circle. First, seeking change on the basis of change of heart was danger-ous ground on which to base social protest writing, since men were not expected to respond to sentimental writing, and men were at the levers of power. Secondly, such an ap-proach set up the family circle as the only acceptable way of life, with the accompanying bundle of affiliated expecta-tions; that is to say, if a reform was not directly related to the traditional family, its worthiness was suspect. This would cause difficulties for arguments for suffrage when only women in certain roles were seen to have credence; even into the Second and Third Waves, women not in traditional roles had to operate from a defensive position. What also is to be considered is that to persuade by feeling on a set of as-sumed standards—for example, the role of family—is to also assume that everyone is similarly moved by the same im-pulses to the same ends. It does not consider that common feelings may not be so common, that particular cultures can dictate core beliefs that may not translate across cultures, and that there are issues that can and should stand outside of other institutions, such as ideas of family.

Certainly, there had been other arguments against slavery—slavery as an offense against God, slavery as an inef-ficient labor system, slavery as incompatible with a nation committed to a philosophy of equal rights. In the early 1840s, when Lydia Maria Child was the editor of the leading abolitionist newspaper, the *National Anti-Slavery Standard,* she sought to expand readership to a "balanced diet," avoiding polemics and the politics of the movement. None of these rationales was on anyone's minds, however, following the success of Harriet Beecher Stowe's 1852 novel *Uncle Tom's Cabin, or, Life Among the Lowly* (the full title of *Uncle Tom's Cabin*), which had begun its life in the *Standard*.

HARRIET BEECHER STOWE AND THE FAMILY CIRCLE

Stowe was a member of a Protestant reform family whose beliefs coincided with those of the Quaker activists, certainly those that revolved around the sanctity of the home. At the same time, Stowe was one of the scribbling women, that is to say, one of the women who looked at professional writing as a way to help support the family. As she later wrote, "I used to say to my faithful friend & factotum Ann [her live-in help], who shared all my joys & sorrows, 'Now if you'll keep the babies & attend to all the things in the house for one day, I'll write a piece, & than we shall be out of the scrape'; and so I became an authoress." Like many other professional women, Stowe publicly represented her writing as an irregular, amateur avocation. However, her writing before *Uncle's Tom's Cabin* did include the kinds of writing that held promise of remuneration, particularly her focus on regional interest at a time when Americans were involved in new attention to self. In 1841, *Godey's Lady's Book* published "The Canal-Boat," a colorful travel account that turned on Stowe's interest in the ordinary. She wrote for *Godey's* about the importance of domestic skills, making fun of her own initial shortcomings, and provided fiction on the same subject. She was coauthor with her sister, Catherine Beecher, of an early book of advice on home economy; at its reissue in 1869, she contributed several chapters on home decoration. Even after she became a transatlantic celebrity following the success of her major work, Stowe returned to professional writing as a columnist for the *Atlantic Monthly* on domestic matters, including advising women to repress those characteristics (fault-finding, irritability, repression, intolerance, and so on) that would interfere with domestic happiness. In 1868 she was coeditor of *Hearth and Home*. These were not subversive activities. Stowe believed in the domestic circle and, as sister to New England's foremost preacher, adhered to the belief of women as a religionist and moral center. Even before Victoria Woodhull exposed the double sexual standard practiced by Stowe's brother, the Rev. Henry Ward Beecher, Stowe and her sister could not but oppose Woodhull's idea of sexual choices for women.

Because Stowe was a member of a famous family involved in reform and its publications, it was logical that her writing career would also include writing for the antislavery publications that were part of her extended circle. They included the *National Anti-Slavery Standard* in Washington, and it was here that she broached the idea of the serialized novel (again, pointing to her knowledge of professional behaviors), making that suggestion, according to a biographer, as an "established contributor." Her proposal that the work be serialized also suggested her awareness of publishing trends, as the success of the novels of Charles Dickens in serialized forms had proved. Moreover, Dickens had also shown the strength of novels of social reform in a domestic frame. Indeed, as with Dickens, it is to be considered that *Uncle Tom's Cabin* owed a large part of its success to Stowe's ability to frame antislavery in the rhetoric of the familiar domestic circle.

Nothing is more telling in *Uncle Tom's Cabin* than that

the incarnation of evil, Simon Legree, is a bachelor and removed from the civilizing aspects of a woman. His unkempt
place of residence—"a weird and ghostly place"—is clearly
devoid of a woman's touch. Topsy is a child who has not had
the benefits of being properly "raised." Uncle Tom chooses
not to escape to freedom not from a mewling acceptance of
his slave status (as later critics would have it), but out of what
Stowe viewed as appropriate religious conviction necessary
as the undergirding structure of the home. Stowe's work also
used a strong dose of examples of barbarism and cruelty that
had characterized antislavery writing since the days of
Quaker pamphleteer Anthony Benezet. Nothing could be
more compelling than the breakup of families as a result of
sale: "Down goes the hammer again,—Susan is sold! She
goes down from the block, stops, looks wistfully back—her
daughter stretches her hands towards her. She looks with
agony in the face of the man who has bought her,—a respectable middle-aged man, of benevolent countenance. 'Oh,
Mas'er, please do buy my daughter!'" Benevolent or not, the
gentleman does not answer the plea, and the child is sold,
along with Tom, to the new master, the infamous Legree.

Such scenes awakened the nation to the issue of slavery
as never before, in some part because slavery was positioned
as the apotheosis of the domestic circle that resonated so
strongly at the time. The response to the book—many unbelieving that such events could occur—led Stowe to write *A
Key to Uncle Tom's Cabin,* aimed at proving that her story was
true to life. In contrast to the novel, *Key* addresses legal prece-
dents, notes slave notices in newspapers, and provides the
economic rationale for slavery. As one Stowe scholar notes,
"Those who wept over his [Tom's] death in *Uncle Tom's Cabin*

were confronted, in the *Key*, with an iron logic that had no room for the sentimental." In short, the novel had not simply burst from her pen in a Linda Sigourney–style "effusion," but, as the *Key* suggested, Stowe had framed the story in ways that were expected to move the American public for political ends. It is not an exaggeration to say that the book would be a lesson for all future reform movements.

THE MOVE TO BUREAUCRATIZATION

By the time Stowe published her book, women had been active in the antislavery movement since the American Revolution, but only formally active from the 1830s when female antislavery societies were founded in New York, Boston, and Philadelphia. These female antislavery societies gave women experience in organizing, writing, and sometimes speaking. The antislavery movement produced several major speakers who not only broke prohibitions against women speaking in public, but who spoke on a subject that incited public wrath and could jeopardize safety. Like Frances Wright and others, abolitionist women were viewed as less than womanly in the outer world, and it is perhaps not surprising that retaining womanliness inside the antislavery circle was important.

The antislavery societies became most connected to fundraising, and this interacted with the belief of its members in the importance of the family sphere. The Philadelphia Female Anti-Slavery Society had begun ambitiously, canvassing door to door for signatures on the ever-present antislavery petitions, supporting a school for African American children, and recruiting new members, including African American women. But within 20 years, the focus had changed. The society's major activity revolved around organization of the annual fundraiser, the antislavery fair, and the production of domestic products sold at the fair. By 1846, an organizer put out the call: "All the usual articles of needle work will be in demand, and a much larger supply than heretofore of the products of the garden, the dairy, and the farm." Men now conducted the petition drives, managed publications, and organized speaking tours.

Why this shift occurred had to do with several influences, including, as Jean Soderland argues, a female strategy to maintain their society's power and autonomy in the larger abolitionist movement by the money it could raise. But the demands and the priority of the domestic circle must be counted as among the reasons, especially since its sanctity was one of the abolitionist arguments. And by moving to a less public mode, sympathetic women could participate in abolitionism by that most acceptable of domestic arrangements, the sewing circle. Sewing circles in any case offered female sociability, as described by one early member when "our small number eight or ten, who repaired to a school-room because it was central, each with her supper of nuts and cakes brought in pocket, eaten at twilight while we walked in the yard,—then a few more hours' work by the glimmer of candles." Women did not have to choose between social activism and the demands of the domestic circle, but melded the two and could find some pleasure in the practice as well.

The experience of the Philadelphia group was of importance in the later construction of the women's movement by way of yearly conventions. One of the founders of the 1848 Seneca Falls women's rights convention was Lucretia Mott, who with her husband James was one of the leaders in the Philadelphia Female Anti-Slavery Society as it shifted to a bureaucratic model that used its members' energies sparingly by way of the fairs. Elizabeth Cady Stanton herself was in close contact with Mott during the years leading up to the Seneca Falls Convention. Not surprisingly, the early women's rights organization was similarly conducted along lines of yearly conventions that, as in the antislavery societies, served to maintain ongoing leadership and other activities rather than moving into mass organizing itself. Indeed, the founding of the National Organization for Women in 1966 followed the same model. This approach to reform organization put less importance on the door-to-door canvassing that characterized labor and political organizing. For early feminists, organizing might still be conducted, but by letter writing—a mode that was apt to extend a skein of contacts horizontally, to those already known, rather than develop new circles.

Given the constraints made necessary by the beliefs in responsibilities to home and hearth, Stanton, using whatever tools were at hand, was more likely to be aware of other ways of reaching audiences, including through the growing mass press. She utilized press contacts in getting press attention to the Seneca Falls Convention and continued to maintain a close eye on how the movement was covered. "Henry brought me every item he could see about you," she wrote to Susan B. Anthony in 1856. "'Well,' he would say, 'another notice about Susan. You stir up Susan, and she stirs up the world.'"

SENECA FALLS CONVENTION

The history of the Seneca Falls Convention in 1848 is well known—the idea was sparked because of objections by the

American Anti-Slavery Society to female membership and a similar rejection of women at the World Anti-Slavery Convention in London in 1840. At that meeting Elizabeth Cady Stanton, attending the convention on her honeymoon, came to know Lucretia Mott, and they had discussions that led to formation of an advocacy society for women. The immediate prompt to the Seneca Falls Convention was Stanton's visit to the Motts and a handful of friends. The Declaration of Sentiments was drawn up around the family table of one of the five women, Mary Ann McClintock. (That table is now in the Smithsonian Institute as if to emphasize the domestic underpinnings of the start of the movement.) A notice sent to the Seneca Falls paper appeared the day before the convention.

> Woman's Rights Convention—A convention to discuss the social, civil and Religious rights of woman will be held in the Wesleyan Chapel, Seneca Falls, New York, on Wednesday and Thursday, the 19th and 20th of July current; commencing at 10 A.M. During the first day the meeting will be held exclusively for women, who are earnestly invited to attend. The public generally are invited to be present on the second day, when Lucretia Mott of Philadelphia and other ladies and gentlemen will address the convention.

Some historians have underrated Stanton's skills and experience in establishing the initial convention, including the eight years of discussion with Mott that preceded it and the consciousness about its public presence when it did occur. Eleanor Flexner, for example, writes, "Having drafted the notice, the women were at a loss as to how to proceed." In actual fact, Stanton and the woman around her had long been involved with persuasive techniques as part of their reform backgrounds, and the idea of a convention posed no great difficulty. Moreover, Mott was clearly mentioned in the announcement because her name was expected to give the convention legitimacy. Finally, it is naive not to recognize that Stanton was aware of the attention that would be given to the "Declaration of Sentiments," a statement that so clearly referenced the Declaration of Independence. When Stanton wrote the "Declaration of Sentiments and Resolutions" as a rewritten Declaration of Independence, she was taking her cue from William Lloyd Garrison's *Liberator,* whose position on the U.S. Constitution as a flawed document was well known. The document also set women's rights outside of the domestic frame into a political one—the first to do so since Mary Wollstonecraft's *Vindication of the Rights of Women.*

But to the press of the time, the declaration was hardly a serious document. As Miriam Gurko finds, subsequent editorials were denunciatory. In one, the convention was "the most shocking and unnatural incident ever recorded in the history of womanity." Greeley's *Tribune* tried to be objective and opened its columns to Stanton's pen. But to Stanton's particular delight, James Gordon Bennett's *New York Herald* printed the entire Declaration of Sentiments—although the purpose was not necessarily to flatter. To Stanton, however, the attention was "just what I wanted. Imagine the publicity given to our ideas by thus appearing in a widely circulated sheet like the *Herald.* It will start women thinking, and men too; and when men and women think about a new question, the first step in progress is taken." Altogether, Stanton was pleased: "There is no danger of the Woman Question dying for want of notice. Every paper you take up has something to say about it."

THE ROLE OF PUBLICITY

Stanton, like twentieth-century feminists, had faith in the mass press, and she also lived in the new age of publicity. Although people have tended to remember Alice Paul's picketing of the White House during World War I as the major propaganda campaign of the suffrage movement, what is clear from the accounts of the yearly conventions collected in the six-volume *History of Woman Suffrage* is that suffrage proponents from the beginning were conscious of the mass press and courted it by increasingly sophisticated means. At the yearly conventions, state organizations reported on the suffrage positions of their local papers, knew women who worked for them, and regularly sent out what would now be called news releases. Although it has come to be a mantra that the mass press uniformly ridiculed suffrage, the *History* increasingly includes many examples of flattering coverage of the yearly conventions by local papers (perhaps written by the women reporters who were profiled in the state reports). Support by the press was considered necessary in the state-by-state campaigns. In the difficult 1867 Kansas campaign, when the American Equal Rights Association sought a referendum for the enfranchisement of African Americans and women, the *History* notes, "The editors of the *New York Tribune* and the *Independent* can never know how wistfully, day to day, their papers were searched for some inspiring edito-

rials." After the movement's split into two wings, press attention was sought by the Anthony–Stanton wing assiduously.
Susan B. Anthony's attempt to vote in 1873, for example, was
a test case that cannot be separated from the national press
attention it engendered. Indeed, in the early years, Anthony
seemed as much a proponent of press attention as Stanton. It
was Anthony who led a six-month campaign in Philadelphia
seeking to connect suffrage with the nation's 1876 centen-
nial. It culminated with efforts aimed at having the Declaration of Sentiments read out loud alongside the reading of the
Declaration of Independence. When an invitation to the
platform did not occur, Anthony and Matilda Josyln Gage
pushed their way through the crowd—"hustling generals
aside, elbowing governors"—to the front to present a scroll
of the Declaration of Sentiments to a bewildered master of
ceremonies. The national press did not ignore the interrup-
tion. The *New York Tribune* considered it "discourteous" and
said it prefigured "new forms of violence and disregard of
order." The *New York Evening Post* was sarcastic. The *Times*
was almost thoughtful: "It is easier to ridicule the woman
suffrage movement than to answer the arguments advanced
by some of the leading advocates of the question." It was
classic agitation propaganda that would be useful in the
Second Wave.

    In its varying forms, organized suffrage from both
wings conducted public relations campaigns as part of overall strategy. Eventually, techniques included suffrage parades,
in-house publications, a press of their own, article writing for
commercial magazines, mailings to newspapers, and instruc-
tions to convention delegates on how to maintain good press
relations. In the 1906 convention, delegates were told the

"golden precepts": "Keep the paper fully informed of all suffrage news. If there is something unpleasant in it and the reporter tells you that the editor and not himself is responsible for it, smile and believe him. Take the reporter into your confidence and let him absorb the impression that you trust him implicitly."

THE CHALLENGES TO DOMESTICITY

The Seneca Falls convention established a tradition of annual meetings that, like the antislavery fairs, were periodic and allowed the women to continue with the duties of the domestic circle. But such conventions did not attract every independent woman, particularly those who were on the fringes of the accepted reform movements of the day. Prompted by strong personalities and outside of definitions of the domestic circle, the outsider women were not shy about proclaiming their own individuality, sometimes with little regard for or consciousness of the commonalities of women. Such women, particularly those who had public voices, posed particular problems for feminists who had been influenced by the antislavery movement that considered domestic life sacrosanct. Organizational feminism, while presenting rhetoric that aimed to speak for all women, had strategic decisions to make about its responses to women who operated in their own spheres. The press corps was eager to make the most of any division.

Women had challenged authority in several fields before the Civil War. This was also the case in the area of journalism; Anne Royall started the first of her two newspapers

in 1831, when she was 61 years old, after an early widow-
hood, subsequent disinheritance, and a writing life that included travel across country by horseback and stagecoach.
Accounts of her, in her time and since, have tended to revolve
on personal characteristics—her quickness to take offense,
her argumentative nature, her "posturing and pretenses," her
favoritism, and her bluntness. She persisted in petitioning
Congress's Pension Bureau for Revolutionary War benefits
connected to her husband. She mounted a campaign against
the "evangelical threat," but when she shouted insults from
her boarding house window at a group going to church in
1829, she ended up in a trial on a charge of being a "common
scold." Later she was named a "public nuisance" and "a common brawler." Nonetheless, she was able to make friends with
John Quincy Adams, and subsequently the characteristics of
persistence and frankness served her well in the "Pen Portraits" of Washington politicians and for the political investigatory functions of her newspaper, *Paul Pry.* That newspaper
financially failed in November 1836, only to be replaced in
December with a second newspaper, the *Huntress,* based on
the same principles of investigation that characterized the
first newspaper. Journalism historian Frank Luther Mott
saw her work as the forerunner of "the modern Washington-
gossip columnist," a characterization that tends to minimize
her work.

Nonetheless, despite the breadth of her interests, the
courage of her style, and the considerable amount of public
criticism she underwent in her life, Royall did not join the
suffrage movement and even railed against dress reform. "Let
men look like themselves, and women look like women."

Her lack of support was not mourned in the women's community. She was rather a warning on the limits of acceptable behavior. At her death, it was the negative aspects that came to be her final summing up. At her death in 1854 at age 86, the *Washington Star* was the only newspaper to note her passing. "To the hour of her death she preserved all the peculiarities of thought, temper and manners which at one time rendered her so famous throughout the land."

While Royall is remembered in terms of "virago," it might be considered that the facts of her life—her travels around the new nation as its storyteller—might easily have been framed heroically, and that her accounts of the new nation, appearing at the same time as Alexis de Tocqueville's vaulted accounts, may have become equally celebrated. But they did not; and, indeed, characteristics that in a male context might have been footnoted, omitted, or even viewed as evidence of power and genius have instead been cast as the major and central detriment in her life story.

Like Royall, Jane Grey Swisshelm was a woman who did not fit easily into organized feminism. She came to feminism by way of the antislavery movement after a stay in the slave state of Kentucky. But as a Conventer, a strand of Presbyterianism, she was outside of the hub of the East Coast, Quaker, and Congregational antislavery establishment. Nonetheless, as had other women of similar leanings, she turned to writing to earn money in difficult times and as a means of protest. When both of the Pittsburgh antislavery newspapers she wrote for ceased publication, Swisshelm began her own abolitionist newspaper, the *Pittsburgh Saturday Visiter.* The newspaper succeeded without affiliation with any of the antislavery organizations of the time, allowing her editorial independence. Later, separating from her husband and taking her daughter with her, she moved to the Midwest and founded another antislavery newspaper in St. Cloud, Minnesota.

Like the Calvinists and Congregationalists, Swisshelm took an absolute position on slavery and wrote in their emotive, denunciatory style. In 1850, observing the debates on Henry Clay's compromise bills on slavery, she wrote to Horace Greeley (for whose paper she was writing a column): "It is very easy for you or any other Northern gentleman to make a bow to a Southern gentleman and in the spirit of the 'most generous compromise' agree that he may tear a mother from her babes and set her upon the auction block to get money to buy a race horse or gold chair, and banish her, forever, from all she had known or loved."

Swisshelm's editorial independence, however, allowed her to take on other issues, including those addressing women—at least, those that Swisshelm supported out of her own life experiences, such as her agitation for reform of property laws that disallowed married women from ownership. In 1840, she had prosecuted and won a suit that gave her the right to receive her share of the money for property left by the death of her mother. She also was separated from her husband (later divorcing him for desertion, although she was the one to leave) and believed in education for women as a guarantee against this possibility.

But her commitment to property rights for married women or education for girls did not lead her to embrace other aspects of the feminist canon. In *Saturday Visiter,* her column, "Letters to Country Girls," advised young country women on issues ranging from behavior and etiquette to hygiene and farming. She could be mocking in tone, and in one column she advised a housewife who was beaten by her husband to be less provoking. Her religious beliefs led her to support plainness for women, and, despite the courage of her own life, she believed that women were essentially frail and needed to be protected. Writing in her autobiography late in life, she said, "My glory is in the distinctions of sex; we should rather be whipped or traded off than be deprived of the protection and attention we claim in right of our sex." In women's matters, she urged reform only: "Take away legal difficulties little by little, as experience should show was unwise, but never dream of doing the world's hard work, whether mental or physical; and heaven defend them from going into all trades."

She clearly exasperated Stanton, who, in 1850, let her frustration flood: "She seems to think that the All-wise did not give us a complete outfit for the voyage of life—that there are foes to be subdued and dangers to be encountered, which we have no will or muscle to meet, and no charge of compass to guide us."

It speaks to the strength of the image of the virago that Swisshelm and Royall routinely are remembered in journalism history while Mary Clemmer Ames is not. Ames, however, began a writing career in 1859 as a contributing editor to small papers. By 1866, she was writing the "Woman's Letter from Washington" for the influential religious weekly, *New York Independent,* and then for Brooklyn's *Daily Union.* She refused to use pen names for her work, the practice of the time. She argued, however, that women were of a higher moral fiber than men and thus were ideal for the job of observing political leadership. She gathered material from her large number of male contacts, but also by sitting in Congress's woman's gallery so she would not seem to ape male behavior by sitting in the reporter's section. Such a decision was an early indicator of the complex understanding of self developed by women journalists of the time—arguing change for women as they sought to maintain difference.

FOUR

THE STRAINS ON SISTERHOOD

In the Second Wave, feminists pioneered what was called "consciousness raising," the idea that women had first to acknowledge the reality of their status before change could occur. Early in the suffrage movement, organizers faced the same problems. Even women who had worked in antislavery did not automatically transfer their efforts to suffrage. As Martha Solomon notes, "The transition from public activity in behalf of others to work in their own interests was difficult. Most women only reluctantly acknowledged their own oppression." Suffrage publications became important in building a movement, which not all women agreed was necessary.

In the separate and private space offered by suffrage publications, away from dominant ideology or fear of ridicule, women could explore questions of women's rights and, importantly, build community. Linda Steiner finds that suffrage publications "identified, legitimized, and sustained a community of *new* women," that is, women who were seeking to go beyond constructions of their gender by outside forces. "Suffrage papers," she writes, "articulated new values, suggested new dreams and provided new perspectives on women's experiences, in the effort to evolve a new definition of womanhood and to carve out a new social order." The Female Moral Reform Society considered joining the suffrage movement but eventually declined, not only in fear that its own focus would be submerged in a larger agenda, but that it would lose the considerable role its newspaper played in providing a "safe house," a virtual home for its scattered readership that offered a place where women could express their most private thoughts in a supportive environment. In the same way, suffrage publications not only functioned in the necessary work of organizing, but also served other expectations, including social ones, reflecting the personality and outlook of the editor and the subscribers she attracted.

However, the tendency of women's publications to propose different versions of feminism as they served a wide range of support functions posed difficulty for the formal parts of the movement that was constructing itself along political goals. Ideas could conflict; the lack of a well-funded major organization put power in the hands of editors who were only loosely associated; and the expression of conflicting views in a public forum—no matter how private its contributors considered it—allowed the mainstream press to interpret discussion as division. These may be characteristics that occur in the development of all new movements, but it is a chapter that can have repercussions for the political goals that formal organizations seek.

Moreover, in the post–Civil War era, Elizabeth Cady Stanton and Susan B. Anthony were operating on the national stage with few supports. The movement was further strained by the introduction of an alternative newspaper that only loosely followed the sisterhood model in favor of a personal campaign that was associated with women's rights but not defined by it. This was *Woodhull and Claflin's Weekly,* which had as its aim to make Victoria Woodhull the first woman president of the United States. The newspaper's association with the seamy side of major figures of the time and Woodhull's iconoclastic standards caused dissension and defensiveness in the feminist community, played up stereotypes, and, despite its color and energy, served as a diversion and, probably, an impediment to the eventual goals of the movement. Despite Woodhull's early embrace by the mass press, the explication of her ideas in ever-enlarging forums did not serve to move the general audience toward their acceptance but rather fixed her as a warning example. Moreover, the suffrage movement already had plenty of dissension.

By the conclusion of the Civil War, women had been involved in nursing, spying, organizing, and lecturing. Mary Livermore, for example, helped raise substantial amounts of money during the Civil War as part of the U.S. Sanitary Commission and worked closely with Mary Ann Bickerdyke, chief of nursing under the command of General Ulysses S. Grant, the U.S. president who perhaps more than any other before him allowed women participation in a war. Women's contributions in the Civil War included the founding of a new women's league devoted to the collection of signatures—some 400,000 at the final count—on a Congressional petition on behalf of the Thirteenth Amendment. The Sanitary Commission, providing hospital and medical services, similarly brought Northern women together in war work (and finally provided some authority for the nation's first physician, Dr. Elizabeth Blackwell) that developed organizational skills and introduced women to national actions. In the case of Livermore, it was seeing women in war work that turned her into a feminist activist. "Knowing, then, the qualities of woman and her courage and bravery under trials, I can never cease to demand that she have just as large a sphere as man has."

Less clear is whether that service moved women forward in their fight for parity or whether it actually served to emphasize a return to the home after war, as it did after the American Revolution and postwar World War II. Two researchers suggest that images of women in Civil War newspapers indicated that women's wartime work "heightened visibility and appreciation for what they could contribute outside the home." The researchers also note that the most frequent image of women in news coverage during the war was "ornamental," providing support and cheerfulness. Also to be considered is a survey of advertisements during the war in which women "were overwhelmingly cast in domestic roles."

What the war certainly accomplished was to move attention from the political questions of woman's rights under discussion in the prewar press. While a number of publications such as Elizabeth Aldrich's *Genius of Liberty* in Cincinnati had addressed woman's rights as part of their overall reform attention, researchers note three other prewar newspapers connected to the women's rights movement: *Pioneer and Woman's Advocate* in Providence, Rhode Island, published by Anna W. Spencer, argued for education and labor reforms; Amelia Bloomer's *The Lily* moved from temperance to women's rights when it "confronted women with their own powerlessness." *The Una,* of Providence, Rhode Island, was published by Pauline Wright Davis and is notable because of its efforts to include concerns of working and immigrant women, and indeed to recruit them as readers. However, just one suffrage newspaper, the *Mayflower,* printed and published by Lizzie Bunnel in Indiana, maintained publication through three years of the Civil War. Janet Cramer found that women as equal to men was its most frequent focus while the antebellum images of women confined to the domestic sphere were rejected. However, the newspaper failed, a combination of wartime economy and women's attention to the war. Bunnel predicted that the women's service in the war would not matter in the end. "The fact is men have rather more than got their hands full with this war and they welcome woman as a powerful and generous ally [but] . . when they are done with us, they will turn us over to our former occupations and abuse us just as handsomely as ever."

Her prediction was true. Postwar editors picked up the cry of the earlier editorials—postwar suffrage was "meaningless and foolish"; efforts on its behalf were to "vote and hustle with the rowdies of the polls." Negative perceptions translated into visual images. When Susan B. Anthony's sketch appeared in *Harper's* in connection with her arrest at a voting booth in 1873, it was with the downturned mouth and unbending visage that has come to be her major visual representation. At a time when visual imagery was coming into power—even Abraham Lincoln had made regular visits to the portrait studio of Mathew Brady—Anthony's image was predictive. A later recollection of her noted, "Forty years ago, Miss Anthony was described as a sort of virago and man-hater."

The camaraderie of abolitionists and the women's rights groups of the war years ended in reactions to a proposed Fifteenth Amendment to the U.S. Constitution that made it clear voting rights were to be extended to males, including the newly freed slaves, but not to females. Anthony and Stanton's group believed if women could not ride into enfranchisement alongside the former slaves, the opportunity would be lost—for a hundred years, Stanton thought. The group most associated with former antislavery activists saw the Fourteenth Amendment as "the Negroes' Hour." The final split occurred when the Radical Republicans, including their female supporters, seeking to pass a Fifteenth Amendment, chose to exclude women. It became clear that the antislavery advocates had accepted women's issues as an addendum to the antislavery fight, not as a bargain.

As the rift deepened, Anthony accepted financial support from a questionable source, George Francis Train, who was rumored to have supported the South in the war. The shock of the reform community that Anthony would accept Train's contribution gives evidence to the notion that women's behavior had no room for expediency even in a political fight. The money went to underwrite the reform publication of *The Revolution* as the organ of the Stanton/Anthony views. Here, Stanton and Anthony expressed views, some of which contributed to feminism's racial polarity. Stanton could argue in problematical terms: "Think of Patrick and Sambo and Hans and Yung Tung who do not know the difference between a Monarchy and a Republic, who never read the Declaration of Independence or Webster's spelling book, making laws for Lydia Maria Child, Lucretia Mott, or Fanny Kemble." Anthony was rhetorical and angry: "I will cut off caution: this right arm of mine before I will ever work for or demand the ballot for the negro and not the woman," she argued early in her newspaper's run.

Stanton was no less angry when the former abolitionist Gerrit Smith did not sign a petition for the enfranchisement of women on the basis that it did not also call for "the removal of the political disabilities of the Negro man." In a newspaper tirade, Stanton took her former colleagues to task, charging that white male suffrage had not led to the protection of white (or "Saxon") women any more than black male suffrage could be expected to protect black women. But she was on treacherous ground that called on stereotypes in one example, pointing to the case of a 14-year-old girl who had been charged with infanticide in the death of a child born as a result of a rape by a black farm worker. She compared it to a similar case of infanticide charges connected to a white father to make her point that men, black or white, were the danger, not vulnerable girls. "Society, as organized to-day under the man power, is one grand rape of womanhood, on the highways, in our jails, prisons, asylums, in our homes, alike in the world of fashion and of work." Universal suffrage, she argued—that is, black and female suffrage linked— offered the most practical promise for the passage of voting rights for both: "Although those who demand 'Woman's Suffrage' on principal [sic] are few, those who would oppose 'Negro suffrage' from prejudice are many, hence the only way to secure the latter is to end all this talk of class legislation, bury the negro in the citizen, and claim the suffrage for all men and women, as a natural, inalienable right."

Stanton was not laying out any new territory in the article. The question of color was part of Stanton's 1860 address to the New York state legislature on the pending bill for female suffrage. The prejudice against gender, she told the assembly, was as strong, if not stronger, than that against color. "The Negro's skin and the woman's sex are both prima facie evidence that they were intended to be in subjection to the white Saxon man." Similarly, men had never been the protectors of women—and it was hypocritical to argue that women should not be subjected to the jostle of the polls "when alone in the darkness and solitude and gloom of night," she wrote, slipping into the affective rhetoric of the temperance movement, "she has trembled on her own threshold awaiting the return of a husband from his midnight revels."

However, the split with former abolitionist comrades was irreconcilable, and it led Stanton and Anthony to use *The Revolution* not only to challenge their former friends on the subject of suffrage but to set out a philosophy in which women alone would be its focus. The masthead called for "Men their rights and nothing more; women their rights and nothing less," a sentiment put even more strongly in the proclamation from its editors: "While we would not refuse man an occasional word in our columns, yet as masculine ideas have ruled the race for six thousand years, we especially desire that *The Revolution* shall be the mouth piece for women." In their paper's short history, Anthony and Stanton addressed the spectrum of issues related to female discrimination: low wages of working women, the economics of prostitution, marriage and sexuality—indeed, many issues that had not been addressed frankly in the prewar period because of the influence of the male abolitionists, who had argued that issues related to marriage affected both sexes and should not be included on a women's rights platform alone. As Bonnie J. Dow finds, "*The Revolution* was different because its editors did not conform to politically popular or expedient positions by pursuing their objectives; instead, the journal reflected the uncompromising and often controversial ideas of its creators." Although the later postwar women's movement would become known for its sole emphasis on women's suffrage, in the first years of the period Stanton and Anthony addressed the substratum of the domestic circle and its intersections across class lines. It was Susan Anthony who in 1868 founded an organization that sought to bring together feminism and trade unionism. And it was Elizabeth Stanton who discussed the sexuality of the marriage bed and analyzed the exploitation of women in marriage as she argued for more liberalized divorce laws. These were approaches consistent with the uses of an alternative press, although, as Steiner notes, the inconsistency of their discussion brought about attacks and damaged the aim of the newspaper's recruiting goals. "*Revolution*'s editors wished to attract and organize a national or even international audience. To the extent that they achieved this 'publicity,' however, they sacrificed opportunities for private rehearsal.... Hostile critics gleefully pounced on each indication of inconsistency and discord."

POSTWAR SUFFRAGE NEWSPAPERS

In 1870, another single-focus suffrage publication appeared, *The Woman's Journal,* edited by Lucy Stone and representing the American Woman Suffrage Association. Rather remarkably, given its visual representations of feminism, *Harper's*

Weekly gave the *Journal* high marks, noting the paper's single-mindedness with approval: "The *Woman's Journal* is a fair and attractive paper in appearance; while the variety and spirit of its articles, and the dignity, self-respect, good-humor, and earnestness of its tone, will show how profoundly mistaken are those who suppose that folly and extravagance are necessarily characteristic of the discussion of the question." The Boston press was particularly sympathetic to its homegrown feminism. Boston's *Transcript* (itself once published by a woman), in a reference to the still-publishing *Revolution,* saw the *Journal* as the appropriate choice: The new paper was "to be positive and progressive rather than controversial and complaining."

Established as a joint-stock company, with men included, the *Journal* seemingly had a stronger financial basis than Anthony's paper with its reliance on the vagaries of Train. However, in 1889, Lucy Stone wrote to her daughter, "The *Woman's Journal* money was never so low as it is now." Indeed, the newspaper struggled for many years. Nonetheless, the *Journal* was the longest-running of the suffrage newspapers and, to some, it was the "voice" of suffrage. It early collapsed at least two existing newspapers into it, including Mary's Livermore's *Agitator,* as it drew Livermore to the editorial chair. Its main goal was that of suffrage in the belief that once the ballot was obtained "all the blessings of the subsidiary goals of social, economic and educational equality would flow." Although the ballot was to be the ultimate solution for a panoply of injustices against women, the argument for the vote included the specificity of the ills it would cure—laws that permitted men to beat women, prohibitions on women's ability to own property and to serve as guardians of their children in marital disputes, and many others. The *Journal,* even as the conservative sister, still urged reform across many platforms—prostitution, bigamy, rape, proper care of infants and children, abortion, factory work, equal pay for equal work, advances in the professions. Local enfranchisement was the place to start, and the *Journal* kept abreast of the nation's changing laws. But suffrage was the underlying need, and the *Journal* took on the responsibility of educating its readers in the process of laws, the circulation of petitions, the process of door-to-door canvassing—a directive tone that was not out of place in a commercial print culture that consistently provided advice for women. Like Anthony and Stanton, Lucy Stone was not unaware of public presence, once producing a celebration of the Boston Tea Party as an event to bring attention to female suffrage. Interestingly, Stone's daughter, Alice Stone Blackwell, and Stanton's daughter, Harriot Stanton Blatch, both became active suffragists and both put much of their efforts into press relations.

All suffrage newspapers struggled for readers and financial support. Pleas for payment were often a theme in most small newspapers of the time, but the woman's press was additionally hampered by the fact that the women subscribers usually had no independent income. Abigail Scott Duniway of Oregon's *New Northwest* got involved in a running battle with the husband of a reader who would not pay the subscription. Duniway sent him a bundle of the papers with a reprimanding note meant to chastise him into payment; the husband sent them back COD. Duniway sued the postmaster. The postmaster's son, editor of another publication, had the final word, publishing a slander against her that caused yet another contretemps. Duniway also tried less confrontational tactics; she was a widow with children to support. Another paper, *Woman's Standard,* told readers that those who did not pay would not find a place in heaven.

To succeed, the founder/editors had to have a driving force: Duniway of the *New Northwest,* Livermore at *The Agitator* and *The Woman's Journal,* and Clara Bewick Colby of *The Woman's Tribune* had to have the passion and personality to attract writers, editors, and office workers at little or no pay. Not surprisingly, the force of their personalities was not left at the composing stick. Suffrage positions were not consistent, which, in the case of Colby and Duniway, led to a feud that began over differing views on temperance. Duniway referred to Colby as one of "the self-imported Eastern Suffragists"; Colby sought to unseat Duniway from her organizational position.

Colby took over the *Tribune* when the state suffrage organization in Nebraska could no longer support it. She moved it to Washington state and Portland, Oregon, and the personal responsibility she had for the paper strengthened her editorial hand. She shaped the newspaper along lines of general news, as she saw it, and reportage of suffrage news in a personal voice aimed to give her readers who were not in leadership circles a first-row seat. But her emphasis on expanding her readers' horizons brought a rebuke from Anthony. "You must realize that the *Tribune* as managed of late years, carries but very little for even the most earnest suffrage women. All that you put in it about the mysteries of Eastern religions, the reform dress, etc., etc. you could just as well get into the daily papers and it would go to a great many more people who really need it. Our suffrage women get enough of all that in their ordinary papers, and don't wish to pay a

separate woman's paper merely to have that kind of reading."
Still, all the suffrage papers put together would not challenge
Anthony as much as *Woodhull and Claflin's Weekly*.

WOODHULL & CLAFLIN'S WEEKLY

Many of the ideas of Stanton and Anthony in this period
were not so different from those of Victoria Woodhull, who
with her sister, Tennessee Claflin, established *Woodhull &
Claflin's Weekly*. The newspaper was established as part of
Woodhull's campaign strategy that led her to announce herself as a candidate for the 1872 presidential election. But her
"free love" position, a seemingly chaotic private life, her
early history as a medical clairvoyant, the mentorship she
and her sister received from famous and wealthy men, and
two very public trials were among a long list that troubled
suffrage leaders, including Stanton, an early advocate, who
almost entirely wrote Woodhull out of the first formal feminist history.

Woodhull did not come to feminism by abolitionism,
temperance, or reform in general, but by a challenge to the
gender order of the time, as a gold speculator in 1869. Her
financial wizardry on "Black Friday," which made her a millionaire; the novelty of a stock brokerage firm operated by
women; and the sisters' relationship with the powerful Cor-
nelius Vanderbilt came to the attention of the *New York Herald* in a favorable, even flowery article. What followed were
weeks of publicity for the "queens of finance," the "bewitch-
ing brokers," and the "female sovereigns of Wall Street." Visits
to their new offices, including one by Walt Whitman, received press notice. The sisters continued to polish their im-

ages, inviting Whitelaw Reid and other journalists to their evening soirees where they dazzled, charmed, and captivated all who attended. The attention brought the sisters to the notice of the suffrage leadership. Anthony on behalf of her newspaper arrived on the firm's doorstep for her own interview. Two favorable articles appeared, the second even more fulsome than the first: "The new firm Mesdames Woodhull, Claflin & Co., who have made such a sensation in Wall Street [will] stimulate the whole future of women by their efforts and example. They are full of pluck, energy and enterprise and are withal most prepossessing in personal appearance, in manners, and ladylike deportment; moreover, they know what they are about and are calculated to inspire confidence by the sound sense, judgment and clear-sightedness they show in financial matters."

For Woodhull, financial fame was simply a first step in her presidential campaign, which she announced by way of a letter to the *Herald,* arguing her already successful career as a stockbroker indicated that she was an individual of action. "While others argued the equality of woman with man, I proved it successfully engaging in business; while others sought to show there was no valid reason why women should be treated, socially and politically, as being inferior to man, I boldly entered the area of politics and business and exercised the rights I already possessed." The *Herald*—a sense of mentorship and discovery undoubtedly part of the reason— responded affirmatively. It urged women to vote for Woodhull—to show their might "independent of any of these petty organizations," presumably the suffrage groups. The contents of the subsequent *Woodhull & Claflin's Weekly* were often written by her circle of male admirers, but it was

Woodhull's voice that called for education for women, economic parity between the sexes, prostitution as an economic issue for women, women as medical workers, women exploited by dangerous beauty products such as hair dye, and the necessity for all women to know the issues of the world in order to be good wives. She also followed the activities of women lecturers, turned her newspaper into an early muckraking journal as well as covering arts and poetry and financial news. In some ways the *Weekly* continued the focus of *The Revolution,* which had failed by 1870, putting Anthony personally in debt for $10,000. In contrast, the success of the Woodhull newspaper was remarkable. Frederick Hudson, in the first modern history of American journalism, summed it up in 1873: "a 16-page paper published by two sisters who seem capable of accomplishing what they undertake."

The *Weekly* provided an account of Woodhull's political maneuvering as she moved from the belief that a Sixteenth Amendment for women's suffrage could be achieved (the proposal remained in committee) to a strategy that claimed that the language of the Fourteenth and Fifteenth Amendments to the Constitution, in which citizenship is described as by birth or naturalization, should be interpreted to include women. A congressional act or judicial pronouncement of such an interpretation obviated the need for an additional constitutional amendment that had been the focus of suffrage. Although the notion had been proposed before without much support from the suffrage organizations, Woodhull, who had charmed Anthony as much as anyone, brought Anthony's organization to the cause.

Under the guidance of the powerful General Benjamin Butler, a member of the U.S. House of Representatives from

Massachusetts and a member of the House Judiciary Committee, Woodhull received permission to present the argument to the committee in person at the same time the suffrage convention was meeting in Washington, in January 1871. The morning suffrage session was cancelled so women could attend the hearing. Anthony made special arrangements. Newspaper reporters had been invited. At the age of 32, Woodhull made a ringing and charismatic call for female enfranchisement.

The *Herald* and the *Tribune* gave her credit. "There is no disguising the fact that the women suffrage advocates are making headway in Washington." Greeley's *Tribune* noted, "All the past efforts of Miss Anthony and Mrs. Stanton sink to insignificance beside the ingenious lobbying of the new leader and her daring declaration." A personal audience with President Grant suggested hope that he would bring pressure on the committee for a favorable response. He did not; the committee's majority report was negative. Woodhull gave the anti-Grant *New York Sun* an interview that called his administration "weak and corrupt."

But the new approach had energized the suffrage movement and placed Woodhull at the cynosure of press attention. She rented the largest hall in Washington and filled it. Suffrage leaders shared the stage, grateful for the energy, attention, and finances she brought to the cause. Her lecture was considered a great success. Press reports were close to adoring, and Stanton wrote to her: "We have waited 6,000 years, and the time has fully come to seize the bull by the horns, as you are now doing in Washington and Wall Street." The *Herald* remained Woodhull's friend: "She seems to be the head and front of the movement now, having pushed the oth-

ers aside, who never could manage to stir up public enthusiasm and enlist prominent politicians in the cause as Mrs.
Woodhull has done."

But Woodhull and the *Weekly* were also representing
other aspects of reform that Stanton, for one, had long cham-
pioned. "I read your journal with great pleasure," Stanton
wrote. "It is the ablest women's journal we have yet had, discussing, as it does, the great questions of national life." And
Stanton sought to stem the gossip about Woodhull's private
life: "Women have crucified the Mary Wollstonecrafts, the
Fanny Wrights, the George Sands, the Fanny Kembles of all
ages, and now men mock us with the fact, and say we are ever
cruel to each other. Let us end this ignoble record and hence-
forth stand by womanhood. If Victoria Woodhull must be
crucified, let men drive the spikes and plait the crown of
thorns."

It was not men who drove the spikes but two sisters,
Catherine Beecher and Harriet Beecher Stowe. (A third sister, Isabel Beecher, stood by Woodhull until the end.) Offended by her sexual mores and defensive of the rumors that
circulated about their brother, the Beecher sisters conducted
a campaign of their own. Stowe, in fact, mocked Woodhull in
her novel, *My Wife and I,* which appeared as a serial in *Christian Union.*

Meantime, Woodhull brought modern sensibilities of
campaigning to her effort, seeking out the approval of the
elite leaders while building grassroots support through her
Victoria Leagues. At the convention, she was surrounded by
the suffrage leaders she had courted, although not from the
Boston group. In a fiery speech she called for a reform platform for women beyond suffrage, concluding with the same

fire as a familiar Garrisonian abolitionist: "We mean treason; we mean secession. We will overslaught this bogus republic and plant a government that derives its power from the due consent of the governed." The delegates called it the "Great Secession Speech." Once again the New York press applauded.

The Bostonian suffrage wing, represented by Lucy Stone and supporter of *The Woman's Journal,* had long regarded the Woodhull household arrangements as being close to a menagerie. Their opinion seemed to be supported when in May 1871 Woodhull's mother sued Woodhull's husband for alienation of affection. The ensuing trial revealed Woodhull may or may not have been officially married, disclosed previous and ongoing lovers, and described a household that included the alcoholic ex-husband, late-night male visitors, and two children (one mentally disabled) amid the coming and going of the clan's various relatives. As the trial unfolded, Stowe put it all in her serialized novel. The tide of public opinion shifted. Horace Greeley returned to his original position against suffrage on the basis that "my conception of the nature of the marriage relation renders my conversion to woman suffrage a moral impossibility." The *Weekly* responded less stuffily, by claiming Greeley's own home was a "domestic hell." Woodhull then sent her defense to the *New York Times,* claiming there was a double sexual standard for men and women, a veiled reference to Boston's Rev. Henry Ward Beecher, which provoked another noisy episode. But her public defense led female supporters to return to her.

The episode encouraged Woodhull's interest in putting together supporters across the various platforms her newspaper represented, including her spiritualist base and labor reformers, to establish a new national reform party, the Equal Rights Party, which would nominate her for president of the United States. Stanton was in favor of the new thrust, but not Anthony, who directly (by turning off the gas at a suffrage meeting at one point) discouraged suffrage involvement in the new party's convention.

Woodhull was clearly aware that her lectures on sexual emancipation for women were popular and brought press coverage. Her speeches increasingly included the subject, in part to ensure profitable tours. However, the real line she crossed was to align herself with labor. The *Weekly* had been the first U.S. periodical to publish Karl Marx's "Manifesto." It is to be noted that *Harper's* published Thomas Nash's cruel cartoon of Woodhull as "Madame Satan" not as a result of her lectures on sexual freedom but when it was clear her alliance was with the International Labor Party. A harassment campaign began; loans were called; she was evicted from her house. The press attacked. Although at one point ill enough to be thought dead (the narrative of her life often parallels the era's sentimental fiction), Woodhull rallied her paper to expose what had been the object of gossip—the adulterous affair Henry Ward Beecher, the nation's most famous preacher and president of the rival suffrage organization, had conducted with the wife of his confidante and associate, Thomas Tilton. Woodhull herself had had an affair with both. Tilton, however, had come to acknowledge Woodhull and her politics while Beecher refused to publicly acknowledge her in any way.

The *Weekly* sold 100,000 copies with the story, although it was not reprinted in one mainstream paper. And more chapters were to come. Shortly after its publication,

Woodhull, her sister, and her husband, managing editor of the paper, were arrested on federal obscenity charges. New York's moral crusader, Anthony Comstock, ensured the federal charge by sending the paper to himself through the mail to comply with the letter of the law. The sisters were thought dangerous enough to be jailed to await trial while the other sisters, the Beechers, continued their defamation campaign: Woodhull was no more than a common blackmailer and "insane" to boot. Woodhull's letter of protestation to the newspapers, once so adoring, that had published the Beecher tirade, was rejected, while the Beecher attack was reprinted throughout the country. She turned to the *Weekly* to present her own account. Despite her defense, the upcoming suffrage convention did not invite her to speak.

In June of 1873, a judge exonerated all three. *The Sun,* which had not raised its voice during the episode, apologized: "For the wrong which has been done to these women, they have no redress. The injury is irremediable."

By that time the 1872 election was concluded— Stanton and Anthony having supported Grant and the Republican Party, which promised "respectful attention" to women's issues in its party platform—Anthony believed progress had been made, but not Stanton. "I do not feel jubilant over the situation," she wrote to Anthony. "In fact, I never was so blue in my life." The Republicans lost even respectful interest in the women's movement after the U.S. Supreme Court ruled in 1875 that suffrage was not a right of national citizenship but a privilege granted by states. Comstock later had a New York obscenity law named after him and, as Woodhull predicted, it became a tool for the suppression of a wide range of reforms. Stanton let it be known that Woodhull's version of the Tilton/Beecher affair was accurate but remained cautious about too close a connection with her.

Woodhull returned to the lecture circuit in the spiritualist circles from which she had emerged, again on the subject of sexual emancipation. She could, as her major biographer, Lois Beachy Underhill, noted, "still sell out the house." Finances improved, but the *Weekly* was finally closed for good in 1876. Woodhull and her husband divorced. Still, the Woodhull story had more to come. Woodhull, her sister, and the extended family moved to Great Britain, where the sisters married wealthy and well-connected men in what were by all accounts matches of affection. Woodhull lived as a lady of the manor into a generous old age. Her participation in the suffrage wars of the post–Civil War era was soon forgotten.

What are we to make of the rise and fall of Victoria Woodhull, the role of the press, and Woodhull's interactions with suffrage feminism? Was she simply a bizarre side story in the world of American politics (a not so unusual tale for third-party candidates in any U.S. election, even to present times)?

Woodhull put into relief Anthony's decision, after the break with the abolitionists, not to align woman's rights with other groups. Anthony prevailed over Stanton's early belief that the suffrage movement could be built with political partners from the reform parties whose politics grew from the same root. By the time Anthony had reconceived that position, and, indeed, sought to unite suffrage with the powerful temperance and club movements, she was joining hands with political philosophies far more conservative than those she and Stanton had expressed in *The Revolution*.

Clearly, Woodhull was author of her own personae and

conscious manipulator of the press of the time. Her own publication served her well. She utilized it to maintain her standing in the reform community and as a corrective device when she was manhandled in the mass press. In the Tilton/Beecher affair, she turned the paper into a weapon of attack and a voice in her own defense. But social movements continue to struggle with issues that Woodhull brought to the forefront—including those of allowing leadership to accrue to the charismatic individual who is the choice of the mass press; the ease with which the mass press can give and retract support; and the role of reform publications in the discussion of ideas and policy.

For Victoria Woodhull and Tennessee Claflin, the split in the movement positioned the Lucy Stone wing as morally superior to the Stanton/Anthony wing, encouraging arguments for reform on the role of women as moral leaders. Woodhull and Claflin excoriated the Bostonians in their newspaper: "Then [before the split into two organizations] Mrs. Stanton and Miss Anthony were good women and true. Now they are not fit for the excellent Bostonians to mingle with at all; they will have nothing to do with anything either of these ladies associated with." Mary Livermore, they pointed out, the new editor of *Woman's Journal,* eschewed support from those "that hold more advanced social ideas than are considered admissible by the clique of which she is chief." Indeed, they were "not even to be permitted to so much as approach the platform upon which 'the immaculates' stand." Livermore "has contracted the disease of respectability and can abuse as vilely as the most pious of former times."

Respectability, indeed, was at every turn.

FIVE

DOMESTICITY AND ALL ITS IMPERATIVES

What Victoria Woodhull identified was the new importance of Victorian respectability permeating the postwar world. While it ostensibly was based on the role of piety as the undergirding principle of women's role in the home, respectability functioned as an ordering device for an industrialized and divided postwar world. Respectability was not simply about maintaining social position, but rather signaled an orderly and acceptable way for movement toward a change in status. Respectability did not have to be a closed door in American society, but might even be acquired. The burgeoning mass media world was pleased to offer directions.

The press and the new magazines provided a national chorus to the notion that woman's role was to be the chief keeper of the family circle. As it was newly interpreted, that meant women were to be shoppers, consumers for the goods that industry produced in great abundance and that, thanks to an expanded rail system, could be distributed across the nation. In this industrial world of exploding consumer choices, the job of the housewife was to be a kind of chief financial officer for the home, buying the products that would serve the domestic sphere. Not only did this provide new markets, purchase promoted an orderly society. Consumption offered workers immediate rewards for their day-to-day work, put attention on their own well-being rather than the problems of the rest of society, and provided definitions that were already in the culture and easy to accommodate.

THE STRENGTH OF THE DOMESTIC CIRCLE

As early as 1854, the single Susan B. Anthony saw the impending strength of the domestic circle as a new absolute, noting that a male lecturer on "Home Life" had remarked, "'It is here in the home that *most* men and *all* women's chiefest duties lie.'" Twenty years later, Philadelphia's *North American* intoned, to no one's objections: "Public opinion has perseveringly set up the home of the domestic circle as the chief object to be provided for, looked after, cared for and rendered comfortable, pleasant and attractive." Indeed, after the 1870s, arguing for reform outside of the family circle seemed increasingly difficult. Elizabeth Cady Stanton's lectures on liberalized divorce laws were reargued on the basis that the sacred responsibility of motherhood was jeopardized by unhappy marriages. The temperance campaign, once a tent that included woman's rights, drew adherents on the basis of the dangers to the domestic circle of drinking, and prompted emotional campaigns of victimized women and children that rivaled the emotionality of antislavery rhetoric. The new political initiatives that flooded the country in the second half of the century—unionism, socialism, anarchism, and Marxism—were not so likely to make it to the national stage when portrayed as destroyers of the family, which was increasingly conflated with the ideology of the nation itself.

However, the radicalism that existed just behind the scrim of respectability provided no outpost for women's rights. Although "the bourgeoisie" was despised in radical circles, radical politics were slow to take on women's labor concerns, much less women's rights. Socialist men promoted a culture of "manliness" in male-only clubhouses and the construction of solidarity by way of brotherhood. The German radical writer August Bebel warned in 1883 that poorly paid working women were destructive to working women's family lives, but the answer was not "to banish woman back to the house and hearth, as our 'domestic life' fanatics prescribe . . . but . . . to lead woman out of the narrow sphere of strictly domestic life to full participation in the public life of the people." These were not words taken to heart by socialist newspapers. The women's page of the most successful of the socialist papers, the *Milwaukee Leader,* did not differ remarkably from the same section in the mainstream *Milwaukee Journal.* Outside of the radical communities, the immigrant men who filled the labor needs of the industrial machine similarly operated in masculine worlds, and they expected women to operate in theirs. The religious and foreign-language presses that served the groups were not organs for domestic rearrangements, but were committed to maintaining ethics, values, and usefulness.

Women themselves adopted the culture of domesticity in varying degrees, but most often in terms of the larger service to the home. Although often derided, women's affiliations in women's clubs, garden clubs, and reform organizations were not so much about promoting women in the home as women's role in the larger world. Josephine St. Pierre Ruffin, for example, established the National Association of Colored Women, linking thousands of middle-class black women. Ruffin used her publication, *Woman's Era,* to showcase the strength of African American women and, as Rodger Streitmatter notes, "encouraged her readers to break out of the traditional women's share to become knowledgeable about public affairs issues." Similarly, the General Federation of Women's Clubs and the Women's Christian Temperance Union, which both eventually adopted suffrage, were most about what became known as "moral housekeeping," extending republican values to society at large through very practical efforts of housing and factory reforms.

Reform activity by way of women's clubs was conducted amidst a media campaign that sought to portray women's clubs as meddling, its members grim and masculine-appearing, and their unfortunate husbands as Milquetoasts in their thrall. An 1893 cartoon featured a man with a nose ring and chain being led by a woman, with the caption, "The wedding ring, as Sorosis [a women's club] would like to see it worn." Such images reappeared in the 1970s with the rebirth of feminism. But from 1889 to 1919, Edward Bok, editor of *Ladies' Home Journal,* unremittingly campaigned against women's clubs as part of his general opposition to women's suffrage. He particularly ridiculed club study programs, saying "to inculcate the love of the beautiful and pride of the home in the mind of the young is far more important than ... what Caesar did."

He could also have said that study clubs did not inculcate consumption. The *Journal*'s publisher, however, was clear. Cyrus H. K. Curtis asked a group of manufacturers: "Do you know why we publish the *Ladies' Home Journal?* The real reason, the publisher's reason, is to give you people who manufacture things the American women want and buy a chance to tell them about your products." The promotion of domestic ideology that did inculcate consumption was most useful in varying male centers of power, none more important than the politicians and capitalists of the late century. While capitalists sought immigrants to fill the labor needs of the industrialized nation, both capitalists and their politicians feared the ideas they brought with them. Newspapers and women's magazines played an important role in emphasizing virtues that were helpful to the running of the industrial machine. Mass media found their most useful contribution to the stability of the nation was in shaping demands. This kind of journalism had ramifications for the presentation of women in the popular press and how women would perceive themselves in the culture; and, while the emphasis on the home prepared the way for women journalists, women journalists were faced with the incongruity of writing about the home from outside it.

The home gained its authority from its connections to a certain kind of Protestant domestic virtue, representing, as Colleen McDannell says, "larger visions of morality, aesthetic, class and civilization." Homes became symbolic even in their design and layout, constructed to emphasize what were considered the separate needs of the family, with specialized spaces for each of the activities supposedly appropriate for men, women, and children. Indeed, *Ladies' Home Journal* even supplied examples of approved houses and sold architectural plans as one of its services. "Home" carried both instrumentalist and metaphoric meanings in Victorian America but certainly was less connected to the geography of where you came from than as a place that could be "established." For a price, Victorians could purchase a structure that embodied the respectability of the time and furnish it in ways that evidenced their commitment. Home may have been in the heart, but it was surely in the pocketbook.

ADVERTISING AND ITS MESSAGES

Fueled by industrialization, transportation, and an advertising industry that promoted its goods in ways that resonated in the culture, money spent on U.S. advertising increased tenfold in the years between 1870 and 1900. By the postwar period, city newspapers had become major contributors to the advertising industry, thanks to new audiences supplied by city populations and the need to reach them by the makers of industrialized goods. Joseph Pulitzer is credited with establishing women's sections to provide the demographically desired audience for the new advertisers. Although the women's sections appeared at a time of women's involvement in reform, they emphasized fashion, and only later club news as women were hired for the new departments. Pulitzer took the editorial content one step further when he consciously placed particular advertisements next to relevant copy and sketches of the latest ready-to-wear advertisements and pointed out where the garments written about could be purchased.

It was the department stores, however, that would be most influential in cementing the shopping woman into the national consciousness. Like the shopping experience itself, advertising messages from department stores promoted women's role in the domestic circle as a separate and special function of her gender.

Scholars of American consumption vary in their interpretations of the stores—were they simply new ways to manipulate women consumers, as Stuart and Elizabeth Ewen argue, to separate women from their own abilities and allow themselves to take direction from commercially based interests? Or, as William Leach suggests, did the culture of consumption have a "transforming" effect on women? Leach writes that the stores provided an "emancipating impact" on both working and middle-class women by releasing repressive tendencies as stores sought to trigger purchases by emotion and desire rather than rational decision-making. As a result, women, he writes, became more secular and public and came to a sense of individualism by way of consumption. The role of department stores even stretched into feminist ideology, moving from an understanding of women's independence by way of productive work to one that demanded "greater sensual gratification and experience." And, indeed, giving credence to some part of Leach's argument, feminists were to grasp the new principles of display as the feminist parades in the new century became awash with sashes, silken banners, floats, and spectacle represented in the celebratory symbol of Inez Milholland on a white horse.

In New York, A. S. Stewart's department store was the first major store to follow the Paris model, which substituted one large store for the multiple specialty stores that had served women shoppers. Its adoption by U.S. retailing was at a time when the enclosed, safe, and even luxurious environments of department stores provided an oasis in a period of urban unrest. The sense of protection was strengthened as stores adopted policies of fixed prices and guarantees of their merchandise—no need to barter at outside stalls. Moreover, the new tools of marketing pictured middle-class life by way of plate-glass windows and accessible store tableaus, settings wherein customers only had to imagine themselves. From New York, the concept spread to all American cities. In Philadelphia, advertising copywriters learned how to tap into the female market with such success that department stores across the country had subscriptions to Philadelphia newspapers so their advertising copy could be examined. The copywriters of the store that bore the name of its founder, John Wanamaker, shaped the department store as a separate nation composed for women; here, women could exercise their vote simply by purchase. In this protected environment, women were wooed and cajoled, spoiled and waited upon, advised and supported in their efforts to purchase whatever was needed in their role as the professional manager of the home—proper clothing for its members, furnishings for its rooms, and multiple attendant articles. These were important directives in a city that invented savings and loans associations so that workers could purchase homes of their own. Keeping up with mortgages and paying bills for furnishings as well as, for some, the obligations of church and synagogue had the additional benefit of keeping workers off the streets in a city known for its prewar rioting. Big cities across the nation found this a useful model.

From the perspective of shopping women, the added value of department stores was to be put at the center of a catering environment, reminding them at every turn of their special value. The price of privilege was women's role as consumers. In tones that were variously familiar, caring, and respectful of customers' good sense as choosers, the Wanamaker advertising was still, for example, didactic rather than persuasive. In a technique that was to be adopted by broadcast writers, the ads liberally used the word "you," meaning its female readers, in a confidential *entre nous* tone that camouflaged the fact that thousands of other readers were reading the ad at the same time. How could the store sell gingham so cheaply? "Not going to tell you. The makers don't want us to tell. We'd like to tell *you,* but the merchant's reading every word we print." The ad writers were all-knowing about their readers: "Are you tired of hearing of bargains? We imagine not, so long as the bargains are real bargains." The underlying sense was one that Wanamaker's was looking out for its customers the way other stores did not: "Carpets and matting vary enough to make it worth your while to study them in several stores before buying."

Hundreds of department stores across the country reiterated the domestic rhetoric in advertising, and it helped develop a long-lived tradition of advertising aimed at women that was detailed rather than broad. Women were seen to have the leisure and the interest to read detailed advertising copy, whereas men were not and were thought to respond to broader messages. In the advertising for department stores, the style served the manufacturers and retailers of the day, but its price for women was one that allowed the freedom to choose only from an agenda composed by others. Department store doors literally shut out other considerations such as the partnership gratifications of home productions or meaning outside of consumption. You were what you bought. Women might not be able to vote, but they sure could buy.

MAGAZINES AND THE SELLING OF BRAND-NAME PRODUCT

For magazines, the growth of brand names provided the same kind of bonanza that department stores had provided for city newspapers. Some of the companies that had produced goods and foods for local audiences found they had the opportunity to sell to a national audience when national magazines and goods could reach new audiences by the extended rail system. Food products could also become nationally distributed, thanks to developments in canning and freezing. By 1857, Gail Borden had developed safe canned milk (earlier versions had poisoned consumers), and, as mechanization improved, the production of cans was exponentially expanded—6,000 cans an hour by the end of the century. To match customers with the availability, Borden eschewed advertising based on what had been called "portable food," a reference to what was considered its major benefit. Instead, canned milk was advertised as "cleaner, purer and fresher than anything else otherwise available to city residents." Prompted by the same thrust of safety and security, H. J. Heinz began to package condiments in clear bottles to prove they were not adulterated. Biscuits, which once were purchased by the plunging of hands deep into a biscuit barrel, were wrapped in cellophane and packaged in square boxes suitable for shipping, helping to establish the corporate career of the Nabisco Company. The actual packaging of food products may or may not have been sanitary (workers, after all, had to put the biscuits in boxes), but the messages of packaging were all about safety, and mostly from the contaminants of a changing society. Soap manufacturers in particular were frequent advertisers and could play on racial themes. One Pear's soap advertisement featured a bare-breasted woman of color fanning a languorous and reclining white woman.

These messages were now distributed to women across the nation, thanks to billboards, advertising cards, and the women's shelter magazines of the 1870s. As in the department store advertising, specialty ad writers (most of them men) attempted to put at rest possible notions that using packaged food rather than home-produced food was a dereliction of housewifely duties; women were assured they were ensuring cleanliness and saving time in the kitchen that could be used for other domestic and child-centered activities.

These were all seductive messages to the nation's women, and not just middle-class women. Department stores often gave the patina of serving middle-class clientele, even as they sold to working women who saw themselves as moving toward a new place in life. Women could establish respectability by her choices of products, do their duty as guardians of the home by purchasing products that promised safety, and be spoiled at the same time.

THE HOME IN PRINT

While the new men's magazines of the time were organized around special interests such as business or hunting, the new women's magazines were almost exclusively conceived as vehicles to carry advertising. *Hearth and Home* was established in 1868 by the advertising firm of Pettengill, Bates, and Company, early predictors of the connections between products and women, with Harriet Beecher Stowe as its celebrity editor. The major shelter magazines—*McCall's, Good Housekeeping, Woman's Home Companion,* and, by 1883, *Ladies' Home Journal*—followed.

It should be noted that the editors of today's women's magazines are clearly aware of the connection between editorial content and advertising to the extent that some articles are sometimes assigned to attract and please particular advertisers, generally a late twentieth century development. Editors of shelter magazines in the nineteenth century, while committed to the principles of women in the home, were not monolithic in their subservience to advertisers, any more than large amounts of department store advertising ended investigative reporting by newspapers. These threads of independence had to do with efforts to professionalize reporting and writers by forming national organizations—sexsegregated as we shall see, but undergirded by a belief of the practitioners that advertising and editorial aspects of publishing should be separate. The necessity of turning out a strong editorial product abetted the tradition, and many would argue that when competition among media products largely ceased at the end of the twentieth century because of product placement, cross-promotional arrangements, and pressure from managers to design editorial products to fit advertising, the pattern was set for the decrease of audiences for mass products. Even with those cautions in place, however, the overall message of the home shelter magazine set out particular patterns of behavior consonant with the domestic circle and its perceived benefits.

CHANGES IN CONTENT

Women had made their first entry into commercial publication by giving housekeeping and fashion advice. Sara Willis Parton, "Fanny Fern," had become such a national institution that her death in 1872 resulted in front-page coverage. However, the woman thought to be the first woman hired in a newsroom was Jane Cunningham Croly. She began as a freelance writer using the pen name "Jennie June" for a women's column called "Park and Side-Walk Gossip." By 1857, the column had received some syndication—another development of the press that ensured the mass distribution of messages about women's role. The widespread use of syndicated material in general indicated that the message did not have to change wherever it was placed, and it was an economical way to fill the pages of the expanding women's sections. Croly was eventually hired by Pulitzer to run his new women's department while she continued to contribute to *Mme. Demorest's Mirror of Fashions* and other publications. In the next decades, she published three collections of newspaper columns, a cookbook that became an icon in the field, and a book of advice to working women. In the same period, in Boston, Sallie Joy White recognized the impulses in the culture and took a course in home economics to prepare herself to write on the subject; she embarked on a lengthy career at the *Boston Herald,* where she wrote a popular column under the name "Penelope Penfeathers."

By the turn of the century, Joseph Pulitzer's *World* had experimented with women's pages, including society items, gossip columns, and columnists providing advice and guidance on manners and behavior. The rise of columns of advice to the lovelorn was another indication of private concerns coming to public view. Arthur Brisbane of the *World* is credited with taking the idea from the women's magazines. Under the pen name "Beatrice Fairfax," Marie Manning began "Advice to the Lovelorn" in 1898. Within a few months, she was receiving 1,400 letters a day. "Dorothy Dix," Elizabeth Merriwether Gilmer, became the highest-paid columnist in the nation, after she had utilized the syndicates to build her career.

The use of pen names for women, which had begun a century earlier to represent female modesty, gave some indication of the commercial nature of the nation, as the names became brands that could, indeed, go beyond the life of the original holder, or become a façade for a series of writers who did not even have to be female. Bok was for a time the writer of the *Journal's* advice giver, "Ruth Ashmore," after an earlier career establishing a syndicate to distribute "Bab's Babble" and similar material. The spread of the columns by way of the well-known brand names in syndicates, newspaper chains, and national magazines helped construct a national culture of, if not shared values, certainly equally distributed ones.

Advice-giving in general became endemic, and the domestic sphere spread as far as the garden, which became a new area of expertise for women. Grace Tabor, writing for the *Woman's Home Companion,* was the doyenne of a cluster of female advice-givers on the subject. But advice was most promoted by editors of the shelter magazines, which, like Bok, took on the role as the defender of the home. While reforms addressed external dangers threatening the home—alcohol, prostitution, child labor—advice-givers, including Bok and other male editors, saw the enemy within, the importance of women keeping busy with tasks at home: "[W]hat a certain type of woman needs today more than anything else is some task that would 'tie her down.' Our whole social fabric would be better for it. Too many people are dangerously idle."

The Human-Interest Story

In addition, new, more sophisticated developments in journalism served to make sure women appreciated their home responsibilities. The use of the reportorial interview, for example, permitted entry into the homes of the well-known. Heroes were now likely to be successful businessmen, such as Horace Greeley, whose various biographies were the most successful books of the day. But to be useful to members of a society on the make, rise-and-succeed accounts had to provide a behind-the-scenes explanation of how success had been achieved. As rise-and-succeed narratives entered newspapers and magazines, human-interest stories discovered the helpful wife, giving evidence to the notion that women's real power was in the home. In what Charles Ponce de Leon calls the "master narrative," male success was equated with the devotion and the day-to-day attention given to him by the woman in the home, domestic detail that in previous times was considered of no interest or no business of the reading public.

Traditionally, the home life of the nation's leaders was

only of interest when it could be made into political fodder—Thomas Jefferson's slave mistress, Alexander Hamilton's paramour, the legal status of Andrew Jackson's marriage, and in this period, a presidential campaign that included charges Grover Cleveland had fathered a child outside of marriage. But press interest in domestic arrangements allowed politicians to take the initiative to present themselves in tune with national life. The *Munsey's* profile of Chauncey M. Depew was in terms of his "Home and Home Life." Later, "The Home Life of William Jennings Bryan" in the same magazine profiled its subject in terms of "simple American domesticity." Theodore Roosevelt's family was part of his substantial press apparatus. "The families of few presidents have awakened so much interest as the American people feel about the wife, daughter and the interesting group of children now in the White House," according to *Ladies' Home Journal,* which profiled them all. When questioned about the liveliest child, Alice, Roosevelt famously responded, "Listen, I can be president of the United States, or I can attend to Alice." Already the muscular hero, Roosevelt did not eschew his role as family man.

The human-interest story in its domestic dress opened doors to areas that had been off limits to respectable journals. In less respectable journals, actors and actresses, for example, had been profiled in ways that played upon what was generally considered their too-open lives. When Pulitzer drama reporter Alan Dale interviewed the French actress Anna Held for an article replete with illustrations and the headline, "Mlle. Anna Held Receives Alan Dale, Attired in Nightie," it was denounced as yet another example of the sensationalist press, but its subject matter called on long-held attitudes toward actresses, in this case compounded by American assumptions vis-à-vis her nationality. Still, publishers of the time were discovering that theatrical celebrities made good subjects if they could be sanitized by domestic detail, a view promoted by the growing sophistication of theatrical agentry. Thus, *Ladies' Home Journal* headlined one article on Ethel Barrymore "at Home and at Play" with many illustrations. The magazine took the bull by the horns when it headlined its two-page "Actresses as Housekeepers" with an underline that just hinted at the real popular belief: "There has long been a popular belief that actresses are not good housekeepers. Here, however, are a number of actual scenes of the home life of actresses of today, showing how they take an active interest in their households." For the unbelieving, the *Journal* provided a dozen photographs, including "Miss Cross Making Fritters" and, again, Barrymore, who employed servants but who did not shy away from dusting her own books, at least when a photographer was on hand. Actress or not, Barrymore was clearly the all-American girl, even to designing her own dresses. The article was part of a whole series devoted to actors and actresses in their private worlds, which, as it turned out, appeared to be not so different from those of the readers. "Sweet, unaffected" Annie Russell, for example, kept house for her brother, liked fresh air, and had little taste for society. The wicked world of the stage had been domesticated in large part because unmarried actresses had been brought into the home by way of American girlhood. Since Bok was not so sure about the independent "New Woman," who was both grown up and unmarried, his answer was to extend girlhood well into young womanhood.

The rise of photography in telling the story of the actresses reflected the growing influence of the visual image. As manufacturers discovered that branded products with recognizable icons helped build loyalty, advertisers also found that visual imagery in general was powerful. In the general condemnation of yellow journalism in the 1890s, one speaker argued that the "most potent of the facts in the success of yellow journalism is the pencil, not the pen. In nine cases out of ten the reading matter is not so much to be deplored as the suggestive and demoralizing pictures." There was, however, nothing to be deplored in the work of magazine illustrators whose images of glorified domestic circles were found both in advertisements and in cover illustrations for the new magazines.

By the end of the century, illustrations often came from the hands of female illustrators, such as Jessie Wilcox Smith, whose idealistic family portraits were popular with the women's magazines and advertisers, and she provided work for both. In 1897, Alice Barber Stephens, the "dean" of the new cohort of women illustrators, provided six full-page illustrations for the *Journal*'s series on "The American Woman." Three of the illustrations showed women inside the home in ways that Bok approved; the other three showed women outside the home and stretched his taste. "The American Girl in Summer" represented a casual grouping of young women, not girls, on a lawn. After its appearance, Bok appeared to have second thoughts. He warned that summer encouraged the loss of deportment. "It is a very fine line which divides unconventionality in a girl's deportment from a certain license and freedom of action, which is so fraught with danger—a very, very fine line."

There could be no better guide to respectability and its

gender meanings than the *New York Times*. Purchased by
Adoph Ochs in the 1890s, the *Times* built circulation by appealing to the new petit bourgeoisie. Its campaign, "It Will
Not Stain the Tablecloth," was intended to position the paper
as the alternative to the yellow press, driving home the point
that the *Times* was suitable reading in the home and echoing
Harper's Monthly, which had already promised, "Our rule is
that the Magazine must contain nothing which cannot be
read aloud in any circle."

The *Times* rejected the techniques of the sensational—
stunt reporting, celebrity reporting, and advice columns—to
draw female readers. But the paper surely had at its doorstep
the Gilded Age and its handmaiden, society reporting. Unlike
the outsider style of society reporting of the sensational press,
the *Times* adopted a façade of reporting the events as if its
reader were participants in the social whirl—although its
readers, then and now, included more outsiders than insiders
and the "old rich" insiders had no need or desire to be reported on. Still, the *Times* set itself up as a kind of arbiter in
reporting on the lives of the rich and famous, even as its subscription drives were focused on the schoolteachers and the
lower end of the managerial class. In the 1890s, it added the
regular column "Her Point of View" that was less about the
doings of high society than household hints mixed in with
informal, amusing anecdotes that assured readers of their
own importance.

However, the necessity of appealing to the managerial
class and the perceived role of women in that class seemed to
lead to coverage of women in terms of the home, even to
household hints. Well-to-do women were presented in traditional roles when that was not always the case, and the *Times*

eventually had to face the reality that many suffragists were women of means. Still, the myth of the well-to-do and traditional roles for its women persisted, and the *Times* did not hire women for its city staff and did not open its columns to nondomestic subject matter very often. The *Times* provided a flattering profile of a woman who, after her son's illness, had invented soap bubbles safe for children, an appropriate extension of her role. "In the home, generations of husbands and sons have relied upon 'mother' to tide them over all its emergencies." "A Study of the Army Woman"—of women married to men serving in the army—found she was a woman of character and endurance, evidenced by the fact she had to give up "delight in the home." Such stories were not so different from the those appearing in many of the women's magazines, but the *Times*'s coverage of women was less leavened by stories of women outside the domestic circle until the suffrage marches occurred. Extensive evidence still has to come, but even *Ladies' Home Journal,* with an editor who was strongly antisuffrage, may have featured women outside the role of domestic success more than what appeared in the elite newspaper press of the time.

The Home at Risk

Of all the advice given to women, none was more consistent than the importance of childbearing and the fear that women were not living up to the need for it. This was surely the fear of "race suicide," as it was called by Theodore Roosevelt, in light of the declining number of births in white Protestant families compared with the large families of the immigrant poor. *Good Housekeeping* warned a reader that sterility was often the comeuppance for those who used birth control.

Readers wrote in to tell an earlier correspondent that if she continued to remain childless by choice, her husband "would lose interest in her." When Edward Bok permitted the *Journal* to discuss venereal disease, it was in the context of concern that men who had contracted gonorrhea from prostitutes ran the risk of infecting their wives and causing sterility. The New York purist Anthony Comstock led a movement that prevented even discussion of birth control, resulting in the banning of Margaret Sanger's publication and to her flight to Great Britain to avoid legal charges.

We know from the considerable scholarship on late Victorian views of physicality and sexuality that women's anatomy was, as one physician put it, "built around the uterus," which led to the notion that potential fecundity was related to every function of the female body. The use of the word "injurious," as in a 1910 Lyman Abbot article in the *Ladies' Home Journal* "Will the Vote Be Injurious to Women?" could be interpreted quite literally at a time when physicians fully believed that brain activity was to risk infertility. The "great uterine manifesto" of the era was Dr. Edward H. Clarke's *Sex in Education, or a Fair Chance for the Girls.* Clarke argued against female education because of its physical danger: "Women beware. You are on the brink of destruction." Women, he demanded, stop studying. "Science pronounces that the woman who studies is lost."

So, too, was the woman who rode the bicycle. The introduction of the bicycle complicated the concerns about fertility, as riding astride was seen as damaging to a woman's reproductive center. Advertisements for bicycles emphasized the role of the bicycle in maintaining health of women, with its subtext that riding a bicycle would not damage women's ability to have children and might even improve the chances. But the fear of physical damage to females was prominent enough that proponents of bicycle riding such as Frances Willard felt it necessary to routinely caution that women should take the advice of their doctors before taking up the sport.

Bicycle riding also contributed to one of the dramatic fears of the period—like the vote, the inchoate, hardly to be expressed notion that it forewarned the annihilation of masculinity. The bicycle was not only a metaphor for the increased mobility of getting away from the home, but young women who rode bent over their handlebars in the "scorch" position for fast riding might be doing so for the sexual pleasure promoted by the position of the seat. Bicycle seats were redesigned to eliminate the possibility. Handlebars were raised and women were shown bicycling in rigid, upright positions, decorously dressed in long skirts.

Bicycle riding was also related to longstanding notions of dress reform. From the middle of the century, dress reform had been on the women's agenda. The columnist Fanny Fern suggested that women periodically adopt male clothing for both health and as a disguise that would allow women freedom of movement into evening hours. Amelia Bloomer made the most headway and gave her name to apparel that was adopted for a time by many women. Elizabeth Cady Stanton adopted bloomers, at least for a time, after her dress caught on fire in the kitchen (a common occurrence for women and one of the arguments for reform) and she had to be chopped out of it by the vigilant Anthony and a pair of scissors.

The concern with dress reform continued through the

nineteenth and early twentieth centuries, now brought to the forefront by women—not necessarily suffragists—who adopted male attire. These included the editor and cofounder of the literary magazine *The Critic,* Jeannette L. Gilder. Gilder routinely dressed in a mannish mode, not trousers, but jacket, tie, and stick. Her portrait so dressed appeared regularly in the literary press, and in one profile she was quoted as saying that she "had never worn evening dress in her life, and never expects to." The style of dress spurred Ida Tarbell to note that Gilder "carried to perfection the then feminine vogue for severe masculine dress: stout shoes, short skirt, mannish jacket, shirt, tie, hat, stick." But Gilder was an antisuffragist friend, so Tarbell was quick to add, "But the masculinity was all on the surface."

But no one, it appeared, was entirely what she seemed to be. Despite the many illustrations of women and children that were so popular with the mass magazines, the most popular illustration of a female in the first decade of the twentieth century was not one of a mother and baby, but rather its opposite, the single and powerful "Gibson Girl," the work of illustrator Charles Gibson. So popular was the image that it moved from its debut on a 1903 *Ladies' Home Journal* cover to be replicated, often with the addition of a chiseled "Gibson man," in many of the popular periodicals: *Century, Scribner's, Harper's, Cosmopolitan, Good Housekeeping, McCall's, Leslie's Weekly, McClure's, Life,* and *Collier's.* The image was reproduced on plates, silverware, pillows, tablecloths, scarves, even wallpaper; it was found on music sheets and advertising posters while manufacturers produced shirtwaists, skirts, corsets, shoes, and hats inspired by her look. The image was so popular that Gibson has been credited with defining an entire era as "intuitively absorbing the yearnings of the time and crystallizing them into captivating pictorial images." There seemed no overt negative messages for the hegemony of the time, since the Gibson Girl was portrayed with the rounded figure and abundant hair that portended fecundity and was often paired with a suitable man, both images projecting characteristics of Anglo-Irish profiles and white-toned skin.

But what complicates the Gibson Girl is the power she had over men. Carolyn Kitch finds many examples of the Gibson Girl posed not just with the suitable Gibson man, but with miniature men—as if the onus is on the male not being up to the task of fulfilling the needs of the Gibson Girl, not the opposite. "Though the Gibson Girl is often hailed by historians as one of the first representations of the independent woman, her independence was frequently presented in the form of cold and cruel power over men. Gibson's beauties quite literally played with men." Viewed as a male-produced image, the Gibson Girl was only one of what Kitch calls the "distinctive motif of domineering and destructive women emasculating weak and powerless men."

We might consider then that trousers, bicycle riding, deportment, the New Woman in the guise of the Gibson Girl, and, increasingly, the call for votes for women (not even counting the disappearance of the American frontier and the rise of white-collar managers!) comprised a bundle of male-related anxieties that put the survival of "the race"—most often construed as the white masculine gender—at the heart of domestic ideology. The headline of an 1894 *World* story was the frightening "Will Women Grow More Masculine? A Woman Physician Discusses Dr. Shrady's Proposition to the

Effect that They Will Do So." The headline was likely to be what was remembered even though the woman physician assured, "The woman who is sensibly educated and employed will be a healthier woman than any other, and that will mean more healthy emotion."

Indeed, as the call for dress reform increased and gored skirts were found useful for riding bicycles, the world of magazines seemed to enlarge attention to plush and full gowns and swooping hats as the proper dress for women of English-Irish ancestry. Women in the home with children, women in dresses whose folds overflowed from their laps with such abundance they seemed to serve as anchors, and women clearly identifiable as a racial type comprised a new holy trinity that was found in the coverage of social events in newspapers, in advertising, on the covers of magazines, and in illustrations for magazine fiction, all putting before the public the preferred (at least by the media makers) gender characteristics. As late as 1915, women artists who contributed to a show to raise money for suffrage felt the necessity to proclaim their allegiance to the fecund nation. "There are babies, babies everywhere," according to one New York review.

However, despite all this energy placed on the promotion of domestic ideology, there could be no doubt that some women were moving out of the domestic sphere into education, into law, into medicine, and, indeed, into journalism, the field that provided so many directives for women to stay where they were. Writing for the domestic sphere was the entryway for women journalists, and, for some, it was also the Trojan horse into the forbidden encampment.

SIX

NEGOTIATING THE
NEWSROOM

To the naked eye, women in journalism seemed ubiquitous: A flurry of articles proclaimed that women had vanquished the dragon of the newsroom. Biography, popular fiction, and quality monthly and newspaper articles said the woman journalist was coming into her own. "[T]hey are to be numbered in the thousands," according to Margherita Arlina Hamm, later a war correspondent during the Spanish-American War. "To-day they are reporters, translators, copy-readers, interviewers, proof-readers, staff-writers, publishers, business managers, advertisement solicitors, book-reviewers and musical critics."

The federal census supported the general contention. Between 1880 and 1890, the number of full-time women journalists increased from 288 to 1,888, and by 1900 more than 2,000 women were employed in journalism. Moreover, a quick look around the profession could identify Gertrude Battles Lane, editor of *Woman's Home Companion,* the closest competitor to Cyrus C. K. Curtis's *Ladies' Home Journal;* Jane Cunningham Croly, the columnist "Jennie June"; sisters

Mary and Elizabeth Bisland, representing a syndicated columnist and the legion of female freelance writers respectively; Elizabeth Banks at the *World;* Helen Campbell, writer of a series of articles on child poverty for the *New York Tribune;* Elizabeth Jordan, Margaret Welch, and Margaret Sangster, editors of *Harper's Bazar* (the original spelling, later changed to *Bazaar*); Josephine Redding, editor of *Vogue;* Juliet Wilbur Tompkins, editor of Frank Munsey's effort at a slick magazine, *Puritan;* Marie Mattingly Meloney, editor of *New Idea Woman's Magazine;* and Kate Upson Clark, editor of *The Housewife. McCall's* had five female editors between 1884 and 1911. In 1906, Willa Cather moved to New York to work for *McClure's,* eventually becoming managing editor. At the end of the first flurry, in 1910, Emma Bugbee began her half-century career with the *New York Tribune.*

Outside of New York, Marion McBride was at the *Boston Post;* Sallie Joy White, the *Boston Herald;* Jane Meade Welch, the *Buffalo Courier.* Women editors included Mrs. John A. Logan of *Home* magazine in Washington, D.C., which despite its name, emphasized international affairs; Annie L.Y. Swart of *American Woman's Review* in St. Louis; F. Beulah Kellogg of the dressmaking magazine *Modern Priscilla* in Boston; Nella Daggert of *Home* (a common name), also in Boston; Mrs. S. T. Rorer, of the cookery magazine *Table Talk* in St. Louis; and Dr. Mary Wood-Allen of the child-care magazine *Mother's Friend* in Ann Arbor, Michigan.

In the newspaper world, Genevieve Forbes Herrick was at the *Chicago Tribune;* Teresa Howard Dean was working for the *Chicago Herald* when she was assigned to cover the Sioux ghost dance and became an activist for Native American rights. Ellen Mackay Hutchins ran the *New York Tribune's*

Sunday edition. In 1896, Isadore Miner ("Pauline Periwin-kle") became the first women's editor of the *Dallas Morning News*.

But the West Coast was the most amenable for women reporters. Florence Finch Kelly, who had experienced "adamant walls of negation" in Boston, found less prejudice against women reporters in the West. Most famous was Win-fred Sweet, who, under the name "Annie Laurie," was Hearst's *San Francisco Examiner*'s most famous "stunt reporter." Stunt reporting demanded women reporters take on physical challenges in the pursuit of sensational stories and provided one of the few alternatives to the women's pages. But Sweet, according to Kelly, was "a capable newspaperwoman in straight honest newspaper work and probably would have been equally successful without the 'stunt' decorations." Similar positions were held by Mabel Craft at the *San Francisco Chronicle* and Marjorie Driscoll at the *Los Angeles Examiner*.

Women could also be found as writers of specialty columns on topics such as architecture, fly-fishing, livestock, and horse racing as well as the traditional fields of books, music, gardening, and home decoration, along with the stand-by of advice. "Victoria Earle" was the pen name for Mrs. E. W. Mathews, an African American writer who contributed to the mainstream press. The craft had at least one news photographer; in 1903, Jessie Tarbox Beals was working as a staff photographer for the *Buffalo Inquirer and Courier*.

One female publisher of a national publication existed, Miriam Leslie, who edited, with great success, *Frank Leslie's Illustrated Weekly* and other publications in the group. Eliza Nicholson, since 1870, was publisher of the *New Orleans Picayune*. In 1890, Kate Field, a popular public lecturer, established a political magazine in her own name, *Kate Field's Washington.* Jeannette L. Gilder was a founder and editor of *The Critic.* Lilian Whiting was editor in chief of the literary newspaper *The Boston Budget.* The muckraker Ida Tarbell was a founder of *American Magazine.*

Women were involved in a multitude of nonmainstream publications. *The Journalist* magazine in 1889 named a dozen African American writers, including journalists Gertrude Mossell, editor of the women's department of the New York *Freeman* and contributor to Philadelphia's *Echo;* Lillian Alberta Lewis, writing as "Bert Islew" for the *Boston Advocate;* and the "Princess of the Press," Ida Wells Barnett, publisher of the *Memphis Free Speech,* already recognized as famous. Women worked on suffrage publications, in the religion press, and on newsletters; they edited private literary magazines and worked on many small publications. A correspondent to the *New York Times* objected that the newspaper had summed up women in journalism only in terms of editors of women's departments of large newspapers. "[T]hey do all kinds of reporting, from millinery openings to National political conventions," and much in between.

On one of his infrequent trips to his *Herald* newsroom, James Gordon Bennett was unpleasantly surprised by the changing newsroom. "Who are these females?" he is said to have snapped. "Fire them all."

The surge of activity of women in journalism led to the establishment of women's press associations. Sallie Joy White of the *Boston Herald* and Marion McBride of the *Boston Post* took the lead in founding the New England Press Association. The National Women's Press Association counted some 700 members by the turn of the century. A Congress of Press

Women of the World met in Chicago in 1893 and showcased midwestern women journalists, the first step to its ultimate world membership goal. But press clubs proliferated at the end of the century in cities and regions across the nation, in Utah, in the South, in Cincinnati, in southern California, and in Texas. The popular belief that women could do journalism as well as any man spurred a fad whereby groups of club women took over the publication of local newspapers for the day to raise money for charity. In Orange, New Jersey, that included a "Man's Page."

"Ours is another era," proclaimed editor Sangster. "We have changed the point of view." The *New York Times,* despite its own hiring policies, remarked: "Women are succeeding and have succeeded, in every branch of journalism from the mere setting of the type to the absolute control of a great publication." The *Journal of Social Science* asked "Is Newspaper Work a Healthful Occupation for Women?" It was hard work, for sure, according to Margaret Welch, the New York editor. Women were at a disadvantage for their inability to withstand pressure, but her answer was an unmitigated "yes": "As an occupation for women, newspaper work is no longer an experiment." In a *Ladies' Home Journal* discussion, Foster Coates, city editor of *New York Journal,* admitted pay discrepancies existed and in some newspaper offices "there was a prejudice against women" but was nonetheless optimistic that the barriers could be overcome: "The latch-string of every editorial door in this country is hanging on the outside. Woman has only to step boldly over the threshold and begin her career. There is fame and fortune for her there."

How had women arrived at this nirvana of employment outside of the home despite overwhelming cultural messages that reinforced the opposite? The explosion of women's shelter magazines and the proven ability of women was clearly one reason. In the newspaper world, which sought to emulate the success of the magazines, women also entered the field by virtue of their gender as advice givers, as society reporters, and, in the sensationalist press, as stunt reporters. Stunt reporting, despite its excitement, may have most relation to gender of all.

STUNT REPORTING

Female stunt reporters can be admired for their ability to survive and flourish in the most difficult of worlds, made even more difficult when Joseph Pulitzer hired more than one female stunt reporter for the *World* so they could compete against each other. While it would seem they advanced the role of women in the profession by proving that there was nothing that women could not do, another interpretation is to consider that female stunt reporters, by doing the opposite of what women were expected to do, actually reinforced women's appropriate role.

In the 1880s, stunt reporting was an aspect of sensational reporting, which had had a long history in U.S. newspapers and in which women had played some role. In the 1830s, James Gordon Bennett of the *New York Herald* promoted circulation by publicizing a scandalous anti-Catholic book that purported to be the account of a young woman who had to flee a Montreal monastery or be party to sexual debauchery. After *Charlotte Temple, Awful Disclosures* by "Maria Monk" was another best seller before *Uncle Tom's Cabin*. The book supported a rash of anti-Catholic prejudices of the day (although Bennett himself was Catholic) in a traditional pornographic story setting. In the same period, Bennett made the murder of a prostitute Ellen Jewett a daily story. The account of the murder was endlessly repeated, including salacious details that worked to reinforce positions on the danger women opened themselves to when they stepped beyond the acceptable; in other words, Ellen Jewett deserved what she got.

Joseph Pulitzer and William Randolph Hearst refined Bennett's techniques. In the Sunday-supplement war, Hearst did not shy away from headlines such as "Pretty Annette's Gauzy Silk Bathing Suits" or "White Woman Among Cannibals," both of which called upon mythic notions of womanhood, the seductress and the victim respectively. Pulitzer promoted the Spanish-American War by making the imprisoned daughter of the Cuban consul the victim of a suggested rape. The eminent war correspondent Richard Harding Davis reported on the imprisonment in less than accurate ways while the renowned illustrator Frederic Remington picked up on Davis's tacit suggestion to inflame passions at the Spaniards' treatment of innocent young womanhood. The May 4, 1898, *Puck* satirized the campaign in its cartoon, "The Duty of the House: To Save Her Not Only from Spain, but from a Worse Fate."

More than any other publisher, Hearst is considered to have provided the incubator for the female stunt reporter. As his contemporary, Ishbel Ross, put it, "Hundreds of them passed through his doorways, some to lose their jobs with staggering swiftness; other to build up big syndicate names and draw down the highest salaries in the profession." Stunt reporting began with male reporters, but it was not until publishers Hearst and Pulitzer hired female stunt reporters that the readers' interest was piqued in the mixing of long-held attitudes toward women—women as objects of danger, for example, at a time when women were supposed to be protected. Stunt reporters could be put in clear physical danger, but a Pulitzer or Hearst reader might sympathize with a woman in danger at the same time he was considering that she was responsible for her own plight, much as a reader of Bennett's juicy prostitute story might consider that Ellen Jewett's end was in some sense deserved.

Moreover, as the profession as a whole was turning toward a production style that all could learn, women stunt reporters were expected to write in a highly charged, individual style. "[T]he reporters at the *World* and for the Hearst Papers had to turn in spice and color," Ross writes. "The women there were in hot competition to get a story or die. They had to show their feelings in their reporting."

The gender of women reporters was also manipulated outside of stunt reporting. Most reporters were expected to report in ways that carried out the ideology of the newspaper owners; for women, this meant the reiteration of common wisdom that was not so helpful to women overall. In a rather pedestrian assignment in 1909, Winifred Black Bonfils interviewed Upton Sinclair, socialist and the muckraking author of *The Jungle*. Sinclair was appalled that the interview to promote his theatrical troupe resulted in the headline, "Upton Sinclair Sorry He Wed. Says Ceremony is a Farce." But "Annie Laurie" would not have kept her job had she not written an article that connected socialism to the overturn of society's institutions.

Bonfils was better known for the big headlines. Her first

story for the *Examiner* occurred when she got herself admitted into the San Francisco Receiving Hospital and provided the front-page exposé, "A City's Disgrace," with its insinuations of male staff members' lewd sexual advances. The story led to a long series of similar exposés achieved by some kind of risk-taking and, in a fulsome style, called for civic reform in a manner that was ostensibly and in a self-congratulatory way aimed at moving readers to action, when, indeed, readers had little ability to achieve the changes.

Bonfils was also first to be called a "sob sister," a term given to her by journalist Irwin Cobb during the sensational 1907 Harry Thaw murder trial, which she and Dorothy Dix, Ada Patterson, and Nixola Greeley-Smith (granddaughter of Horace Greeley) chronicled by sentimental description of its principals. The name came to describe a whole genre of writers even up to recent times when magazine writers who specialized in tales of personal trauma were routinely called "agony writers." There was no affection or respect in the term, and sportswriters or male columnists who wrote in the vernacular, other examples of a marrying of content and style for circulation purposes, did not have derogatory terms applied to them. Rather, the name served to define female reporters, and by implication the female readers they were supposed to attract, by their perceived nature as female, only able to write in emotional terms because that was what their nature demanded. Bonfils hated the term. "I am not a 'Sob Sister' or a special writer. I'm just a plain, practical all-around newspaperwoman. That is my profession and this is my pride. I'd rather smell the printers' ink and hear the presses go round than go to any grand opera in the world."

In popular memory, Elizabeth Cochran, the "Nellie

Bly" for Pulitzer's publication, has become most famous of all stunt reporters. Pulitzer's announcement that Bly would beat the 80-day, around-the-world trip by Jules Verne's fictional hero gained the attention of the editor of *Cosmopolitan,* John Brisben Walker, who was seeking to put *Cosmopolitan* on the map in popular ways. He gave Elizabeth Bisland, the magazine's book editor, a day's notice to ready herself for a round-the-world challenge going in the opposite direction.

It was an odd match—Bisland, the southern-born literary editor, against the experienced Cochran, although Bisland may have won if she had not been mysteriously misinformed about an important travel connection that cost her four days. Still, Bisland was not a natural stunt reporter, nor street fighter, and her eventual account turned out to be a travel book ("It fills my soul with passion that I, too, am an Anglo-Saxon," she declaimed at the sight of Great Britain), hardly an account about the headiness of competition. Cochran gave the prize to Pulitzer and his circulation war, while Pulitzer made Cochran a national celebrity by a massive cross-promotional campaign that extended beyond the pages of the newspaper into games and lotteries. On her return, Cochran was met in San Francisco by a special train that traveled much like a presidential entourage to return her to New York. Cochran subsequently left the industry for marriage and business interests, returning to pick up her career for a short time. She died at a relatively early age, a rather lonely figure. Bisland turned to magazine writing of an anti-suffrage nature. Her obituary remembered her as a society matron—not a word about the episode that had snatched up the nation's attention.

What is interesting about the publicity in connection

with Cochran's around-the world stunt is that it was, and remains, routinely represented by one visual image—a full-length portrait of Cochran, alone in an otherwise empty frame, dressed in an unflattering checkered coat and clasping her small suitcase. One might compare this image to the flattering portraits of Bisland or to one of the multitude of portraits of another celebrity reporter of the time, Richard Harding Davis—usually decked out in paramilitary gear. In her unattractive checkered coat, Cochran's image is hardly one of power; were the image not so well known, she could easily be mistaken for an Ellis Island immigrant—her background has been erased and her future is hardly assured.

BEHIND THE MYTHS

Florence Finch Kelly believed the female stunt reporters "dealt a serious blow to the progress women were making in the profession." Stunt reporting was a product of the yellow press, "with its incessant noxious appeal to whatever is base and evil in human nature." Women in the field also provided a flood of warnings. The former stunt reporter Elizabeth Jordan, writing in *Lippincott's Magazine,* saw such reporting as the "dark side." Women stunt reporters had to have extraordinary physical and mental sacrifice, even as Jordan acknowledged the pull of the field: "It is a peculiarity of the work that its slaves are willing slaves, who would not throw off their shackles if they could. Even the failures, and there are many of them, feel the fascination of the life and cling to it with pathetic determination long after hope has departed." Haryot Holt Cahoon, warned that stunt reporting—"gutter journalism" she called it—was bound to be short-term and ultimately disappointing. No matter her energy and talent, she predicted an average four-year career for the fresh-faced out-of-town young women who had visions of becoming another Nellie Bly. "Whatever work her editor lays out for her, that she stands ready to do, whether it is figuring in a balloon ascension or a fire-escape descent, posing as an artist's model, camping all night on a millionaire's grave, trotting round the globe in eighty days, or, in short doing any of the things that are beneath the notice of any man on the staff, or, to put it more mildly, 'outside of a man's province.'" As heady as the experience, women should hold themselves aloof from "becoming burnt offerings upon an altar where the sacrifice avails nothing."

Beyond the problems of stunt reporting, women reporters suffered at the hands of many other difficulties. In the January 26, 1889, issue of the *Journalist,* dedicated to women reporters, Flora McDonald pointed to how women journalists were isolated by the nature of the profession and their own rarity. Perhaps worst of all were the society reporters. "She is in the swim, but not of it." Physical demands of the job were often noted. Sangster advised good food and massage.

But nothing was more upsetting than discriminatory salaries. Rheta Childe Dorr, who came of age in the New York journalism of the 1890s at the *New York Evening Post,* recalled, "It was a mark of ability to be asked to join the staff, a mark of special ability if you were a woman, because in those days very few women could get a job on a newspaper anywhere. Yet because of my sex I had to accept a salary hardly more than half that of any of my male colleagues. Moreover, I was given to understand that I could never hope for a raise.

Women, the managing editor explained to me, were accidents in industry. They were tolerated because they were temporarily needed, but some day the *status quo ante* (women's place is in the home) would be restored and the jobs would go back where they belonged, to the men." A Philadelphia writer described the experience of women in the newsroom: "Their abilities were questioned, their intentions suspected, their reputations bandied from sneering lip to careless tongue and on every hand they were met with discouragements."

And, finally, no matter how much the stunt reporters risked life and limb, as Ross summarized, it made little difference to the newsroom culture: "[I]f the front-page girls were all to disappear tomorrow no searching party would go out looking for more, since it is the fixed conviction of nearly every newspaper executive that a man in the same spot would be exactly twice as good."

Edward Bok put the question "Is the Newspaper Office the Place for a Girl?" to 50 male and female editors and found problematical answers: "Reserve and dignity form the armor of the successful newspaper woman. She must expect from her men associates none of the courtesy of the drawing-room, and she must make them understand from the first that they may expect from her only the perfectly cool, professional manner a business woman should wear," according to one female editor. A male editor simply said he was cutting out female staff because they "disorganized" the male staff.

Optimistic accounts of women in journalism notwithstanding, women in editorial offices and newsrooms were accepted slowly and, if not used as stunt reporters, they were placed in the developing women's sections. Gilder did a sur-

vey of colleagues in journalism and concluded the happiest
women were freelancers who combined their work with
families, a position not out of tune with her antisuffrage position. Sangster, a proponent of women in journalism, encouraged women to remain on a "natural ground of vantage,
covering everything which nearly or remotely affects the
home." As modern research indicates, the majority of hiring
was a result of the need for women by the exploding numbers of shelter magazines and for women's pages. But even
where opportunity existed, these were not necessarily the
kinds of jobs that attracted women to the craft. Writing in
Current Literature—one of the several monthlies fascinated by
the subject of women in journalism—Eleanor Hoyt warned
that although "the newspaper girl" had become a stock character in fiction, "in the realm of fact, our newspaper girl may
be called upon to write lotion recipes for the cure of freck-
les and settle the doubts of Lovable Lizzie, who wants the
question and answer department to tell her how she can
show her affection for a young gentlemen without running
after him." In her first job, on the woman's page of a Milwaukee newspaper, Jordan wrote, "It is a miracle that the stuff I
had to carry in 'Sunshine' did not permanently destroy my
interest in newspaper work." Elizabeth Banks turned to sensational reporting but was frustrated by the arrogance of the
society women she was charged to cover. Ross thought that
the life of a society reporter "was particularly cruel," traveling to events on trolleys, expected to underwrite the costs of
dressing properly, and treated poorly by those she was told to
cover.

Disallowed to compete for the jobs held by men at the
next desk (if women were allowed in the newsroom), paid

substantially less than those men, and sometimes treated in unkind ways by their fellow journalists and even their subjects—daily life for women in journalism was difficult. The opportunities so frequently heralded for women in journalism in the 1890s turned on reporting tasks that were expected to represent women in the most traditional ways.

THE SUFFRAGE QUESTION

It is telling that in the dozens of women Margherita Arlinna Hamm profiled, just one woman, Mrs. George Pusifer Porter (no given name provided) was described as a "strong supporter of the woman's cause," in her capacity as a leader of the Maine Federation of Women Clubs. Of the women professionals of the period, a handful of them were directly active in suffrage. Lilian Whiting was one of them, but after a period of time spent as editor and reporter. Kate Field endorsed suffrage as a lecturer, not a daily worker. Rheta Childe Dorr and Ida Husted Harper went to work for suffrage after mainstream careers. Ruth Hale worked as a freelancer. June Cunningham Croly was only the most famous of journalistic women to be involved in the nation's substantial club movement. While the club experience provided organizational training, women in the club movement had to endure ongoing attacks and ridicule—a favorite theme of Edward Bok at the *Ladies' Home Journal*. This experience was a dampening one and may have discouraged the press clubs from adopting suffrage positions. At a time when women in journalism were exhorted to use their positions to agitate for other reforms, suffrage was not one of them. One of the conundrums of the period is that women in journalism, as a group, did not—or, perhaps, could not—embrace suffrage, and, in some individual cases, such as Jeannette Gilder, Elizabeth Bisland, and Ida Tarbell, distanced themselves entirely from the cause.

Suffrage posed a difficult negotiation for the first wave of women in journalism, who were fighting to make a place for themselves in a profession that did not want them. They were expected to maintain notions of women's difference in their daily work even as they were held to expectations that were demanding, and, as much as any other women of the age, they were having to make decisions about their own identity. It is an issue that remains relevant. What negotiations have to occur for a worker to perform in an institution that in the larger world may actually represent views antithetical to a class of people the worker is seeking to serve? In the period roughly from 1880 to World War I, women faced the questions of the day with various strategies. In face of the difficulty of mounting organized support of suffrage, what has not been acknowledged is how everyday workers helped fashion a world that made suffrage a next logical step.

For the dozens of women working in journalism on mainstream publications, the day-to-day difficulties of the job were hardly to be borne, and silence on personal politics was likely the wisest choice if they wished to retain employment. Moreover, the process of finding and keeping jobs in journalism left nothing over for other kinds of activity for women who may have believed that survival in the field was contribution enough. But with that caveat made, it is relevant to consider issues other than gender that contributed to the disconnection of women journalists—although not all— from the kind of political activity that consumed so many other women. As Linda Steiner concludes, women in nine-

teenth century journalism in the United States universally attributed barriers to success to gender alone—disregarding, or
not wanting to acknowledge their discomfort with, the class
issue that was part of life in a newsroom and affected women
most of all. As Ross described it, "They [women reporters]
are seldom lazy. But the highest compliment to which the
deluded creatures respond is the city's editor acknowledge-
ment that their work is just like a man's. This automatically
gives them a complacent glow, for they are all aware that no
right-minded editor wants the so-called woman's touch in
the news." And she might have added, why would a female
reporter not want to be mistaken as a member of the class of
people who had power? Still, the power of the men in the
newsroom was only marginally superior to their own and
was just as anxiety filled.

ANXIETY IN THE NEWSROOM

At a time when journalism for men was just emerging from
a period when its practitioners were increasingly "divorced
from the rum shop and the beer saloon" but when reporters
were still thought to be better equipped if they had real
knowledge of the world than if they had a higher education
degree, it was difficult for men to know who they were,
much less know exactly how women fit. Were reporters a
member of the professional class, like law or medicine, with
demands for service to ideals? Were reporters simply craft
practitioners doing the bidding of owners? Male reporters
were not so sure. On the one hand, male-only journalist
organizations reified working-class bonding rituals—
backslapping and drinking and sharing a common cynicism

and, just as important, not associating with the weakest link, women who had no power to offer. Male reporters may have thought of themselves as a kind of hybrid, charged with bringing working-class suspicions to jobs that made sure those in control were kept on short leashes. It is telling that reporting grew in status as a result of the Civil War, when male reporters performed in clearly masculine roles, risking life and limb to report danger, not unlike the cowboy icon that also developed in the post–Civil War period. However, the campaign to professionalize, as exemplified by the *Journalist* magazine and the organization of Sigma Delta Chi, had overtones that meant giving up lower-class masculine behaviors for those of a class reporters were committed to oversee, not to imitate. No wonder that male "college boys" were ridiculed by old-time reporters or that the newsroom spittoon was slow to disappear.

For male reporters, the entry of women into newsrooms further challenged notions of both job and masculine identity and, because women reporters were there for management goals, may have furthered simmering class antagonisms. Women were expected to be genteel creatures, but a newsroom was not a genteel place; indeed, in the views of many working reporters, it could only operate successfully if reporters eschewed the gentility that consumed the nation. If women were to be accepted as genteel, there could be no escaping the notion that the newsroom was less a place for a working-class culture, for its male purveyors, or, indeed, for working-class sensibilities in covering the news. But not to accept women as genteel was similarly complicated. For working-class male reporters, definitions for women were limited. No wonder, then and later, that women in newsrooms had to be accepted as pals, as men in their own right. "You're a tough guy, Mary—and a first-rate newspaperman" was the highest accolade, as long as it could be parsed out sparingly.

For women, newsroom issues were also fraught with unspoken issues of class. Given their salaries, women in newsrooms were not middle class and found it difficult to maintain even illusions of middle-class status. Moreover, women in newsrooms may not have come from middle-class backgrounds or—more likely—may have arrived from middle-class families who had fallen on hard times. But the expectation of the period was that they should at least have the accoutrements of genteel behavior, dress well enough to cover society events, and have some knowledge of middle-class issues for women; these were certainly necessary for someone working in women's sections or on women's magazines. Although the popular press talked about pluck and perseverance as necessary characteristics for women in journalism, one woman whose work was turned down was told by the editor that she lacked "sufficient cultivation." At the *New York Times,* Midy (Marie) Morgan was permitted to cover livestock, not only because of her depth of knowledge, but because, as a large and ungainly woman, she was thought to fit the job as a kind of middle gender; it was unlikely she would have been employed as a society reporter.

For the most part, we might say that women in journalism occupied an awkward position between working-class and middle-class ideologies, as did many other new working women; this is one reason the messages of department-store consumption were so powerful. However, women in journalism daily had to face the working-class atmosphere of the newsroom even as they practiced their craft in ways that promoted a way of life in which they themselves did not participate. Women in journalism went to work to find out all they were not: they had not the leisure, and often as single women, did not have the marriage status to participate in reform by way of the club movement; their salaries were not so far above the factory women of the time; they were abjured by many of their male colleagues, concerned with their own place; opportunities to rise, if any, were limited.

Altogether, these were difficult issues of identity for the First Wave of women in daily journalism, and it is not so surprising that social networking by way of professional organizations became one solution, connecting them with the formidable middle-class club movement. Like those organizations, women in professional journalism organizations worked for civic reform on a basis that women had a special obligation to community but one that was compounded by their role in journalism. As Agnes Hooper Gottlieb notes in her study of the Women's Press Club of New York, its members took on reform activities because they believed their abilities to catch the ear of the public gave them a special obligation to serve. Amouretta Beecher told the group that members had "high responsibilities because we speak to the world." Women were urged to use "their influence through the press" to advance public education, to take on preservation of the forests by way of their writings, to help working women obtain housing. Phebe Hanford, an early suffragist, ordained minister, and author of a book extolling women's achievements, nonetheless urged members to do their "best work . . . in a womanly way." Engaging in reform work as

other women did was a way women journalists could connect to a broader women's community even if that meant less
attention to their own concerns.

Moreover, Frances Willard, head of the powerful
Women's Christian Temperance Union, believed that
women's special nature would eventually change journalism
anyway. Willard argued that there was a place for women in
journalism because "the spiritualizing process which it has
undergone has opened its doors to her." It is unclear exactly
what part of 1886 journalism was spiritual, but for Willard it
was a matter of time. "For here, as everywhere, she seems des-
tined to soften asperities, to sublimate coarseness, to eliminate the last reminder of barbarity." Indeed, in an example of
how women regarded their own power in the time, Willard
predicted that women in journalism would mean "Less space
will be given to the prize-fight, and more to prize poem; the
murder trial will be condensed that the philanthropic convention may gain a wider hearing; the wholesale verdict
against political opponents merely because they are such, will
be modified by an attempt to show some faint approach to
justice." Willard's role for women in journalism was "uplift."
"[W]omen's opportunity in journalism is just what it is in the
great world. She has a *role* peculiar to herself. The niche she
is to fill would remain empty but for her arrival."

These were complicated imperatives for the new professional woman, expected to demonstrate her ability to
compete in what was a man's world, for less money, and yet
bring about change because of her innate womanliness. Importantly, these messages of womanly virtue were also middle class. Thus, to be active in concern for her own livelihood

over higher moral purpose not only carried the risk of putting her essential womanliness at risk, but promised a shaky middle-class identity. Such warnings were not so easy to ignore in the inhospitable setting of a newsroom, and those reporters who did ignore them, such as Winifred Black, embraced journalism—for all that it had to supply—with a lifelong ferocity.

For other female journalists, the easier road was to adopt the societal approved role, adopting reform positions of "moral housekeeping" but stopping short of outright support of suffrage, which would have endangered their jobs and certainly made them even more objects of ridicule. Women journalists who did support suffrage turned to other means to advance the cause of women.

STRATEGIES

First, women journalists could point to their own success, and one function of the press organizations was to provide acknowledgment. In their frequent articles for the mass and professional press, Flora McDonald and Margherita Arlinna Hamm, each associated with professional groups, served as publicists for women in journalism. Furthering their efforts were the journalists themselves. One reason that women in journalism did get a fair amount of attention in the period is that women journalists used their skill and industry know-how to write about the field. It was, tellingly, less a subject of interest for male writers. In the Second Wave, professional women writers used their skills to put feminism on the media agenda. In the earlier period, most professional writers did not, publicly at least, make the connection between their own status and that of women in general. Instead, women in journalism found individual strategies to mitigate the tension of the times.

Involvement in professional organizations could be helpful to career building, but Jane Cunningham Croly was only the best known of women journalists who saw benefit in the power of utilizing the separate sphere, in this case by women-only professional organizations. For Croly, women-only organizations provided a place of support and sustenance for individual women and a collective face to the world at large.

For women who recognized systemic connections, the tools of their trade had subversive possibilities. Women journalists on women's magazines and on women's pages had a degree of autonomy that could be used to advance suffrage. Women's pages were the place where clubwomen's activities were chronicled and their leaders and their successes were acknowledged in ways that did not occur in news columns. As suffrage leaders pulled club and society women into their ranks, women's page reporters covered their activities assiduously.

Some journalists, such as writer Helen Campbell, sought to utilize the reach of a major newspaper to bring attention to women's concerns about the overall reform impulse in society. Some of those reporters, Helen Hunt Jackson and Rheta Childe Dorr, left the day-to-day profession for full-time attention to reform. And a few journalists—Ida Tarbell the most significant—simply rejected any call but her own. Finally, Miriam Leslie gave money.

Women Helping Women: June Cunningham Croly
Born in England, Jane Cunningham Croly, the columnist
"Jennie June," was throughout her career deeply involved in
organization building. She called the first woman's congress
in the North in 1856 and the second in 1868. When the New
York Press Club denied her and other female journalists
entry to a men-only reception for Charles Dickens, she
formed what became a famous women's club, Sorosis, that
emphasized friendship and network building. In 1889, she
helped found the Women's Press Club of New York and later
the powerful General Federation of Women's Clubs at the
turn of the century; she was its first president and wrote its
history.

Croly had a particular interest in economic equality. As
early as 1884, as she told the Packard Club, "Women have a
natural right to be money makers and money spenders, and
it is not a credit to them to make a little money and then sit
down quietly with it, or give it to some man to make ducks
and drakes of. She must not think of making just enough
money for her support until some man comes along to marry
her. If a woman cannot take care of herself, she is not fit to
be married." At a time when striking workers were considered one step from socialists and anarchists, Croly was a public supporter of the Working Women's Society of New York
and was public in her support of women strikers.

Working from Within
Women reporters were not in powerful positions at most
newspapers, but clearly some women journalists used the
tools at hand. One such woman was Marie Manning, whose
nationally distributed column "Beatrice Fairfax" was a dom-

inating feature of American newspapers for thirty years early in the nineteenth century. Manning followed Arthur Brisbane in the exodus from Pulitzer's *World* to Hearst's *Journal* at the time of the Spanish-American War. She joined two other women (Anne O'Hagan and a second woman Manning only identifies as "Bettina the Fearless," "Fearless Child," or just plain "Fearless") in the "Hen Coop," an office outside of the main newsroom where the women's section was prepared. Newsmen who were out of favor were sent to work in their office—"the equivalent of sending a dog to the pound." She describes the three women as "ardent feminists." Manning herself could not but be aware of women's concerns that flooded her desk as "Beatrice Fairfax"—occasionally passing the hat in the newsroom when the mail brought notice of a particularly harrowing problem.

But it was clearly difficult to put suffrage on the agenda in an environment when suffragists were configured as figures of fun or nothing at all. "We girls were all confirmed suffragists," she writes, "but so far as writing about the subject went, our hands were largely tied. The big shots at the paper were not interested in woman's suffrage in the beginning of the 1900s." Stories of suffrage meetings were either discarded or boiled down to a sentence unless there was promise of "fights." "Not only did we watch out for them, but we actually created them, aided and abetted by those splendid pioneer suffragists who had been working for the amendment for nearly fifty years," she recalled in her 1944 memoir. "The moguls never caught on. Doubtless these innocent prevarications never got the movement very far, but it helped to keep our spirits up in the Hen Coop, and it mightily amused those splendid old high priestesses of the movement." After she moved to Washington, Manning did indeed take part in direct lobbying for suffrage, but her experiences at the turn-of-the-century *Journal* may reflect the small subversive battles that women journalists adopted.

By 1911, suffrage was on the nation's agenda and in the nation's newspapers, and, at least in the beginning, the subject was handed over to the females on staff. Suffrage was front-page news with the introduction of elaborate suffrage parades, but in the day-by-day coverage before parades were introduced, it was the women reporters who were most likely to cover the stories of lectures to club women by suffrage leaders. Indeed, one of the many strategies of Ida Husted Harper, the press representative of the National Association of Women's Suffrage, was to mount the kinds of society events that could result in coverage. Seeking suffrage adherents among society figures did the same thing. One such conversion resulted in the 1910 headline in the *Times,* "Mrs. Fish Gone Over to the Suffragists." These were strategies that women reporters could participate in as they could in coverage of the ongoing lectures where, in the manner of society reporting, all who attended were listed. Lists of names—especially as they included the wives of prominent men—were helpful in establishing a middle-class power base in support of suffrage. The *Suffragist,* the newspaper established in 1913 to represent Alice Paul's Congressional Union, similarly adopted the strategy.

As suffrage was more and more part of the daily beat, women reporters attempted to give to suffrage reporting the same kind of attention as any other story. Emma Bugbee and Eleanor Booth Simmons at the *Tribune* covered suffrage activity regularly. When it appeared the 1913 front-page suffrage parade would be covered by a man, *Tribune* management responded to the female reporters' objections and agreed to allow the women reporters to do the entire coverage.

Meantime, whether written about by men or women, the increasing suffrage parades were treated with some respect, prompted certainly by the number of well-known women involved. Mrs. O. H. P. Belmont, as she was known in the suffrage movement (she had previously indulged in the excesses of the Gilded Age as Mrs. William K. Vanderbilt), contributed to suffrage in myriad ways—organizational leadership, writing for the quality monthlies, leading parades in fashionable clothing that achieved press notice, and quietly paying fines for homeless women in New York's night courts. Thanks to figures such as Belmont who were connected to powerful men, the new attention by the *New York Times* to the drama of a parade and the young, attractive, marching feminists in the New York City 1912 suffrage parade was just short of fulsome. An estimated 400,000 to a half million parade watchers were on hand for "a wonderful spectacle"; cheering was "of the complimentary and admiring sort"; the march was composed of "well-dressed, intelligent women, deeply concerned in the cause they are fighting for." It was only below Twenty-Third Street that side comments were "rather inclined to vulgarity." Flattering and impressive photographs accompanied the story. It is not clear if a female reporter wrote the story, but clearly the campaign for legitimacy that reporters had quietly waged had had some success. Moreover, the organizational aspects of the parade—the marchers grouped by occupations and historical periods—provided a metaphor that the goal of suffrage was going to upset the logical progression of society. In 1911, the fashion section of the *Times* devoted a discussion to appropriate wear for marching society, some indication that the press had normalized suffrage parades, if not what they stood for.

The Professional Career

Gertrude Battles Lane is the premiere example of the professional woman of the time, who took the opportunity that was offered her and by enormous effort turned it to the best advantage. Like Croly, Lane arrived in New York determined to find a job, in part to support her parents. Turned down at *McClure's,* she found a position at *McCall's,* thence the *Woman's Home Companion* in 1903. In 1909, she was made managing editor; she became editor in 1911. In 1929, she became vice president of the publishing company itself. At that time, she commented in an interview for the *New York Telegram,* "The opportunities that come to me were based on the fact that the Crowell Publishing Co. gives equal opportunities to men and women. There is no prejudice against women." She explained her success succinctly: "I was a hog to work, and so I got ahead. There's no secret to it beyond that." She was skilled in surviving the firing of her first boss and dealing with less than helpful subsequent management. When she was finally offered the editorship she was in a strong enough position to present the publisher with a list of demands, to which he acceded. But her achievement was based, as she said, on her abilities as editor. She took the *Companion's* circulation into the millions (3.5 million by her death) by a formula as described by Mary Ellen Zuckerman of service departments, nonfiction articles, reform crusades, and fiction. The *Companion* campaigned against child labor, tuberculosis, and dirty grocery stores while arguing for healthier babies, clean fiction, and moral movies. It also published articles on politics. Her reader, she said, "was intelligent and clearheaded. I must tell the truth." Like other shelter magazines, the *Companion* published articles on suffrage, although it was not until 1910 that it suggested editorially that women, as moral guardians of the home, needed the right to vote to carry out those responsibilities—perhaps the most conservative of the prosuffrage positions. Lane may have hired more women than any other editor of the time. And she was well compensated for her work—at her death in 1941, she had one of the highest earned incomes of any woman. She lived well, traveled, and was helpful to family and friends. Although the *Ladies' Home Journal* tends to be most remembered of the major magazines of the period, the *Companion* under Lane was a powerhouse.

Helen Campbell

In an age of muckraking and of women's involvement in reform, Helen Campbell's 1886–87 series on poverty for the *New York Tribune* may not be surprising. But Campbell was writing slightly before the muckraking era was in full swing and writing for a metropolitan paper rather than the quality monthlies most associated with muckraking. Moreover, she was clearly addressing the systemic problems of women in poverty, in a compelling way but not in the wrenching, sensational style of the sob sisters. Altogether she wrote 21 articles in the "Prisoners of Poverty—Women Wage-Workers Earners and Their Lives" series, beginning with women in factories and expanding to housing and the sexual demands put on house servants. But despite the thoroughness of her research (or perhaps because of it), as Susan Henry writes, even at the *Tribune,* still with its Greeley-era liberal bent, the series brought criticism and the paper publicly called her ideas "quite impractical under almost all circumstances."

The series has been useful in helping scholars to understand the period, but it is interesting that no matter how well it was written or how trenchant its analysis of economics, and despite the fact it was published in the influential *Tribune,* "Prisoners of Poverty" mostly seemed to be a management concoction to serve the middle-class reforming-women portion of the newspaper's readership. The series points up the difficulty of trying to attract the kind of mass media attention for women that leads to legislative reforms, which muckrakers were able to secure in other arenas. Women's concerns did not get serious coverage until the Triangle factory fire in 1902 (wherein young women were throwing themselves out of windows to escape) and the shirtwaist-workers, which garnered coverage because of the youth and attractiveness of its strikers. "Prisoners of Poverty" was something of a test case that sought to put women on the reform agenda without placing the suffrage question in the forefront.

Ida Tarbell

The woman who is most connected to muckraking is Ida Tarbell, who did not write about child or female poverty. Her picture continues to grace most U.S. history books as the representative of the muckraking period when she became a celebrity as one of a group of otherwise male muckraking writers for *McClure's* magazine. Beginning in November 1902 and not ending until October 1904, Tarbell's 21-part series, "History of the Standard Oil Company," spelled out in rational and precise prose how John D. Rockefeller had achieved a monopoly in refining, transporting, and marketing oil.

Notably, Tarbell's Progressive politics did not include support of suffrage for women, a position she formed in the wake of the Woodhull scandal. She wrote books about women, including a series on famous women for *American Magazine,* and two works of nonfiction—*The Business of Being a Woman* (1912) and *The Ways of Women* (1915)—that expanded on her antisuffrage position. She sat on the executive board of the New York Association Opposed to the Extension of Suffrage to Women and wrote pamphlets that were sold by the antisuffrage publications. The nature of her celebrity gave authority and entry to antisuffrage articles in *Ladies' Home Journal* and *Women's Home Companion.* But in 1912, when she wrote for *Ladies' Home Journal* a group of articles that seemed to blame independent women for their own unhappiness with the most objectionable "Making a Man of Herself," suffragists called a rally specifically to respond. In 1924, suffrage now a constitutional amendment, she clung hard to her position, asking in *Good Housekeeping,* "Is Woman's Suffrage a Failure?"

Indeed, Tarbell pondered the role of women in society all her life. A single working woman still with family responsibilities even into her later years, she was sympathetic regarding the barriers to working women. She may have seen herself primarily as a worker—the title of her autobiography *All in the Day's Work* is significant. She supported labor issues when women were affected. But she had an antipathy to middle-class reformers that she could not shake. When Al

Smith lost the presidency in 1928, she wrote, "I have always known that you could depend upon my sex for a full measure of prejudice and conservatism, but I did not think it could be so bad."

Rheta Childe Dorr: Challenge

Rheta Childe Dorr suggests the impossibility of wedding radical change to the mainstream press. Her radicalism was fueled by discouraging experiences in getting a job. In her autobiography she recorded her early experiences: "As far as I could see I lived in a world entirely hostile to women; a world in which every right and every privilege were claimed by men. Men exacted everything, gave nothing, throwing contempt into the bargain." She finally secured a position to write articles of interest to women for the prestigious *New York Evening Post,* known for its high road in politics but seeking female readers to meet the demands of advertisers. Dorr interpreted her assignment of "articles of interest to women" broadly. She became politicized by aligning with the Women's Trade Union League that sought an eight-hour day, minimum wage, woman suffrage, and—its most difficult task—politicizing working women themselves. Meantime, the *Post* chose not to give her a raise, noting that any woman reporter could be hired for the same salary. By 1906, she had turned to writing about child labor and working women for the quality monthlies, putting herself (as Barbara Ehrenreich would do in the 1990s) in real-life, working situations. Dorr's first book, *What Eight Million Women Want,* published in 1910, resulted from a series of articles she wrote for *Hampton's Magazine.* Like the Campbell series, it appealed to middle-class readers, arguing that to force women into routinized labor was "destroying the home by taking away from the workers the power to make homes." Even Childe had to adapt her writing to the domestic rationales of that day.

Finally, also influenced by the British suffrage movement, she aligned with Alice Paul's Congressional Union, for which she edited the party's organ, *Suffragist*. She was in the forefront of a party of 500 women at a meeting with President Woodrow Wilson in 1914 to present a resolution for federal suffrage that had been passed by the General Federation of Women's Clubs. In the tradition of the British suffragettes, Dorr stepped forward and challenged Wilson face-to-face for his refusal to back the amendment, forcing a steely Wilson response: "I think that is not proper for me to stand here and be cross-examined by you."

Miriam Leslie

And, finally, there is Mrs. Frank Leslie, a woman who might have been Victoria Woodhull's sister for the way she flouted the domestic conventions of the time. Miriam Follin Squier Leslie inherited from her second husband a publishing empire built from the fount of *Frank Leslie's Illustrated News,* known for its competitive edge, its impressive artistic illustrations, and an early muckraking campaign against contaminated milk.

She learned about journalism when Leslie, separated from his wife, came to live with her and her first husband, Ephraim G. Squier. Both Squiers worked for him and they all traveled overseas together. After a decade of working together—a subject of great gossip—Leslie and Miriam each obtained divorces, married, and lived in a grand style above and beyond the talk and despite a tell-all book from her ex-husband. At Leslie's death, Miriam Leslie had her named legally changed to "Mrs. Frank Leslie" as she set about putting to use her years of apprenticeship to the man whose name she bore. Leslie finally sold the now-profitable newspaper in 1889, just as illustrated newspapers were reaching the end of the line.

Through it all, she was not shy about offering her name, her opinions, or her photograph for publications. She was mentioned in the press on "How to be Beautiful"; the value of her jewels was noted by *Ladies' Home Journal;* she provided a chapter for the book *What America Owes to Women* that put her next to notable feminists such as Mary Livermore. For *Ladies' Home Journal,* she gave advice on "Women in Business Life," noting women had several advantages over men except in the area of "nerves"; later, she wrote a column for the *Journal* meant to address the question, "Are Our Girls Too Independent?" but it had more to do about advice to young women on how to conduct flirtations. She wrote travel accounts and a slightly scandalous book, *Are Men Gay Deceivers?*

At the time of her death in 1914, she had been multimarried, had survived scandal and ridicule, and by her own acumen had enlarged her wealth. Shortly before her death, she changed her will once more, this time to remain true to a promise she had made to the Women's Press Club of New York 30 years earlier. To the consternation of her many relatives-by-marriage and accumulated hangers-on, her will directed that all of her money—$2 million—go to Carrie Chapman Catt to establish the Leslie Woman's Suffrage Commission. It provided the means for the final push for passage of the Nineteenth Amendment.

SEVEN

NEGOTIATING THE NATION

In 1909, Progressives won a major reform battle. Sparked by socialist and labor concerns, some 30,000 young women in northeastern shirtwaist factories went on strike. At a time when the mass press expressed the fear of strikes as close to anarchism and socialism, the young workers and the generation of college women who supported them (although not the labor and socialists behind the strike) gained a sympathetic eye, both from the quality monthly magazines and, more surprisingly, from the mass press. The young women picketers were portrayed heroically, especially after police turned a blind eye when they were abused by gangs of thugs. "Probably public sympathy has been more stirred by the unfair treatment of women pickets than the cause of the strikers could ever have aroused so that the martyrdom of the girls who have been abused, thumped and thrown into the gutter has not been in vain," said an article in the quality monthly *The Survey*. The *New York Times* noted that they had drawn the support of college women such as "Vassar girl and suffrage enthusiast Inez Milholland, arrested for unlawful assembly in the picketing and whose example would encourage other young women to want the right to vote." Daily papers devoted whole columns of news to the workers' struggle; the magazines commented on it; meetings were held in women's colleges and in clubs to hear the story. The propaganda significance of the sympathy raised by way of young women in danger, the press attention that the beautiful and dedicated Milholland attracted, and the usefulness of a middle-class imprimatur could not have been lost on Alice Paul and the Congressional Union for Woman's Suffrage.

The success of the shirtwaist workers' strike resonated with the Progressive politics that believed the multiple evils of a society based on industrialization could be solved, first by exposure. The muckraking writers of the era brought attention to the evils of the time in the important quality monthlies. Major magazines were not complete without series on food adulteration, the problems of poverty, and the abuse of children. Some of the reform initiatives had what could only have been considered intoxicating successes by their proponents. The optimism of the age encouraged the development of independent young women to take an active role in solving problems, as previous generations had taken up antislavery. These became exponents of the New Woman—educated, middle class, and activist, and certainly confident in ways that women had not been before. Inez Haynes Irwin recalled the years between 1900 and 1910 as "full of hope and freedom. Great movements were starting everywhere. In the United States, the loudest voice in the land was that of the liberal. Everyone was fighting for something. Everyone was sure of victory."

While the success of the shirtwaist workers' strike

maintained the Progressives' high energy, in other parts of the country suffrage was being handed defeats from the liquor industry. From the earliest days of Stanton and Anthony's collaboration, suffrage had been associated with temperance. Clara Bewick Colby of the *Women's Tribune* saw suffrage and temperance as twin goals. Temperance supporters, however, were not always suffrage supporters, and it took until the end of the century for Frances Willard to move the Women's Christian Temperance Union (WCTU) to its support. Willard's ability to move the huge organization—much larger than all the suffrage groups put together—to a suffrage position was of major importance.

But in state-by-state elections, the association of temperance and suffrage was not helpful. The liquor industry put major resources into antisuffrage in the fear women would eventually make the sale of alcohol illegal, and, indeed, temperance advocates had that plan. Carrie Chapman Catt, who identified the extent of liquor interests in Oregon's 1906 suffrage election, commented, "Had there been no prohibition movement in the United States, the women would have been enfranchised two generations before they were." Abigail Duniway, editor of Oregon's *New Northwest,* opposed any cooperation between suffrage and temperance, leading to a WCTU charge that she had sold out to the liquor interests. In 1896, Anthony asked Willard not to hold a convention in California where it might injure a suffrage campaign. Willard complied, but suffrage was still defeated.

The second problem was the difficulty of dealing with Willard's argument that suffrage was about the transformation of society, a point of view already an influence on the Stone-Blackwell wing of the suffrage movement and a reason that brought many of the nation's reformers to the cause. By the turn of the century, suffrage leaders were trying to disassociate themselves from the unrealistic notion that suffrage would lead to the solution of all industrial ills.

Finally, Progressives were supporters of African American rights. Progressive writers exposed the evils of Jim Crow laws; Progressive activists worked on antilynching campaigns; and African Americans and Progressives, including white suffrage activists such as Inez Milholland and Jane Addams, participated in the formation of the National Association for the Advancement of Colored People (NAACP) in 1902. From earliest days, male and female African American leaders had been supporters of suffrage, and W. E. B. DuBois argued for suffrage in his challenge to Booker T. Washington's power base. Much of that history came undone in 1912, when Theodore Roosevelt's Progressive Party approved a strategy that permitted the party in the South to be "lily white."

Altogether, these were difficult shoals for any strategist. The suffrage campaign and Alice Paul's final thrust came at a time when the issue of votes for women was diffused among many quarters, had been intertwined with dozens of other messages, and carried implications that were deeply rooted in Americans' ideas of nation. The close connection of suffrage to the agenda of Progressive reform gave to suffrage a wide base of general support, but suffrage also inherited Progressives' powerful opponents, who warned that, like socialism and anarchism, suffrage would contribute to the overturn of the nation's ideals. For Paul, her own gender complicated her decisions. Expected to be a representative of the moral high road because of it, she pursued her political goal as pragmatically as any politician.

As World War I approached, the campaign for the vote was continuing as highly organized and directed from the new National American Woman Suffrage Association (NAWSA), the result, in 1890, of the final coming together of the Stanton-Anthony and the Lucy Stone wings of the movement. By 1910, women had equal suffrage with men in Idaho, Utah, Wyoming, and Colorado. Some form of school suffrage existed in twenty-two states; two states allowed tax-paying suffrage; three states allowed school and taxpaying suffrage; one state allowed municipal suffrage. No form of suffrage existed in nineteen states.

Meantime, women's rights activities were occurring on other stages. Belva Lockwood had mounted two campaigns for the presidency of the United States as a candidate of the Equal Rights Party—the party established by Victoria Woodhull. Elizabeth Cady Stanton produced a major propaganda effort at the end of the century with the publication of the *Woman's Bible*. Stanton's interpretation of the bible was a remarkable risk for its time (as it would be today), tampering with the sacrosanct much as her Declaration of Sentiments had offered a reinterpretation of the sacred text of the Declaration of Independence. It was not well received in either the feminist or larger community, and, indeed, the *Woman's Bible* added to the perception that woman's suffrage was becoming more radical.

THE PUBLIC RELATIONS CAMPAIGN

Susan B. Anthony was one of the leaders of the time who would not connect herself to Stanton's bible project. From the days when she and Stanton tried, unsuccessfully, to introduce bloomers, Anthony had concluded that one campaign at a time was enough. One of Anthony's closest associates, and an individual who shared her single focus, was Ida Husted Harper. Harper is most remembered as Anthony's biographer and author of the final two volumes of *History of Woman Suffrage*. But in the years of the new century, Harper's contribution to suffrage was as press representative of NAWSA. She was a "chairman" of the National Woman Suffrage Press Committee, and then the "editorial chairman" of the Leslie Bureau of National Suffrage Education (thanks to the Miriam Leslie bequest). At a time when the field of public relations was still being invented, Harper was already practicing its principles—like Anthony, seeking to stay on message at a time when there were many opportunities to do otherwise.

It is not surprising that NAWSA put particular attention on the press, since both earlier suffrage wings had promoted a press presence. The report made by Dr. Anna Shaw, the organization's president in 1901, gives some indication of the scale of the press effort, noting that "175,000 articles on the subject [suffrage] had been sent to the press and a careful investigation showed that three-fourths of them had been published. In addition different papers had used 150 special articles, while the page of plate matter furnished every six weeks was extensively taken. New York reported 400 papers accepting suffrage matter regularly; Pennsylvania, 368; Iowa, 253; Illinois, 161; Massachusetts, 107, and other States in varying numbers. Since this question is very largely one of educating the people, the opening of the Press to its arguments is probably the most important advantage which has been gained."

These and the continuing successes speak to the press achievements of the many local leaders. In California, for example, Mabel Craft Deering's report on her role as suffrage press chair for the state became a "readable guide for suffrage campaigns" in other states. By 1913, suffrage press activities in Georgia had resulted in woman suffrage departments at the Atlanta *Constitution*, regular columns on the issues in the *Journal* and the Columbus *Ledger*, and, in 1914, special suffrage issues of *The Atlanta Georgian* and the *Ledger*, altogether a rather remarkable record when the antisuffrage press was mounting its own race-based campaign.

In the last stages of the amendment campaign, however, Harper personally wrote thousands of letters to editors, prepared pamphlets, and furnished a monthly article for the *International Suffrage News* in London. She reported by the end of 1918 that her office was receiving 300 to 500 editorials monthly on suffrage; that most were knowledgeable and most northern papers were in favor of suffrage and the federal amendment, while the South had leading advocates. Harper may have been the most responsible for achieving a respectful place for suffrage in the mainstream publications of the day and setting the stage for Alice Paul's more dramatic publicity.

Like Dorr, Harper had been a reporter who had "gone over" to suffrage on a full-time basis. As a young married woman living in Terre Haute, Indiana, she began contributing to newspapers—for twelve years, she contributed "A Woman's Opinions" to the *Terre Haute Saturday Mail*, and from 1884 to 1893 she provided another woman's column for the *Firemen's Magazine*, edited by socialist Eugene V. Debs. However, it was her work as a press liaison for the California state suffrage campaign that brought her to Anthony's attention.

After Harper moved to New York, her suffrage and professional careers conflated. She took on the women's department at the Sunday *New York Sun* from 1899 to 1903, and from 1909 to 1913 she was a staff member for *Harper's Bazaar* (by then, spelled with two *a*'s). In both capacities she addressed suffrage. She was an indefatigable writer, and her articles appeared in newspapers in Chicago, Boston, Philadelphia, Washington, D.C., and New York. At the same time, she wrote a stream of major articles on suffrage for the quality monthlies. Aileen Kraditor credits her with thirteen articles in half a dozen years, all on suffrage. (At Harper's death in 1931 at age 79, one obituary noted her works filled fourteen large indexed volumes in the Library of Congress.) She found herself in an enviable position for a publicist—considered the expert rather than polemicist for the field she was representing—and the *Times,* no supporter of suffrage, used her as the expert of choice on suffrage. In addition to her major writing, she also took on many of the mundane day-to-day demands of a publicist—writing letters to the newspapers, from thank-you letters to polite corrections; mounting the society events that would bring coverage; and lecturing and participating frequently in suffrage activities in the United States and overseas. She was with Alice Paul when suffragists met with President Woodrow Wilson in 1913, but she did not follow Paul into the Congressional Union.

The suffrage campaign in New York was also energized when Harriot Stanton Blatch, daughter of Elizabeth Cady Stanton, returned to the United States in 1902 after twenty years in Great Britain. She set about revitalization by recruiting working-class women and by organizing parades and dramatic events in the style of the British suffragette (the British called themselves *suffragettes;* Americans were *suffragists*) Emmeline Pankhurst. She was outspoken and quite fearless, and would work with the New Jersey–born Alice Paul, when she also returned from England, where she had been imprisoned and force-fed alongside British suffragettes.

Still, the activity represented by Harper, Blatch, and others fell short for Paul and the younger feminists as the deaths of the women's activists who had come of age during the abolition movement led to examination of the suffrage movement. To the new critics, the New Woman of Greenwich Village, suffragists were using the out-of-date techniques of petition drives and meetings with congressional committees. Rheta Childe Dorr's assessment of suffrage activities did not credit Harper and other activists. In describing the routine of meeting with a congressional committee on the matter of a federal amendment, she wrote, "As a reporter I had attended one or two of these, watching the bored and indifferent men as they listened unmoved to women like Carrie Chapman Catt, Dr. Shaw, Ida Husted Harper, and others, speaking with intelligence and real eloquence. Nothing ever happened, but the women went home feeling that they had done their righteous best."

Paul believed in dramatic events—climbing fences, burning "watch fires" in front of the White House—but closely honed to a political strategy. She considered unrealistic the NAWSA goal to expect that a two-thirds majority in the House and Senate would vote for a constitutional amendment when each member had to come to that conclusion on his own. Paul and her second in command, Lucy Burns, focused on President Woodrow Wilson at a time of Democratic majorities in the House and Senate and the existence of the powerful Democratic caucus, which dwarfed the impact of any individual legislator. In that powerful position, Wilson could insist Congress call for the amendment. "The whole suffrage question," as Dorr described it, "thus reduced itself to winning one casting vote, that of Woodrow Wilson."

Older suffragists were unwilling to adopt Paul's ideas, as they ran counter to the organization's nonpartisan strategy. Moreover, Wilson was a man of too strongly conservative beliefs when it came to women, unlikely ever to favor woman suffrage. But in the new organization that Paul founded, Congressional Union for Woman's Suffrage (CUWS), later the Women's Party, Paul eschewed moral suasion—it did not matter whether Wilson personally ever changed his mind as long as he responded, like the practical politician he was, to the kind of leverage that had been applied by the Women's Social and Political Party in Great Britain.

ALICE PAUL AND PUBLICITY

At the center of Paul's strategy was publicity, but less along the lines of NAWSA's state-by-state letter-writing campaigns. The Congressional Union adopted a power strategy that exerted pressure on the top by way of the example of the British suffragettes. Her strategy was in evidence in the 1913 suffrage parade. When it was broken up by toughs and women were injured, Paul's demand for an investigation received newspaper space across the country. It was symbolic, Dorr writes. "The Congressional Union had set out to 'induce' President Wilson and publicity was its first weapon."

Before Paul established the Congressional Union, she was involved in the NAWSA 1913 national suffrage parade in Washington, D.C., scheduled the day before President Wilson's inauguration to bring attention to the proposed federal amendment. New York suffrage parades had become almost routine—building solidarity among members of the movement and indicating the breadth of support for suffrage by including everyone from socialites to workers, organized under appropriate banners. Women paid particular attention to spectacle and femininity—colorful sashes, floats, and banners. For those along the parade route, a suffrage parade could be as simple as a day out or a time to express rowdyism, which was certainly an ongoing concern in New York, where parade organizers regularly asked for police protection.

For the Washington march, Paul could call upon an experienced cadre of suffragists: 8,000 marchers for an "eye-popping extravaganza" of colorfully attired women, patriotic floats, women on white horses, all-women bands, and cadres of marching women wherein women were portrayed both as feminine and as citizens of the nation. Half a million people were arrayed along the route, which was somewhat longer than the route of the previous year's New York City march. But Paul had no experience with the District of Columbia police. When the drunken rowdies appeared, police offered no protection. Some women were injured. Inez Milholland, on her white horse, forged into the crowd to protect them. As reported by the Associated Press, "Five thousand women marching in the woman suffrage pageant today virtually fought their way foot by foot up Pennsylvania Avenue through a surging mob that completely defied the Washington police, swamped the marchers, and broke their procession into little companies."

The national publicity prompted Senate hearings. A noisy audience of suffrage supporters packed the courtroom as 150 witnesses recounted the attacks and jeers. Called a heroine by the Associated Press, Milholland, photographed astride "Grey Dawn," received national attention. Less noticed in the tumult of the march and its aftermath was Paul's reluctant permission to allow a group of African American women from Howard University to march nor the order to Ida Wells Barnett to march with the black contingent only, which Barnett refused, marching instead with a group of white suffragists. But Paul had surely achieved her goal of publicity by playing on patriarchal sympathies of unprotected women and maintaining ideas of white hegemony.

THE ROLE OF SUFFRAGE PUBLICATIONS

The cluster of suffrage publications introduced in the years after the Civil War served to bolster particular views toward suffrage and the positions of women who promoted them, sometimes straining the ongoing theme of sisterhood. State suffrage organizations had publications. *The Woman's Journal,* long connected to the Stone-Blackwell wing of the movement, became *Woman Citizen,* the official organ of the new national organization, the National American Woman Suffrage Association. In 1888, the *Journal* established a supplement, *The Woman's Column,* edited by Alice Stone Blackwell, the daughter of Lucy Stone and Henry Blackwell. Begun as an attempt to be a kind of news service about suffrage for newspaper editors, it extended its proselytizing purposes by extensive mailings to educators, ministers, political figures, and influential citizens. Like the *Journal,* the *Column* sought to disassociate itself from radical politics in favor of traditional values, images, institutions, and individuals. However, the *Column* has been credited with providing the movement with a sense of unity, promoting a unified effort that led to the re-unification of the two wings. And even within the middle-class ideology, the *Column* took on some wider issues.

Although *The Revolution* died an early death, other publications connected to the Stanton-Wing appeared, including Matilda Gage's *National Citizen and Ballot Box* in Syracuse, New York. Claire Colby's *Woman's Tribune* was also associated with Stanton, participating in the *Woman's Bible* (which she published in her paper, much to the consternation of the conservatives). In addition, a cluster of regional suffrage publications targeted specific audiences. *The Pioneer* served the western feminist; the *Farmer's Wife* (1891–1894) aimed at women on the Kansas prairie. *The Woman's Exponent* (1872–1914), published in Utah, served a Mormon readership and presented suffrage as a further empowerment of the theology. *Progress* (1902–1910) was a western organ for the suffrage association in Warren, Ohio. The *New York Suffrage Newsletter* was a publication from the state organization.

There were also publications that did not have suffrage as their primary purpose, but promoted women in general. Barbara Reed has brought attention to *The Jewess,* the first publication in the United States that served Jewish women. *The Woman's Era* under the editorship of Josephine Ruffin represented the considerable African American club women's movement. Moreover, in the print-heavy culture of the time, we should also consider the plethora of publications emanating from women's clubs, women's organizations, and women's colleges that addressed women's role in the culture.

However, the publication that is most connected to the final success of the Nineteenth Amendment is *Suffragist,* begun in 1913 as the representative of Alice Paul's Congressional Union and edited by Rheta Childe Dorr. More than other suffrage papers, *Suffragist* represented the single focus of Paul's approach, maintaining the refrain that the Democratic president headed a Democratic machine in which all officials were at the level of "buck privates." The president was the focus, readers were told, because it was the president alone who had the power to insist upon a federal amendment. As Dorr wrote, "In 'The Suffragist' I kept this fact constantly before the women." The intensity was maintained by the constant reiteration of present actions. "Alice Paul would never allow me or any of the others to speak of the amendment as a thing of next year or the next. Always it was spoken of as a measure which must be passed immediately."

Suffragist used cartoons as part of its strategy, aligning it with other radical publications to make radical political points. The paper had its own cartoonist, Nina Allender, one of the clusters of female cartoonists of the era. *Suffragist* used cartoons regularly, always on the front page, and this use alone tended to align the publication with the radical, sometimes socialist, publications, which had introduced cartoons as a way of reaching immigrant readers. Paul's readers were far from immigrant readers, but the use of cartoons themselves was a form that carried its own meanings: At the very least, cartoons countered the practice of fine and decorative arts that was the province of the well-brought-up young woman and provided an alternative to the lushly illustrated covers of the women's magazines.

Interestingly, the cartoons and the assertive editorials existed side by side with strategies redolent of women's sections of newspapers—chapter news from around the nation and the publication of long lists of female supporters. These female supporters were, as in society and club news, identified by their marriage status, their husbands' names, and, when they could, mention of their connection to prominent husbands and fathers. Despite the front-page cartoons, there was, indeed, a middle-class aura to the paper—from its advertising, which included advertising for millinery, to its promotions of suffrage balls and suffrage demonstrations that emphasized color-coordinated clothing. But we might consider that in Paul's highly politicized publication, the middle-class emphasis signaled that suffrage—to its readers and to the outside world—had the support of women who had some power in the culture, even if that power emanated from their male connections and their roles in "society." Paul used what levers were available to her, and there was political advantage to be gained from positioning suffrage as supported by the conservative segments of society at a time when suffrage was connected to the most radical segments.

Linda J. Lumsden has discussed how the newspaper supported the White House picketing campaign that aimed to keep suffrage on the presidential agenda. Beginning on January 10, 1917, two sets of six women stood outside the White House gates bearing the placards "Mr. President, What Will You Do for Woman's Suffrage?" and "How Long Must Women Wait for Liberty?" The women were jeered and sometimes attacked. Half of the picketers were arrested, and 168 were jailed in the district workhouse for as long as seven months. Paul was put in a psychiatric ward. The ensuing hunger strikes, as Lumdsen writes, "proved perfect propaganda fodder." "I am afraid this letter is not well written and I am rather light headed from hunger," Mary Winsor wrote in a smuggled note that was printed in the paper. Through it all, *Suffragist* (Lucy Burns now writing many of the editorials after the departure of Dorr), maintained the focus on President Wilson during a war period when dissident publications were being closed for sedition. Lumsden speculates that the newspaper escaped prosecution because it "was insulated partly by the women's elite status and partly by a sense of male chivalry" but also because the paper kept itself on message, away from war criticism.

ANTISUFFRAGE PUBLICATIONS

But *Suffragist* did not operate in the kind of safe and private world of earlier reform publications. The most virulent of antisuffrage rhetoric was found in an active antisuffrage press, whose ideas permeated and even strengthened similar notions in the mass press. *Suffragist* found itself trying to counter antisuffrage arguments in ways that were pragmatic but did not reflect the high moral standards that some women believed women would bring to politics.

Ida Tarbell was the most well known of women antisuffragists. Others were Annie Nathan Meyer, a founder of Barnard College as well as associate editor of *The Antisuffragist* who occasionally wrote for the mass press, and Jeannette L. Gilder, whose argument in *Harper's Bazar* in 1894 that the nation needed mothers of great men more than women in office was still quoted in the *New York Times* twenty years later. Such a statement was in line with the antisuffrage argument, as Manuela Thurner puts it, that the issue "was not women's domesticity, but their effectiveness as nonvoting, yet public spirited citizens and agents of social change." In her examination of the antisuffrage *The Remonstrance* (1890–1920), however, Elizabeth Burt does not find so much a call to change by way of influence in the domestic circle as much as a reiteration of the domestic circle per se; that is, the domestic circle did not have to have an activist rationale. Every issue of the newspaper contained articles "that upheld and defended woman's sphere," or "the womanhood of woman." As *The Antisuffragist* put it, "Protection in the home and immunity from public service and labor, in order that her time and strength may be given to the supreme work of creating anew the human race, or and more, in the image of God, and for a destiny of progress and brotherhood is the most ancient, the most fundamental, right of woman, and one in which the future of the race is deeply involved."

This use of "right" attacked the suffragists' claim that voting was a basic right of democracy by indicating that domestic "rights" (and responsibilities) were of a higher order. The subject of women's domestic "rights" also came in for discussion with the sinking of *Titanic* in 1912, when women and children were first to be saved. The antisuffrage press brought attention to British suffragette Sylvia Pankhurst's remark that the practice of "women and children first" should be abolished in a world where all were equal. The antisuffrage paper, *Militancy of the American Suffragette: the Woman's Protest* (1912–1918), the organ of the National Association Opposed to Woman Suffrage, reprinted a British sermon on the subject: "Men of much use to the world perished in that catastrophe because their inherent chivalry compelled them to give way to women. But Miss Pankhurst is impudent enough to withhold credit for them." This was less a discussion of philosophical difference, however, than an effective propaganda technique, connecting antisuffrage to a tragedy of the moment. The antisuffrage press also picked up themes from the previous century. *The Protest* reprinted an article from the *Woman's Journal* supporting working women but with a headline, "Suffragist Leader Endorses Free Love," a hot-button issue from the days of Fanny Wright.

MASS MEDIA

In her 1901 report, Shaw expressed belief that suffrage was on its way to win the battle of the press:

> The most encouraging sign is the attitude of the Press. Although the country papers occasionally refer to the suffrage advocates as hyenas, cats, crowing hens, bold wantons, unsexed females and dangerous home-wreckers ... these are no longer found in metropolitan and influential newspapers. Scores of both city and country papers openly advocate the measure and scores of others would do so if they were not under the same control as the Legislatures. Ten years ago it was almost impossible to secure space in any paper for woman suffrage arguments. To-day several of the largest in the country maintain regular departments for this purpose.

Whether all the attention was favorable is not clear, but suffrage activity had found a place in the mass media. However, as the antisuffrage movement adopted some of the same publicity techniques that suffrage had developed—including public events, use of well-known women on its various mastheads, and placement of major articles in the commercial press—in the view of the press the point was made that there were clearly two sides to the suffrage argument. Suffrage proponents argued that the two sides were not at all of similar size—like comparing "a minnow and a mackerel," according to Alice Stone Blackwell. Yet, antisuffrage, even in an argumentative form, kept suffrage on the table because it fit in the craft tradition of providing "balance." Similar events occurred in the Second Wave, when conservative organizations, whatever their size, were used to "balance" arguments put forth by the National Organization for Women. As craft traditions also developed along lines of even-handedness, name-calling was not so frequent, but the new craft traditions still allowed a fair amount of latitude in presentation.

THE QUALITY MONTHLIES

Early on, the monthly magazines gave suffrage a head start. For middle-class reformers, the quality monthlies provided their view on the world, and it was the quality monthlies that gave their imprimatur to the suffrage moment by the end of the century as a way to serve the Progressive agenda as well as their women readers. This attention to women's sensibilities was not always the case. Boston's *North American Review* was the most notable quality monthly that provided forum for discussion, beginning in 1879 when Francis Parkman prayed that God would deliver the nation from the specter of suffrage driven by "a few agitators." Parkman's article resulted in an extensive rejoinder from five men and women suffragists. In 1892, another controversy erupted when a doctor voiced his reservations on the basis that a woman's brain was smaller than a man's, to say nothing of the "peculiar neurotic condition called the hysterical is grafted on the organ of a woman." Another spate of responses occurred. By the new century, the *Review* has been persuaded. At Stanton's death, it published Susan B. Anthony's 1902 heroic review of suffrage activity. Later it published an article by Harper calling for suffrage as "a right" for all—one of Harper's attempts to move the discussion beyond the perception of women's elevated morality. Shortly thereafter, the *North American* was the first monthly to endorse woman's suffrage: "We are convinced that the time has arrived when the welfare of the Nation would be most effectually conserved by conferring upon women the privilege of voting and holding office." The endorsement was accompanied by the caveat that suffrage was not so much a right of citizenship "as some would have it" as an extension of womanly responsibilities.

At a time when women reformists were driven by moral housekeeping rationales, the quality monthlies of a Progressive nature often, although not entirely, saw suffrage as an extension of women's abilities as moral leader in the home. In particular, Benjamin Flowers, the editor of *The Arena,* in 1891 ushered in what he called the "Era of Women," a time when women could do nothing less than change the course of civilization. Flowers was criticized as presenting a "beatific vision" of women, or, as one critic put it, "[A]ll women do not have wings under their stays."

Nonetheless, with its many women contributors (a fourth), readers, and editors, the *Arena* lived up to its name for presentations of suffrage, dress reform, divorce, factory labor, and the rights of women in marriage.

The *American Magazine*—the publication started by Tarbell and her fellow muckrakers to present a more radical voice than offered by *McClure's*—began a series on a larger role for women in society. And other monthlies opened their doors to the suffrage question: The *Atlantic Monthly, Lippincott's,* and *Overland Monthly* provided mostly prosuffrage articles and not always with moral housekeeping rationales. In 1912, *McClure's,* the famous muckraking journal that had exposed corruption and graft in the highest places, addressed suffrage in terms of Inez Milholland, "the most effective spokesman of the suffrage cause in America," accompanied by one photograph of her on a horse from the 1912 suffrage parade and another pensive and glamorous profile.

Suffrage had been grist for the humor magazines in the 1870s. *Puck* published the cartoon of leading suffragists as geese in 1878. But times change. *Puck* may have published one of the most unequivocal of the prosuffrage pieces—a two-page cartoon showed a poor woman with many children and sketches of women in factory work. "Shall Women Vote?" asked the underline, with the answer, "No; They might disturb the existing order of things." By 1915, *Puck* used a female cartoonist and a female writer for its satire of the antisuffrage movement, "Madame Anti Makes Her Annual Report." In the same year, *Puck* published the straightforward "A Suffrage Editorial especially written for Puck," altogether a complete turnaround from its positions in the 1870s and 1880s. Surely, penance had been done.

However, the choice of Inez Milholland as the representative of suffrage suggests that *McClure's* was not any more adverse to the glamorization of a subject than the *Times* had been in the shirtwaist workers' strike. However, while suffrage was still a matter of some ridicule in the newspaper press, the quality monthlies represented an increasing base of middle-class support.

THE MASS MAGAZINES

The mass magazines were less eager than the quality monthlies to give their imprimatur to suffrage. Still, the use of balancing articles provided entry for suffrage discussion. In the first decade of the century, the major shelter magazines, including the *Ladies' Home Journal,* adopted policies that represented both sides of the debate. In 1910, the nation's American heroine, Jane Addams, wrote "Why Women Should Vote" for the *Journal,* arguing along moral housekeeping lines, while Lyman Abbot provided a counter-article suggesting the vote would be "injurious to woman." The *Journal's* most famous antisuffrage article was by President Grover Cleveland (whose wife later headed up an antisuffrage association). However, by 1913, Bok had changed from a tactic of positing pro and anti arguments. Perhaps not wanting to alienate his readership (some of whom could vote by this time) and not discounting the pressure from the other shelter magazine, Bok published articles such as Margaret Deland's proposal, "The Third Way in Woman Suffrage: A Plan for Possible Solution of a Vexing Problem." Her "third way" was an intelligence test. "Personally, I am not afraid of the uneducated vote. I am very much afraid of the unintelligent vote."

At the *Woman's Home Companion,* amid the many crusades, Gertrude Battles Lane was finally allowing prosuffrage
articles, including a three-part series with the lead article
written by the professional writer and editor, Anna Steese
Richardson, aimed at the "antis." Antis were similarly
ridiculed in a *Good Housekeeping* article by Dorothy Dix, the
advice columnist who increasingly allowed her prosuffrage
voice to emerge. Writing about "The Girl of Today" for
Good Housekeeping in 1916, Dix took on the editorial voice:
"The modern girl is a suffragist by instinct. She doesn't argue
about equal rights for women. She simply takes them for
granted. She knows herself as strong, as intelligent, as of as
much importance in the world as her brother, and it is un-
thinkable to her that he should have privileges, which are
denied to her, that doors should be open." Also in *Good
Housekeeping,* Margaret Sangster, the editor who had advised
woman journalists to stay close to their native interests, now
supported suffrage. The indefatigable Mrs. O. H. P. Belmont
provided "The Story of the Woman's War" in November
1913. The following month it was "The Women Who Get
Together," a nine-page, prosuffrage article with photographs
and first-person accounts of what it was like to march for
suffrage. The editorial voice introduced the article (and others) in prosuffrage ways.

By the end of the period, four of the "big six" (*Delineator, Woman's Home Companion, McCall's,* and *Good Housekeeping*) came to support female suffrage, primarily on the
basis of women's supposed abilities to clean up society. Only
Pictorial Review, under Arthur Vance (who had hired
Gertrude Battles Lane at the *Companion*) "unequivocally supported" equal rights: "We believe when all is said and done,

that if we recognize women to be human, it follows as a matter of simple justice that they have as much right to a voice in governmental affairs as the men."

THE NEWSPAPERS

Despite Shaw's optimistic appraisal of newspaper coverage of suffrage at the start of the century, it was not so clear that newspapers matched either the quality monthly or the shelter magazines in the depth of attention they gave to suffrage. Outside of club reporting, newspapers were more likely to construct the strongest bastions against women's suffrage because of the male nature of the newsroom, the prejudices of their owners, and the lack of women in positions of power. Unlike the magazines, content was less provided by freelance contributors (although NAWSA provided boilerplate articles), and letters to the editor did not carry the same weight as other editorial content. Moreover, outside of human-interest storytelling as noted earlier, newspaper content was also shaped by the copy desks and by devices of the summary lead, headlines, and choice of quotations. Despite the significant successes of the suffrage press campaign, the already important *New York Times* mitigated the suffrage message, often by manipulation of craft traditions. A lecturer who called for women to receive a regular portion of her husband's salary, for example, had his side comments on the giddy nature of New York girls put as the subject of the headline and lead—a much different story. Some stories seemed driven by conservative ideology. As if providing a service, the *Times* republished the *North American Review*'s highly critical article of women in business. Giving credence to the concerns of masculinity, the

Times reported on an antisuffrage speaker who warned women should work for their country, but "Not as a Counterfeit Man," the characterization of the prosuffrage women that the *Times* chose for its headline. When Brooklyn antisuffragists organized, they received coverage in four articles, compared with the single story at the same time given to the state of New York's hearing on suffrage.

Prosuffrage articles were able to come to the attention of the *Times* by the involvement of prominent women, traditional-style charity events, and the suffrage parades filled with spectacle including that of well-known women walking down Fifth Avenue carrying banners. The lowly regarded society and club news editors found ways to put these stories in the newspaper, although not to the extent some would have liked. In a letter that Ida Husted Harper, public relations expert as she was, likely would not have approved, Harriot Stanton Blatch, writing to thank the *Times* for coverage of an event, concluded with sarcasm, "There is absolutely no doubt that an antisuffrage journal can be a very excellent news sheet!"

As the suffrage arguments became polarized in the years of the new century, the *Times* reflected the antisuffrage technique of challenging the argument of some suffragists that women should have the vote because women, operating on a higher moral plane than men, would not tolerate corrupt government. Antisuffragists were quick to examine places that had granted female suffrage to see if that was the case. The *Times* published results in one case that suggested women's vote had made things worse, providing a four-deck headline that told readers all the things suffrage would not do ("Bad Report on Cities Where Women Vote"; "Investigators

Found Flaunting Vice in Denver and Salt Lake and Bribery at the Polls"; "Child Labor Unprotected"; "Divorce Evil Unchecked, He Says, Drug Stores Sell Girls Liquor, and Women Sell Their Votes"). Carrie Chapman Catt, as president of the National American Women Suffrage Association, found herself at the center of the same kind of storm when she was quoted in *Ladies' Home Journal* that suffrage would eliminate social evils. Catt wrote a letter to the *Times* repudiating the statement. The reporter repudiated the repudiation: Alice Stone Blackwell joined the fray. Nor was the paper shy about stereotyping. As one headline put it, "Woman's Sense of Humor It Is Frequently Alleged That She Does Not Possess Any."

As even family newspapers moved to banner headlines, stories in the mainstream press took on a sensationalist aspect, as in a story about Utah's support of suffrage. That support was widely viewed as a way to increase the state's Mormon power—another of the fears of the age—by having enfranchised women voting as directed by their husbands. In this frame, *Times* readers were informed by way of a 1913 banner headline, "Suffrage Appeals to Lawless and Hysterical Women." The headline's decks connected suffrage to even worst fears—Mormonism and socialism: "Mormonism Introduced the Idea Into the United States, Says Mrs. Rossiter Johnson, and Since Then No Large Body of Thinkers Has Adopted the Idea Except the Socialists."

THE MASSES

For Progressives outside of suffrage organizing, suffrage was one of a plethora of needed reforms, and no publication represented that view more than the magazine *The Masses.* In 1911, just two years after the shirtwaist factory strike, Irwin, already a suffragist, was among a group of similarly oriented New Women to become part of a "revolutionary not a reform" publication. As its editor Max Eastman put it, the magazine aimed to address systemic issues in "frank, arrogant, impertinent" ways. It was a magazine "whose final policy is to do as it please and conciliate nobody, not even its readers." *The Masses* had attitude. Like many of the magazines of the time, it was illustrated not in the color illustrations of the women's magazines, but in black-and-white drawings by a cadre of female artists. Its editorial staff and editorial contributors included famous women, socialistic women, women of color, union organizers, poets, novelists, and anonymous women.

The Masses provided more freedom for women to speak candidly than had any other publication. It was a magazine with definite socialistic leanings but, unlike the puritanical outlook of the socialist press, there was room in the magazine for the expression of sexual frustration of single women and even about the goddess Artemis as lover of her female devotees—topics that, in the earkt 1900s, could be handled in the pages of a few small-circulation poetry magazines. Helen R. Hull, who had written on reform issues for the New York papers, wrote a short story that introduced the issue of abortion. Divorce was tackled, as were the topics of cooperative housekeeping and child raising. When Emma Goldman was convicted of delivering a public lecture on birth control in 1916, *The Masses* printed her courtroom speech. Moreover, artwork by Cornelia Barns, Elizabeth Grieg, and Alice Beach Winter introduced working women to the pages of the magazine in ways that played upon strength and humor rather than pain and poverty. In its six-year run, *The Masses* was the exemplar of free speech, confidence in change, and commitment to the notion that a new generation would bring the success that had eluded an older generation. Votes for women seemed the logical step to achieve the promise of larger reforms. Led by Max Eastman, brother of the suffragist Crystal Eastman and a suffragist himself, and with many men on staff, the magazine was by no means an all-female production, but as Margaret C. Jones writes, the magazine "has to be understood as a feminist magazine not only in name, but for what women themselves made of it."

Yet even *The Masses* was not exempt from the dominant themes of the time. According to a less sanguine view, the magazine was not as forward-thinking as it believed but rather reiterated mainstream notions by romanticizing and sentimentalizing both middle-class and working-class women. Some male contributors to the magazines seemed most supportive of suffrage and the New Woman for implicit promises of sexual partnering without the costs and responsibilities of marriage. And because the magazine, despite its socialistic positions, still positioned woman as morally superior, the argument for equality was never made.

Some suffragists themselves believed woman should have the vote to better carry out her moral sensibilities, most defined in white, middle-class terms. Antisuffragists took up the middle-class argument by playing on the threat of power in hands of ethnic and racial minorities, which had some credence even in white Progressive circles. Connections of suffrage to anarchism, socialism, and unionism were entwined

with ideas of sexuality, race, and power. Indeed, suffrage—
however it was portrayed—was not a single reform, but
rather, to many eyes, was a reorientation of the whole social
order of separate spheres. As Paula Baker writes, "If women
voted, they would abandon the home and womanly virtues.
The differences between the sexes would be obscured: men
would lose their manhood and women would begin to act
like men."

These ideas were popular in mass culture, and not only
in Anglo-Saxon culture but also in the real "proletariat"—
new immigrants and working poor, who were much more
likely to go to the movies than read *The Masses*. The new
short films of the first movie companies, such as those headed
by Thomas Edison and Charlie Chaplin, found suffrage images of ridicule easy to adapt. In response, NAWSA, under
the leadership of Ruth Hanna McCormick, part of the
Chicago Tribune newspaper family, made suffrage films of its
own—setting up equal stereotypes of glorified woman. And
suffrage leaders increasingly ridiculed the antis in the stereotypes that had been developed against club women. Propaganda is never pretty, and suffrage efforts to combat the most
virulent stream had far-reaching consequences.

THE MOST VIRULENT STREAM

What the major press did not reflect directly, even in its anti
arguments, was the most virulent strain of the antisuffrage argument. This was the theme that votes for women meant
votes for African American women and the specter of, in the
phrase of the time, "Negro rule." Those ideas were no more
strongly expressed than in *The Woman Patriot,* published in

Washington, D.C., by the Patriot Publishing Company. One of its contributing editors was Henry Watterson, former reform editor of the *Louisville Courier* who was an avowed antifeminist and, given the nature of the publication, racist too. "Anti-suffragists have time and again pointed out that the Susan B. Anthony Amendment means race peril to the South," according to a 1920 editorial. "It is said that the Negro women will be even more insistent upon suffrage than the men," according to another editorial, despite "devices by which the Negro vote is now submerged." The newspaper noted with pride that in 1890, the "best brain of Mississippi was employed to disqualify the Negro men as voters"; it was not likely that such good work would be set aside by "a few fanatical suffragettes, who do not seem to comprehend that the Susan B. Anthony Amendment would make their cooks and washwomen voters." Under the standing head "Votes for Colored Women!" the *Patriot* passed on a report that indicated "Negro women were reported as outnumbering white women nearly three to one at registration quarters."

As the states in the ratifying column grew, so did anti-suffrage rhetoric. "Go ask the farmer's wife as she sat in her home in fear and trembling. The very vine and fig tree in her yard, Bible emblems of peace, tranquility, domestic serenity— were but the crouching places of lustful Negro awaiting to pounce upon his helpless victim." Racism in the United States was at its peak in the final decades of the nineteenth century and the early part of the twentieth century, and its impact on suffrage was profound; profounder still was the split that would occur between white feminists and African American women. The decision for white suffragists was to assess their responsibility to African American women. The decision for African American women was how much to align themselves with a movement that viewed their involvement as problematical.

THE AFRICAN AMERICAN CONSTITUENCY

The National Woman's Party and the enfranchisement of black women is now a new research area of its own, and NWP policies are generally held responsible for the deterioration into racial polarity of suffrage and its aftermath. Paul may have received too much blame for this direction, since suffrage leaders before Paul took on a rhetoric that argued native-born and prepared white women were being denied the vote while less-prepared men—that is, black, immigrant, and poor men—had expanded, in the phrase of the time, the "ignorant vote." Suffrage advocates put forward complicated rationales that turned on expansion of the vote to white women but did not argue against restrictions for others, an intelligence test, for example. This was a long way from the expansive ideology that had led Josephine Ruffin to join Julia Ward Howe and Lucy Stone to found the American Woman Suffrage Association in 1869.

Ruffin, discouraged with her fight to have her women's club included in the General Federation of Women's Clubs, turned to community organizing; and Mary Terrell Church took over Ruffin's Boston club and became president of the National Association of Colored Women. Terrell did not eschew suffrage organizations and addressed the National American Women's Suffrage Association in 1898 in a call for white women to understand the barriers of race. Amidst all her activities, she was also a clear spokeswoman for the suffrage cause, as in a 1910 article in the *Washington Post* that turned around the white feminist argument that had been used against black men.

> The elective franchise is withheld from one half of its citizens, many of whom are cultured, and virtuous, while it is unstintingly bestowed upon the other, some of whom are illiterate, debauched and vicious because the word "People," by an unparalleled exhibition of lexicographical acrobatics, has been turned and twisted to mean all who were shrewd and wise enough to have themselves born boys instead of girls, or who took the trouble to be born white.

Indeed, in 1910 there still existed the Progressive optimism that had undergirded the formation of the National Association for Colored People by black and white leaders, including white feminists Inez Milholland, Jane Addams, and Mary Ovington; that had brought white women and white journalists to Ida Wells Barnett's antilynching campaign; and that had even resulted in moments when it appeared suffrage could move into a new period. In 1910, the Negro Women's Business League in New York invited suffragist Belmont to address their group. The southern-born Belmont, transformed from socialite to suffragist, spoke in the grand hopes of the age: "I know that unless this cause means freedom and equal rights to all women, of every race, of every creed, rich or poor, its doctrines are worthless, and it must fail in its achievement." If we are to believe the coverage of the day, "Negro Women Join in Suffrage Fight" and "'Many Accept

Mrs. Belmont's Invitation to Become Members of Her Organization."

It was, however, a short moment of hope as the anti-suffrage forces played on fears of black dominance. *Suffragist* sought to mitigate the question by denying the facts of the objection, although not necessarily the premise. As the ratification process neared its close, the newspaper reprinted a letter from the Alabama Woman's Suffrage Association arguing that adoption of the federal amendment would not, as the antis proposed, open the floodgates to "improper voters." Indeed, to adopt the amendment would provide "the same qualifying safeguard now existing in the exclusion of undesirable negro women that we have heretofore exercised as to the exclusion of negro men; and if we have been protected in the past by our constitution against ignorant and vicious negro men, it furnishes the same shield against the same kind of negro women." In "National Suffrage and the Race Problem," the newspaper argued, with a numerical chart to support the contention, that "the enfranchising of all women will increase the relative power of the white race in a most remarkable way."

Media of the time were quick to bring attention to racial divisions in the movement. When Milholland died during the suffrage campaign in 1916, columnist and liberal Heywood Broun, married to feminist Ruth Hale, charged the Woman's Party refused to allow a black speaker at her graveside service lest a southern suffrage campaign be jeopardized. Paul refuted the charge, telling Broun no speakers had been planned for the service at all, nor was any southern campaign planned.

But it was Paul who overruled the initial favorable

decision when asked by Mary White Ovington, a founder of the NAACP, to place the African American speaker Mary B. Talbert on the 1921 Women's Party program. Using a rationale that suggests Paul was seeking to solve a political problem diplomatically, she claimed that Talbot did not represent a clearly *feminist* organization. Ovington did not accede quietly, writing in response: "[I]t is surely eminently proper that a meeting which has as one of its objects the honoring of the great feminists of the nineteenth century should have on its program a representative colored woman. Indeed, I think when your statue of Lucretia Mott, Susan B. Anthony and Elizabeth Cady Stanton is unveiled and it is realized that no colored woman has been given any part in your great session, the omission will be keenly felt by thousands of people throughout the country."

As it turned out, the statue of Mott, Anthony, and Stanton remained unseen in a Congressional basement for more than a half century. *The Masses* came to a quick end during World War I, along with other socialistic-leaning magazines. The war divided the Progressive movement. In its aftermath, after women had once again "proved" themselves amid Paul's unrelenting strategy, the Nineteenth Amendment was approved in both houses of Congress. Despite the best efforts of the antisuffragists to use their strongest card—the race card—the amendment was finally ratified in 1920, the final approval coming from the state of Tennessee, the state where Ida Wells Barnett had begun her anitlynching campaign. As late as 1949, Mary Church Terrell was refused membership in the Washington branch of the American Association of University Women.

═══════════════◆═══════════════

EIGHT

FINDING A PLACE

As the United States readied to embark on a new world role in World War I, a young Kansan found a way to report on her passion for international affairs by covering tensions on the Texas-Mexico border via reporting jobs in El Paso. The work paid off. In 1917, "Peggy Hull" (born Henrietta Eleanor Deuell) persuaded her El Paso editor to assign her to France to cover the war, even without formal accreditation from the War Department. She did receive accreditation, finally (after male correspondents had forced her return to the United States), the first woman to be so designated, and she embarked on a career of international reporting that extended into World War II.

Hull was the best known of a cluster of women who were correspondents in the war—Mary Boyle O'Reilly of the Newspaper Enterprise Association; Alice Rohe, United Press International bureau chief; Mary Roberts Rinehart, Corra Harris, and Corinne Lowe for the *Saturday Evening Post;* and activists Rheta Childe Dorr, Inez Haynes Irwin, and Inez Milholland, a celebrity correspondent for the *New*

York Tribune. Even Mabel Dodge, most known for her Green-wich Village salon, provided a compelling article from Paris for *The Masses* before its pacifist stand resulted in its close. While Edward Bok of the *Ladies' Home Journal* set up a Wash-ington office to coordinate information on how women could help the war effort, Madeleine Z. Doty covered the Russian revolution and many other international stories for *Good Housekeeping.* Edith Wharton reported from the front lines for *Scribner's.*

These were exciting figures for young women coming of age amidst a mass media that more than ever sounded the tocsin of journalism for women. "[W]oman's place is in the newspaper office," declared the *New York Tribune.* Despite all the difficulties that journalism posed for women, journalism as a career, Rose Young wrote in *Good Housekeeping,* at "its highest and best, pulls you out to life, pulls life up to you." Moreover, the young, ambitious woman did not have to pack her bag, like Nellie Bly, for a trip to unknown places. She could find help in the journey by way of journalism schools.

In 1927, one of the female (and rare) professors in the new college journalism programs wrote a text designed ex-clusively for women students. She saw a new era of possibil-ities for women in journalism thanks to the necessity of the "woman's angle" in news products seeking female readers. "A successful newspaper or magazine, indeed, must appeal strongly to women," said Ethel Maude Colson. "The woman writer, then, must regard her natural and intrinsic 'woman's angle,' her natural and intrinsic ability to look at and register life from a woman's view-point."

This looking at the world from the woman's angle was interpreted in journalism schools in the ways that already had been established. Journalism schools trained women to be society reporters and work on small-town papers. Even at a time when the suffrage campaign had involved women in sophisticated political maneuvering at local and national levels and women reporters had proved themselves as foreign correspondents in World War I, political reporting was considered off limits to women reporters. Thus, while feminists argued for equality on all fronts, the nation's press, even with the involvement of increasing numbers of women, proclaimed that women were best suited to long-recognized outposts—advice to the lovelorn, the emotive reporting of sensationalism, and the "women's take" on subjects outside of domesticity—all of which served to emphasize the message of difference.

For women who wanted to find a place in journalism, providing the "women's angle" was the cost of the journey. The women's angle worked well for sensationalist reporters, whose emotive writing led to well-paid careers. Similarly, the women's angle of club news and traditional topics ensconced in women's departments and in shelter magazines provided steady jobs for a multitude of women. In the interwar years, the most recognized of the working women, Dorothy Thompson, Anne O'Hare McCormick, and Inez Robb, moved the women's angle into national commentary in ways that were so far beyond the original boundaries that the women's angle was forgotten. More than 100 female reporters used the rationale of the women's angle to allow them to report from the front lines during World War II, where the angle also disappeared. As the Associated Press (AP) reporter Ruth Cowan said of her World War II experience, "I always had to worry with the women's angle in something, but that was not the real story. I was after the real story."

For many ambitious female reporters, the real story was not a women's story, and, indeed, did not want to be associated with "women's stories" as they were defined by the press of the time. Such women were likely not to see women's status as a class and could be antifeminist in outlook. "I am not a feminist," Agness Underwood wrote in the first line of her memoir. Star journalists such as Thompson and Adela Rogers St. Johns saw their own careers as especially ordained, arguing that most women should stay in the home. Flora Lewis, Paris bureau chief for the *New York Times,* and Mary McGrory, *Washington Post* columnist, did not see evidence of gender discrimination in their careers (although McGrory had had to assure her superior she had no immediate plans to marry). As they told interviewers from the Washington Press Club Foundation Oral History Project, they did not remember observing any discrimination at play in the careers of other women. Although successful themselves, these were not the women to lead the charge for other women.

Agitation for opportunities for women came from women of the middle ranks who sought change in many of the same ways that had been pioneered by an earlier generation. Like Sallie Joy White and June Cunningham Croly before them, Emma Bugbee and Ruby Black worked for the mainstream press in traditional roles while seeking opportunities for women in journalism by organizational means and by aligning powerful women to the cause. Other reporters embraced and expanded on the opportunities that were offered, sometimes managing the leap from women's club news to World War II reporting.

Women who sought institutional change at a faster pace than allowed by the mass press faced a more difficult road. Agnes Smedley, Marvel Cooke, and Charlotta Bass had freer voices but smaller voices in the nation's alternative publications, the socialistic *New York Call,* Dorothy Day's *Catholic Worker,* and Margaret Sanger's *Birth Control Review;* in the nation's African American press; or, like Smedley, in overseas publications. Such associations increased the difficulty of being a woman in journalism. Smedley served six months in jail for distributing birth control pamphlets during the World War I era and was the target of investigation by the FBI during the cold war. Marvel Cooke was similarly investigated as a subversive. In the heat of the McCarthy years, the American Legion questioned the patriotism of Lisa Sergio, an early broadcaster, even though she had fled Italy in the 1930s to escape arrest as an antifascist.

Women in journalism faced their own challenges that were necessarily attached to the context of the times. In the 1920s, as organizational feminism was increasingly connected to socialism, the subterranean fears of American culture took hold in ways that had hardly been imagined. The final ratification of the Nineteenth Amendment arrived during a grim decade that saw the rollback of optimism of the prewar years. The "Soviet ark" transported Emma Goldman and other non–U.S. born radicals to their points of departure, and J. Edgar Hoover was beginning his rise by way of Chicago's "Palmer raids" on remaining radicals. Socialist leaders jailed during war hysteria remained so. The quarterly magazines that had provided voices of reason slipped away, and the promise of radio as a populist voice ended with a federal licensing procedure that served to aggrandize the interests of corporations, considered the most trusted guardians of the public airwaves. Many sectors of the economy remained depressed, but music, film, advertising, theater, and speakeasies celebrated the moment in a synergistic outburst in which popular culture collapsed into messages of consumerism. A new, short-skirted "flapper" image emerged. As in F. Scott Fitzgerald's famous story, "Bernice Bobs Her Hair," Bernices across the nation were fashioning themselves from what they saw in media. New magazines such as *Smart Set* seemed to capture the time. In the new culture of self-promotion, no one was arguing that women were morally superior.

After adoption of the Nineteenth Amendment, Alice Paul's Congressional Union for Woman's Suffrage became the National Woman's Party, which reintroduced the equal rights amendment (ERA) and invoked feminist history by making the announcement of the drive at Seneca Falls. But in contrast to her six-year campaign for female suffrage, Paul was less able to inflame public interest for the ERA. Even Eleanor Roosevelt distanced herself from the initiative. At the same time, women activists were loathe to wait for the ERA in the face of the huge range of discriminatory legislation that the suffrage amendment had not touched. The question seemed to be where to start. While passage of the ERA was the approach that would have covered all discrimination, some feminists chose to put their energies into particular arenas.

The National Woman's Party was represented by its newspaper, *Equal Rights,* which, like the *Suffragist* before it, carried news of the plethora of the nation's women's activities. It may be most remembered for its campaign to eradicate so-called "protective" legislation that prohibited women from working after certain hours but actually served to hinder female employment. The contributors included feminist women journalists such as Crystal Eastman of *The Masses;* Ruth Hale, a freelance journalist in the period; Black; and Doris Fleischman, a pioneer in the developing area of public relations. Fleischman, Hale, and Black were collaborators in the campaign by the National Woman's Party to permit women to have passports in their birth names.

The campaign for the use of women's birth names on passports suggests how quickly the National Woman's Party moved from the single strategy of the ERA to attacking many other wrongs. Black was represented by the National Woman's Party at a formal hearing in 1925 after she refused to use her married name on a passport application. She was given an exception, although the law was not changed.

For Hale and members of the Lucy Stone League, the retention of birth names was an ideological battle about resisting the loss of personal identity, part of the larger battle of feminism. Still, to workers in field and factories, retention of birth names, especially for use on passports, was not so important and not an issue that made working women, even women in journalism, flock to organized feminism.

WOMEN IN JOURNALISM

As stunt reporting had done in the previous century, the sensational and tabloid press of the 1920s and 1930s provided an entry for women in journalism. Mildred Gilman on Hearst's *New York Journal* was sent to the bottom of the Hackensack River in a patched diving suit and to speakeasies to check out adulterated alcohol. Florabel Muir arrived at the New York

Daily News during the middle of the tabloid wars to cover the Ruth Snyder trial (culminating in the grisly picture by *Chicago Tribune* photographer Tom Howard of Snyder in the electric chair as the current was released). Kathleen McLaughlin began her career at the *Chicago Tribune* covering 1920's gangster trials. As "Dorothy Dix," Ada Paterson and Nixola Greeley Smith had covered the "Fatty" Arbuckle and Harry Thaw murder trials during the first part of the century. Adela Rogers St. Johns and her cohort similarly covered the sensational trials of the 1920s and 1930s, none more sensational that the story of the Lindbergh kidnapping in 1936, which was equally covered by tabloid and respectable press. The *Herald Tribune* put its respected "front page" female reporter Ishbel Ross on the story. Lorena Hickok crawled up a mountain path at 2 AM to peer in the windows of the Lindbergh home. When it came to awards, the women who had covered the story so assiduously and aggressively were ignored in favor of a male reporter for the *New York Times,* who won the Pulitzer Prize for revealing that Lindbergh was going to leave the country.

Outside of the sensationalist press, women held positions in the mainstream press, sometimes beyond those of society editor. During the interwar years, Genevieve Forbes Herrick, who had started out as a stunt reporter on the *Chicago Tribune,* segued to a larger role as news commentator. Mildred Seydell was a regional power as a columnist of *The Atlanta Georgian,* with Arthur Brisbane calling her "America's brilliant young genius." Dorothy Ducas, one of the new graduates from the Columbia University School of Journalism, was a Washington reporter for International News Service. Bess Furman was a "flapper reporter" in Omaha during the 1920s, covering politics from a "color" or feature angle; this led to a job with the Associated Press (AP) in Washington, joining a handful of other women including Lorena Hickok, Sigrid Arne, and Beth Campbell. Winifred Mallon was the first female political reporter for the *New York Times.* Ruby Black was hired part time by United Press International in Washington. Hickok, on her own from the age of fourteen, worked her way up in Midwestern newspapers and by 1928 obtained a job with AP for its feature service. She was the only woman assigned to cover Franklin D. Roosevelt when the 1932 campaign opened but became known as Eleanor Roosevelt's confidante. Inez Robb, whose column was carried in 140 newspapers, worked her way up from society editor of the *New York Daily News.* Emma Bugbee, who with Ishbel Ross had begun at the *New York Herald* in an office outside of the main newsroom, was only halfway through her fifty-five-year career in journalism. Florence Finch Kelly was concluding her thirty years of contribution to the *New York Times* "Book Review," while at the *New York Herald Tribune*'s book section, Irita Van Doren was just beginning hers. Cora Rigby was Washington bureau chief for the *Christian Science Monitor,* the first woman in the post. Thousands of women continued to hold the forts of society pages in large and small newspapers.

Magazine journalism remained the most popular arena for women and the place where the Progressive reform impulse of the muckraking period most found a home. Anna Steese Richardson was an investigative writer for the *Women's Home Companion, Delineator,* and *McCall's.* Vera Connolly wrote for *Good Housekeeping* and *Delineator* about working women, juvenile crime, and American Indians. In the 1930s, Connolly and five other women founded a new magazine, *Woman's Day,* an inexpensive magazine sold to women in supermarkets. Carolyn Trowbridge-Radnor moved from managing editor at *Harper's* to a successful advertising career.

THE MOST DIFFICULT ROAD

For women of color, entrance into journalism was even more problematical. Prevented from enrolling in some of the state schools until the 1950s, women of color who sought professional training had little opportunity but on-the-job training on historically black publications. Ellen Tarry "dreamed of going to New York and enrolling at Columbia University's Pulitzer School of Journalism." She managed to get herself from Alabama to New York for the purpose, when she was faced with the impossibility of ever financing the $1,000 for a year's tuition and support. Tarry worked intermittently for the African American press but became remembered as a children's writer.

Opportunities for African American women in journalism in the mainstream press barely existed. One early exception, Delilah L. Beasley, wrote a regular column about the black community that appeared in the *Oakland Tribune* in the 1920s and was instrumental in the establishment of a Negro Press Association, modeled on the Associated Press. But it would be the black press that provided opportunity for women of color, although they were as likely to be the target of gender discrimination in the black press as their white sisters were in the mainstream press. Alice Allison Dunnigan also grew up dreaming of becoming a newspaper reporter. At the age of thirteen, she wrote about church activities for the Kentucky *Owensboro Enterprise*. She contributed to various black publications during her teaching career, and it was not until 1946 that she was hired as a full-time reporter for the *Chicago Defender,* covering Washington. She was offered $100 a month, half of what had been offered the male candidate. Charlotta A. Bass got her start as an "office girl" at the *Providence* [Rhode Island] *Watchman* in the first decade of the century. She bought the *California Eagle* in Los Angeles at a sheriff's sale for $50 and only then took journalism courses at the University of California. With Bass at its head, the paper flourished as an activist organ—frequently the focus of government harassment—into the 1950s.

Marvel Jackson Cooke arrived in Harlem in 1926 with an English degree from the University of Minnesota and was hired as an editorial assistant for *The Crisis,* the prestigious magazine associated with the NAACP. She later was hired at the *Amsterdam News,* the city's leading black newspaper, the first female reporter in the newspaper's history, even as a society editor. Her duties expanded at *The People's Voice,* where she ran the paper as an assistant managing editor, but she was never offered the managing editor post and in 1950 saw the paper close. She became the only African American and the only woman on the staff of the *Daily Compass,* a Leftist New York daily. But even after successful stories (the exploitation of black domestic workers was one, accompanied by a picture of Cooke washing a window outside on its ledge), she recalled she "had a very difficult time with the managing editor," who finally admitted that some racism and sexism was involved. Hazel Garland started work at the *Pittsburgh Courier* as a stringer and finally achieved a staff position in 1946. Her series on rural South Carolina resulted in the prestigious Page One Award. Garland eventually became editor in chief in the 1970s, the culmination of another long road. In the 1950s, Ethel Payne had begun her remarkable career with the *Chicago Defender,* one that would lead to coverage of the civil rights movement and to Washington, D.C., where, as part of the White House press corps in the Eisenhower administration, she had to cope with gender and racial discrimination. As she recounted in the oral history project for the Washington Press Club Foundation, "I think you were ignored to a great extent, as much as possible, and sometimes I used to get so frustrated because I couldn't get to the source of something. I don't think I was that much of a threat to the general press, except on occasions, when they decided that a particular angle was of interest to them. So therefore, when you went after it, you were just given short shrift. They would tell you that either something wasn't available or, 'We've already dealt with that.' You were just put aside. So that frustrated you, too."

On the world stage, no journalist was more important than Anne O'Hare McCormick, who began submitting articles for the *New York Times* in 1921 on a "stringer" basis, eventually winning the Pulitzer Prize in 1937 for her body of work. Like so many other women journalists of the time, McCormick's rise in the journalistic world was unpredictable. As a young woman, she was associate editor for ten years for the weekly *Catholic Universe Bulletin.* At thirty she married and learned about Europe by accompanying her husband on business trips in the aftermath of World War I. That led to her request to contribute occasional pieces to the *Times.* However, it was not until *Times* publisher Adolph

Ochs died in 1934 that McCormick was officially put on staff, since Ochs did not want women, at least officially, on the paper's reporting staff. "We have almost a prohibition against the employment of women on our editorial staff," Ochs explained to a fellow publisher in the World War I period. As Nan Robertson writes, Ochs refused to put McCormick on staff even after she had "interviewed Stalin, Hitler, and Mussolini, when resident foreign correspondents could not get near those dictators."

McCormick had few female predecessors on the *Times*. In the nineteenth century, Midy Morgan had constructed the very specialized beat for an urban newspaper of livestock reporting. In 1927, former suffragist Winifred Mallon began a twenty-seven-year association (on a "special" basis) from Washington, which began with a profile of the wife of the then–vice president. She quickly moved into women's role in politics at a time when Ruth Hanna McCormick was bringing attention to women as national candidates. By the time of her death in 1954 (still "special"), Mallon had covered major stories, including the Federal Communications Commission grappling with expansion of broadcasting into FM radio and television and was twice president of the New York Women's Newspaper Club.

By the 1930s, McLaughlin's work on the *Chicago Tribune* had been observed by the *Times* management, and in 1935 McLaughlin was hired, also on a "special" basis, to cover the considerable activities of club women. It was a change from covering gangland slayings, but, like her compatriot in Washington, McLaughlin put club news in a hard-news frame, including coverage of National Woman's Party efforts on behalf of the equal rights amendment, in ways that had not existed since suffrage activity. The club news beat led to an assignment in World War II as the *Times'* Berlin correspondent and then as its United Nations correspondent (joining Sigrid Arne of AP and Pauline Frederick of the National Broadcasting Company, altogether a new kind of "hen coop").

McLaughlin and Mallon operated in relative obscurity compared with stars such as Dorothy Thompson. In the 1920s, Thompson left for Europe as a correspondent for Philadelphia's *Public Ledger.* Her unflattering 1931 interview with Adolf Hitler led to her expulsion from Germany. In 1936, she was hired to write a column, "On the Record," for the *Herald Tribune,* from which stance she warned against Hitler. But in 1940, she joined a list of journalists connected with the Newspaper Guild to support Franklin D. Roosevelt for a third term, a position that led to a disagreement with the Republican newspaper and ended her career there.

In the mid-1930s, Margaret Bourke-White became a glamorous journalistic figure as photographer for *Life* magazine and later as a war correspondent for *Time.* Bourke-White's national celebrity, her photogenic looks, her marriage to a famous novelist, and her adverturesome life seemed to offer the penultimate career for a woman in journalism.

STORIES OF SEDUCTION

Public discussion about discrimination against women journalists that had been part of the First Wave generation was muted in the interwar years, at least publicly; women journalists were simply grateful to work, turned to organizational networking, or simply denied discrimination existed. Some adopted public positions that were opposite to their own life decisions. Adela Rogers St. Johns argued in a public appearance early in her career that suffrage was failing because it led women to forget their duties to home and family. In her 1937 column in the *Ladies' Home Journal* Thompson, a proponent of the suffrage movement in her youth, argued that women should reclaim their place "as a *conservative* influence" and should stay in the home and "stick to their knitting." Correspondent Irene Kuhn claimed she was "fundamentally a simple woman, who would have been completely happy with husband, home and children, realizing myself in them, content to stand by and do just a woman's job." Underwood followed her "I am no feminist" statement with this one: "If I were asked what I regard as the woman's place, I'd probably give the old-fashioned answer: In the home." She wrote disparagingly of the "girl wonders" in the newsroom. "There is a fallacy by which newspaperwomen, because they are females, are condemned as a class," she wrote. She had not hired a woman because no woman had met the requirements. Underwood herself, however, was hired by the women's editor of the Los Angeles *Record,* Gertrude Price, who had paid her out of her own pocket and mentored her for several years.

How to explain their own choices? Unable to accommodate the difficulties of their "two-ness," women turned to the imperative of a higher call. It was an *Assignment to Adventure,* as Kuhn named her call in the title of her autobiography. Florabel Muir was "immediately bitten by the bug." Underwood said she would have been "miserably unhappy" had she ignored "her calling." For Carolyn Anspacher, who went to work for the *San Francisco Chronicle* after her wealthy family lost its money in the 1929 crash, "Newspaper writing became not only my bread but my wine." She wrote, "It was so exciting, so unpredictable, so fascinating." Muir briefly retired to write short stories, "but I'd been swimming in the swift stream of events too long to be happy sitting on the shore." For St. Johns, "We stayed and worked late because we would rather be together in the city room than anywhere else on earth." She would have "done it for nothing."

The biographical writing of female interwar reporters and many of the later interviews of women who worked in those years suggest that women were not willing to risk the seductive power of newsroom bonhomie and the intensity of daily reporting by too much study or complaint. Unlike the earlier period, warnings of the difficulties that await women in journalism seldom appear in the period. And while the memoirs of Marie Manning (Beatrice Fairfax) and Florence Finch Kelley had room for some rumination on the state of the news industry and the place of women in it, memoirs of the interwar women reporters are uncritical of the institution, focusing almost entirely on memorializing the stories they covered. This was even the case for a woman reporter for a small South Bend, Indiana, newspaper. A spelling bee contest is described: "I hurry back to the office. It is after eleven o'clock Saturday night. I begin to write my story in a state of excitement equal to that of a cheerleader whose team has won in the last minutes of play. The Saturday night editor looks over my shoulder as I write, but not even that dismays me. He takes the copy page by page as it comes from my typewriter and sends it to the city desk to have the headlines written. In half an hour it is all over." The description could have been adapted by any reporter of the period, for any

story. The sensual excitement of the moment, like the popular culture of the time, served to keep difficult questions at bay.

BROACHING NEW FIELDS

In 1934, at WOR in New York, Mary Margaret McBride
began her twenty-year career in radio, an intimate medium
well suited to her Missouri drawl. Her interviews with noted
personalities drew millions of women to the daily announcement, "It's one o'clock and here's Mary Margaret McBride."
However, radio had a set of prohibitions against women
based on the belief that women's voices did not carry authority and were not appropriate for news. (Early microphones
were also blamed; women's voices were considered too light
to be transmitted.) But the need for inexpensive programming found places for women as homemaking experts, and
the home shows became lifelines to women listeners in both
city and country. Lisa Sergio, whose broadcasting career in
Italy had led to her sobriquet as "the golden voice of Rome,"
was unusual in that she found work at NBC at a time when
women's voices were generally considered "shrill and man-
nered" and lacking the "conviction" of the male voice.

Finally, women were making inroads in journalism's
aligned professions of public relations and advertising, although clearly in secondary places. After women's page jobs
on the *New York Tribune,* Doris Fleischman joined Edward
Bernays in his new publicity firm, but in an out-of-sight capacity. "If it had been known I was linked up with a woman,"
he told an interviewer, "I would have been considered an
imbecile or somebody strange." In a 1927 textbook, *How to
Become an Advertising Man,* the author devoted a chapter to

women, noting, in the plus column, their obedience ("Women are naturally obedient. How they do love to be told things!") and their ability to master detail, "little things which drive men to distraction, but which hold women's attention with ease." Women could be disadvantaged by other gender characteristics (too much talking), but ambitious and presumably not-so-chatty young women might succeed if they would start as checkers and file clerks and work from their own base of knowledge. One woman, Erma Perham Poetz, won two Harvard University Advertising Awards in 1923 for a Pet milk advertisement, "Take Baby and Go."

Still, as in the 1890s, the numbers of women in high-profile positions in the interwar years gave to the field a sense that women in journalism were everywhere. But the famous names comprised a tip of the journalistic iceberg; most women remained submerged in low-level, poor-paying, and dead-end jobs, or in no jobs at all. Ruby Black set up an early job bank service for women journalists. Nor were there guarantees once the job was obtained. Judith Cary Waller, the general manager of WMAQ in Chicago, was downgraded to public service director when the station was sold to NBC in 1931. In the late 1920s, Ruth Cowan, writing for United Press International as R. Baldwin Cowan, was fired when her gender was discovered after she answered a phone call from a UPI manager. Marriage could also be reason for discharge; pregnancy certainly was. When a woman was able to survive these barriers, she was likely to be expected to resign, as at the Associated Press, at the age of fifty-five, earlier than men and often without a pension.

The double standards were premised on male notions of women from cultural and professional sources. Women in the workforce during the Depression were suspect in any case, accused of taking a job away from a male family provider. Connected to craft demands, the barriers were enormous: women were not physically or mentally strong enough; not worth training when plenty of competent men were available; women in the newsroom might even weaken the toughness of the newspaperman; female bylines, if at all, needed to be limited lest the publication look like it had been turned over to the hen squad; women could not be sent on dangerous assignments—indeed, women's innate differences made real journalism impossible for women except in those rare instance when women, somehow, were not really women.

Cowan found she had to adapt her behaviors to the culture of a newsroom. She found acceptance by a combination of good work, humor, and a low profile. "It had to be good work. I told myself that. If at all possible, it had to be a scoop." At the same time, "I laughed at things as they went along." Finally, "I didn't disrupt the office." In covering World War II, she stood at the back of press briefings, not bringing attention to herself." No one was exempt from these kinds of negotiations, even the Pulitzer Prize winner Anne O'Hare McCormick. "We tried hard not to act like ladies or to talk as ladies are supposed to talk—meaning too much—but just to sneak toward the city desk and the cable desk, and the editorial sanctum and even the publisher's office with masculine sang-froid." Judging from the memoirs, the greatest compliment was for a female reporter to be described as a "newspaperman." Women in hard news reporting reveled in the acceptance, when it occurred, without great concern if they were the only female so accepted.

For a woman journalist in this period, finding her place existed on two levels: quite literally finding a place to work and, second, finding a comfortable place where her gender would not isolate her from her newsroom comrades. Some women reporters—even those hired to write about "the women's angle"—chose to adopt characteristics of male reportorial thinking, even to taking positions counter to the benefit of other women. But it can be considered that whether women became the hard-drinking, hard-living city hall reporter of the stereotype—and memoirs suggest some surely did—or found some surcease in a belief that society reporting and magazine writing gave them pretensions to the middle-class life, women were attempting to cope with constant reminders of second-class status. Lumsden wonders "about the toll of these pervasive messages of inferiority on women's psyches." The messages certainly contributed to women leaving the newsroom, as Linda Steiner has explored. No sadder case is that of Caro Brown, who won a Pulitzer Prize in 1955 for political reporting, but quit within one week of receiving the prize—quite possibly because of her fear that her work was not good enough and she was resented by her colleagues.

THE ROLE OF JOURNALISM SCHOOLS

Almost forgotten is the fact that it was a woman who set up the first school of journalism. In 1886, Martha Louise Rayne established a private school in Detroit to give practical journalism training to women, a recognition that journalism offered women a place to earn a living. The *Detroit Free Press* scoffed at the idea, but the school existed until the turn of the century. By that time, Joseph Pulitzer was seeking to establish a journalism program at Harvard University, an effort to connect the craft of journalism to the elite culture of the day. The effort failed, and Pulitzer's $2 million endowment was given to Columbia University in New York to establish, importantly, a *graduate* school of journalism, to emphasize that journalism was not simply a craft but, like law or medicine, needed postgraduate training. It was not automatic, but Columbia's journalism program included women from the beginning and, indeed, kept track of women's enrollment and later careers in ways that other schools did not.

Despite Pulitzer's ambitions to put journalism training on a par with training for other professions, for most universities journalism programs were an undergraduate endeavor. The first chair of journalism was established in 1869 in Virginia at Washington University by its president, General Robert E. Lee. By the first part of the century, several institutions offered journalism courses, including the University of Pennsylvania, the University of Washington, Temple University, Kansas State College, Denver University, the State University of Iowa, Stanford University, Rutgers University, Indiana University, the University of Texas, and others.

But even by the end of the century, it was clear that the land grant colleges of the Midwest and West were to have a particular role in journalism education. Undergraduate journalism education flourished best in the state-supported and "working-man's" colleges that attracted the first generation of college-bound student. The University of Pennsylvania soon dropped its practical training in journalism, and the role was taken up by the nearby working-man's institution, Temple University. The state-associated colleges and universities saw in journalism—as in their teaching, social work, nursing, and business programs—a service for their communities that would provide immediate jobs for their graduates. Additionally, state press associations, whose members benefited from a regular supply of trained news workers, encouraged many of the colleges and universities to establish journalism programs. As the University of Missouri announced when it founded the first School of Journalism in 1908, "There is a constant call for reporters, editors, special writers, correspondents, publishers, ad-writers, men in all departments of journalism, in city and country, on daily, weekly and monthly journals. It is to supply this demand, in the interest of the state, to furnish well-equipped men for leadership in journalism with high ideals and special training." In 1920, the school emphasized that the institution was to provide "the greatest possible service to the profession of journalism in general, and the journalism of Missouri in particular." The template was generally followed as both individual courses in journalism and formal journalism programs were established in other state colleges and universities. By the 1920s, programs were well distributed enough to have warranted the formation of a national journalism education organization, proving to university administrators the subject was worthy of inclusion on a college level and to the industry that college-trained young people would benefit them. By the end of the decade, more than 5,000 students were being formally trained and, by the mid-1930s, more than 500 institutions were participating in journalism education and could offer themselves for "accreditation" to mark them as institutions whose schema of courses had been approved by the professional body.

The move to professional journalism training by way of the low tuition of the state-supported schools fit with the attraction of the profession to students from families with limited resources. For both men and women, journalism offered the opportunity for a white-collar occupation, located between the working-class occupations of many of the students' families and the professional status to which the field aspired. But from the beginning, pushed by the press associations and newspaper organizations that supported them, journalism programs emphasized the development of skills for entry-level jobs rather than professional management for eventual leadership.

The West and Midwest had certainly produced radical leaders during the Populist and Progressive eras, and the general characteristics of journalism education as it evolved did not mean that the newly trained journalists turned into lackeys. Indeed, the role of the investigatory reporter was enhanced, in some ways funneling Populist impulses into the new frame. But the new programs—much like the programs for public school teachers, health worker, and business graduates of the same colleges—-were more likely to encourage beliefs in the established order rather than to inculcate notions of change. Journalism education programs had their basis in the mainstream beliefs of the period in which they were founded. Exhorted to join a "profession" that provided service rather than leadership, journalism students were to take their place as watchdogs of society as it existed—the necessary mechanics for the nation's operational machinery, but not its designers. The outlook did not position journalism programs to be agents for change for the status of women in the profession any more than they challenged the other systemic issues that crossed the paths of reporters in their daily work.

Women were instead moved toward the arenas where it was thought they could succeed. According to accounts of the University of Missouri's early history, women invited as guests "told of women's success in writing fiction, poetry, features, general and departmental news and syndicated material; in owning and publishing and editing various types of publications; in all phases of advertising work and publicity." Given that opportunity in "poetry" is high on the list, perhaps it is not so surprising that the new programs tacitly trained female students to fit into the secondary opportunities that awaited them in the field. Women staff members of college newspapers were not so likely to be editors (although Ruby Black was the first female editor of the *Daily Texan* at the University of Texas); women were not allowed to join student chapters of Sigma Delta Chi (nor the professional group); journalism texts ignored women; few women professors existed, and male professors, who earlier may have been working journalists, could bring old newsroom prejudices into the classroom. Since women faculty were primarily in the women's news areas, female students did not get recommended for the same kinds of jobs as male students. Indeed, women students were not allowed to interview for some jobs (especially in advertising) when recruiters came to campus— a practice that existed into the 1960s at the University of Missouri. Like the male employers in the field, the journalism schools expected that women were not serious about long-term work, instead looking for lively interim jobs until they got married. In its first twenty years, Missouri's female graduates who did not find jobs were taken out of the school's placement figures on the premise that they had chosen to opt for "housekeeping." Moreover, the university disallowed women of color (and men of color) from enrolling until the 1950s. Lucile Bluford was denied admission in 1940 on the basis on race. Fifty years later, by then editor of the *Kansas City Call,* she was honored by the university that had denied her admission.

Private universities with practical journalism training programs—Columbia University in New York and Northwestern University near Chicago—were less common. Originally there were no plans to accept women into Columbia, because Pulitzer had made no such recommendation and the college was not coeducational. The first dean did not even think women should vote. That position changed after Virginia Gildersleeve, dean of Columbia's sister school, Barnard College (the home to many graduates who entered journalism), expressed disapproval, although whether that was the determining factor is not so clear.

Grudgingly opening its door to women, Columbia University's Pulitzer School of Journalism operated in the belief "that women would be content to receive instruction principally in the field of domestic interests." The women, however, were not so content. "They even displayed a marked hostility toward editing women's pages and confining their time and talent to things of feminine interest only. Instead, they demanded the same general training in reporting, copy-reading, feature writing, and the rest of it, as the men secured. Thus, most of them were turned out by the School equipped as well as the men to deal with the daily grind of newspaper work."

Equal preparation did not translate into equal jobs. Women with Columbia degrees were most likely to find jobs on trade publications, on small-town papers, or in the aligned fields. By 1926, 19 percent of the jobs were in the magazine industry, in part "as a result of the conservatism of the newspapers editors, who take few women for general work," said an early historian of the program. The Columbia survey found "women have been unable to secure reportorial work in or near New York." Five of the responding women had found reporting jobs, just two as straight reporters on Brooklyn dailies. Still, women continued to flood the school's admissions office, although the field was always described in gendered terms. In 1929, reporting that women at the school numbered half of all students, the director talked in terms of men. Reporting and copyediting "were young men's jobs." The lackluster record of women in the field led another dean, in 1932, to announce plans to restrict admission only to those likely to be most successful. "I think the school should not encourage women to believe that there will be unlimited opportunities when we know the opportunities are limited." In 1935, when the university established its one-year professional program, it was with the proviso that women would be admitted only in proportion to their expected opportunities. As the most recent historian of the school remarks, "The underlying assumption, of course, was that there would be few future opportunities for women as journalists; hence, few women were admitted."

In the Depression 1930s, it was easy to rationalize discriminatory hiring when women with full-time jobs in any field were viewed as taking jobs away from male heads of household. But as late as 1953, a very different economic period, only ten to twelve spots were reserved for women. Maureen O'Neill received one, to be told after graduation by an editor at the *Daily News,* "We haven't hired a woman since the last World War and we're not going to hire another until the next World War." In 1957, she landed a job at *Newsday,* where she remained for thirty-eight years. Columbia's exclusionary model also applied to its professorial hiring. Phyllis T. Garland was hired as a full-time lecturer in 1973. Garland, an African American graduate of Northwestern's journalism program in the 1950s and a female editor of the *Pittsburgh Courier*—no stranger to "firsts"—was given tenure in 1981, the first female to receive that status. By that time, women comprised 55 percent of the enrollment, although no women had achieved the rank of full professor. Joan Konner became the first female dean in 1988. It had been a long road.

The second school of journalism was founded at Northwestern University in 1912 thanks to a monetary gift from the *Chicago Tribune,* whose founder, Joseph Medill, came to be represented in the school's name, the Medill School of Journalism. The connection between the school and the *Tribune* may have been one reason why the record for female hiring at the *Tribune* improved from the time when Edna Ferber was told, "We don't hire women reporters. We'd rather have men do men's work."

By the mid-1920s, the *Tribune* boasted about its number of female reporters and was even given favorable mention in the publication *Equal Rights.* The *Tribune's* star was Genevieve Forbes Herrick, a Northwestern graduate. Elizabeth McLaughlin, who in her ten years on the *Tribune* covered Chicago's mobsters of the 1920s to investigations of housekeeping, said the *Tribune* "gave its women reporters precisely the same chance the men had and it was wonderfully appreciated."

One may speculate that these opportunities for women on the *Tribune* may have had to do with the flood of talented women who entered the Northwestern program, the energy of the Midwestern media market as a training ground, and the role of Ruth Hanna McCormick, wife of the publisher, Medill McCormick, in the period. Ruth McCormick was a suffragist and political activist, and her husband in his subsequent career as a legislator was a supporter of women's suffrage activities. As Donald G. Godfrey has explored, wives and family members of important media figures may have played substantive roles in opening up opportunities for women. Iphigene Sulzberger, for example, the daughter of *New York Times* publisher Adolph Ochs, played a role in the long-overdue hire of Anne O'Hare McCormick.

In the 1930s, under the publisher Colonel Robert P. McCormick, the *Tribune* resisted progressive impulses in general and the social agenda of Franklin D. Roosevelt most of all. McCormick believed women were different in nature, including having a proclivity to talk too much. This was a trait difficult to curb and could pose libel problems for newspapers, McCormick told a Columbia University audience, but women "had been getting away with it for years." In the school that carried the *Tribune* name, such views fell on fertile ground. In 1939, Northwestern's Professor Roland Wolseley assured newspaper managers that journalism programs were intent on weeding out incompetents, misfits, and women, although fortunately his student and later *New York Times* reporter Nan Robertson was not one of them.

Professional training did not make entry for women into the field much easier in large part because of continuing attitudes against women by editors. As late as 1937—decades after the establishment of the first journalism programs—the National Occupational Conference reported that substantial numbers of women graduates of journalism programs were not placed, even when jobs remained vacant. Indeed, the report confirmed that some schools had had two and three times as many requests as they could supply. The requests, however, were for male graduates, and journalism schools did not challenge the quotas. "While editors are competing for the services of her brother journalism student, many still look askance at the female of the species, the school directors aver." Out of twenty-one schools, 85 percent of the male graduates were placed; 64 percent of the female.

These kinds of barriers lead to an understanding why relatively few female journalists trained in college journalism programs became national figures. When successful women journalists, that is, women in major positions, are counted in the interwar period, a relatively small number emerge as graduates of the new schools of journalism. Charlotte Ebener held a graduate degree from the University of Wisconsin and went to work for the International News Service to cover the Chinese civil war. Mary Margaret McBride, a Missouri graduate, succeeded in the goal of getting to New York for work. Inez Robb, another Missouri graduate, was a successful columnist and war correspondent. Marguerite Higgins, a graduate of Columbia University's school, became a well-known war correspondent. Campbell, an AP reporter in Washington, came from the University of Oklahoma. Clearly, the list is not complete. But the dozens of their female classmates had very different careers or no careers in the field at all. Preparing students for employment by way of the "women's angle" was to prepare students for niche positions that were not so likely to go further. Journalism schools did not put themselves on the line to combat gender discrimination, and the female students were not inculcated with the same ideas of their own importance that existed in the elite women's colleges. Ruby Black, the national president of the journalism honorary Theta Sigma Phi, early recognized that journalism schools were upholding rather than challenging entrenched newsroom traditions: As early as 1924, in a full-page essay in *Equal Rights,* she wrote, "The schools of journalism should be pioneers in breaking down sex prejudice in the profession. Unfortunately, they are not." Few women were on journalism faculties, few in high positions, and women were discouraged from teaching classes that male students would take. Most disturbing, "few professors have the courage to recommend women when an editor, however unconsciously, asks for 'a man.'"

STRATEGIES FOR CHANGE: THE ROLE OF ORGANIZATIONS

June Cunningham Croly was the first to recognize gender organizations as way to support professional women in journalism. By the 1920s, the club she founded in New York, the

Women's Press Club, continued to promote the role of female journalists by providing scholarships for women at Columbia and by establishing banquets and awards to bring
attention to female journalists. In 1922, the older club was
challenged by the founding of a similar organization, the
New York Newspaper Women's Club (now Newswoman's
Club of New York), which included many of the leading
women reporters of the day, such as Bugbee, McLaughlin,
and McCormick, as well as the long-standing first vice president, Helen Rogers Reid, eventual publisher of the *New
York Herald Tribune*. Outside of New York, the New England
Press Women's Association, founded by Sallie Joy White in
the nineteenth century, remained in existence, as it does
today. From her Chicago base, Helen Stanley Malloch of the
Illinois Woman's Press Association helped establish the National Federation of Press Women in 1937. In Washington,
the National Women's Press Club was founded in 1919 from
a gathering in Cora Rigby's *Christian Science Monitor* office as
an alternative to the men-only membership requirement of
the National Press Club. The organization simulated the
men's organization by inviting serious speakers to address the
group on newsmaking subjects, but in 1932, the many
women who were in Washington to cover social activities re-
grouped into yet another women's organization, the Newspaper Women's Club, which was founded by *Washington Star*
society reporters Margaret Hart and Katharine M. Brooks.
The new organization put its efforts into charity events and
"roasts," but its real purpose was to trade professional information among members, a practice it continues today as the
American News Women's Club.

On the West Coast, the impulse for mutual benefit resulted in the forerunner of what would be the largest organization devoted to women in journalism, now the Association for Women in Communication. It began as Theta Sigma Phi, designed as a female equivalent to the male-only Sigma Delta Chi. Chapters blossomed, including student chapters in most of the nation's college programs. Its publication *The Matrix* provided support and sustenance for women in their newsrooms by awards and notice. Women in broadcasting joined in the Association of Women Broadcasters in the 1920s, affiliated with the National Association of Broadcasters (NAB). NAB ended the affiliation in 1950 after some years of bad blood, at which time the Association for Women in Television and Radio was formed.

Black of Theta Sigma Phi sought jobs for women by helping establish a job bank and pressuring schools of journalism to be more active in promoting women for jobs. The activist Texas Press Women's Association had sufficient influence that its 1913 resolution led to the organization of the School of Journalism at the University of Texas the following year with women included. But changing women's status in the profession was not necessarily the focus of women's press organizations as much as was the role of socialization and the usefulness of the organizations to individual careers. Beth Campbell, working for the Associated Press in Washington as a rare general reporter in the 1930s, found that she helped others as a natural expression of collegiality that she did not relate to gender. "I don't think you do it because they're a woman or a man. At least I didn't."

For two important women, however, change for

women in journalism came by using the levers of power very
consciously.

STRATEGIES FOR CHANGE: WOMEN
IN POWER

Campbell as one exception, the beat for women reporters in
Washington was not politics, but the "women's view" of politics, which generally meant coverage of politicians' wives,
none more impressive than Eleanor Roosevelt. Roosevelt
regarded herself as a news person. She had been forced to resign from her role as editor of *Women's Democratic News* when
her husband was elected governor of New York, but as first
lady she reestablished her journalism career as an editor of a
Bernard McFadden publication about babies, a contributor
to magazines, and, beginning in 1936, the writer of a syndicated daily column, "My Day," for United Features. She was
surely aware of the challenges facing women in journalism
and, as Maurine Beasley has detailed, she used her power as
first lady to promote the careers (and in some cases, simply
to ensure continued employment) of the women who covered her. Roosevelt recalled, "Unless the women reporters
could find something new to write about, the chances were
that some of them would hold their jobs a very short time."
Beginning on March 6, 1933, with thirty-five women reporters attending, Roosevelt conducted regular Monday
morning press conferences for women reporters only, as part
of what came to be the Eleanor Roosevelt Press Conference
Association. Reporters at various times included Bugbee of
the *New York Tribune;* Bess Furman of the Associated Press;

Kathleen McLaughlin of the *Chicago Tribune* and the *New York Times;* Winifred Mallon of the *New York Times;* Ruby Black, representing her own news bureau at the time; Marguerite Young of the *New York World-Telegram;* Martha Strayer of the *Washington Daily News;* Ruth Montgomery of the *New York Daily News;* Ann Cottrell Free of the *Chicago Sun* and *New York Herald* (and later the first woman in the Washington bureau of *Newsweek*); Frances Lide of the *Washington Star;* Malvina Stephenson, a contributor to various papers; and Ruth Van Deman, a home economist specialist on an educational radio program and a magazine writer. Roosevelt did not provide political news, but her activism nonetheless made her a source of news, and the prestige of her role made it difficult for editors to refuse coverage. Moreover, Roosevelt was a great supporter of women reporters, associating herself with women's news organizations, attending their events, and even providing prizes for women reporters, all activities that resulted in press coverage that spotlighted women in journalism. In return, the women reporters cared for and protected her image. One of the reporters, Ruby Black, wrote a biography of Eleanor Roosevelt, and the relationship between Roosevelt and Hickok, as their correspondence attests, was affectionate and even loving.

Less well known are the contributions to women in journalism by Helen Rogers Reid. Reid was one of a few women publishers of a major publication in the interwar era. Some women were publishers of small newspapers they had inherited. Others included Molly Warren Wison, editor and publisher in Wichita, Kansas. Oveta Culp Hobby learned the news business at the *Houston Post* after it was purchased by her husband and eventually came to lead it. Eleanor Medill

Patterson, granddaughter of Joseph Medill of the *Chicago Tribune,* took over the failing Hearst publication the *Washington Herald* in 1920, doubling its daily circulation by features such as a women's page along lines of what appeared in fashionable magazines. She is also credited with substantial female hiring (up from two), but also with going through women reporters "like she was eating popcorn." She had no illusions about women's difficulty in the profession but, as imperious and competitive as she was, her boss—as she said in an early editorial—was clearly "Mr. Hearst," and she was most interested in circulation and results. By the time she was the paper's owner, World War II put her Hearst-bred isolationism under attack.

But it was Helen Rogers Reid whose contributions to women in journalism were formidable. In Richard Kluger's assessment, "[S]he sponsored more women in positions of responsibility on the *Tribune* than on any major U.S. newspaper." Reid came to be copublisher, then publisher, of the *New York Herald Tribune* by marriage into the family of the newspaper's owners, the wealthy Reid family. Elizabeth V. Burt describes Reid's working-class background in Wisconsin— one of eleven children—her education at Barnard College in New York, and her first position as social secretary to Mrs. Whitelaw Reid. In that capacity, she traveled with the family and made contacts in the United States and Great Britain, where Whitelaw Reid was ambassador to the Court of St. James. After her marriage in 1911 to Ogden Reid, the family heir, those contacts were useful for the suffrage movement. With her sister, Florence Rogers Ferguson, a suffrage leader, Reid is credited with raising $500,000 for the final suffrage campaign in New York.

Reid learned the newspaper business by apprenticing herself to the advertising department, seeking to attract suburban women to the paper by focused advertising. But she had a particular interest in women reporters as evidenced by her long association with the New York Newspaper Women. She put her beliefs to work in her position. She hired Irita Van Doren, literary editor of the liberal *The Nation,* in 1924 and made her Sunday book review editor in 1926, which led to a forty-year career at the paper. In the same period, Reid made Marie Mattingly Meloney, former editor of *The Delineator,* editor of the new Sunday magazine. She and Meloney established the speaker series that came to be known as the Herald Tribune Forum, which drew its first audience from club women and eventually became a three-day event broadcast across the country. When the paper was looking for a food editor, Reid hired the legendary Clementine Paddleford, a writer who turned food coverage from the ordinary into the superlative (as in apples: "The teeth crack into the brittle flesh, a winy flavor floods the mouth—the soul of the apple blossom distilled"). She hired the columnist Dorothy Thompson to provide a counter voice to Walter Lippman. She made it possible for Marguerite Higgins to cover World War II and then intervened at the highest levels so Higgins could stay on the front lines. She used her government contacts so that Sonia Tomara, at the *Herald Tribune*'s Paris edition, could become one of the first women to be an accredited war correspondent. She encouraged Dorothy Dunbar Bromley to transform the woman's page from social notes to social commentary. She set the stage for Judith Crist to become the nation's first ongoing female drama critic for a metropolitan paper. When Marie Torre went to jail in 1959 to protect her sources, Reid was behind her.

Richard Kluger, who offers the most complete account of the history of the newspaper, overlooks one important Reid hire, that of Ruth Gruber, a Jewish woman, who was employed at a time of anti-Semitism in general and, according to Kluger, a particular brand of anti-Semitism practiced at the *Tribune* and by Reid. Kluger points to Reid's family correspondence in the 1920s, her refusal to acknowledge the discriminatory nature of the paper's classified advertising, and her hire of a Jewish advertising salesman primarily to target Jewish-owned retail establishments amid an otherwise dismal record of hiring Jews for high-level positions. But as Beverly Merrick has detailed, this profile stands in contrast to Reid's hire of Gruber.

Gruber was a remarkable young woman who was born in Brooklyn and received a Ph.D. at the age of 20 from the University of Cologne. In 1935, at the age of 23, thanks to a fellowship from the New Jersey State Federation of Women's Clubs, she traveled to the Arctic, and her accounts were published in the *Herald Tribune*. When her book appeared in 1939, a member of the U.S. House of Representatives accused her of writing Communist propaganda, but she was publicly supported by Reid and Secretary of the Interior Harold Ickes. During the war years, Gruber's assignments from the *Herald Tribune* led her to specialize in coverage of displaced war refugees, including the voyage of the boat *Exodus* to relocate Jewish refugees to Palestine, work that became a book and helped inspire the film *Exodus*. In the 1940s, the columnist Westbrook Pegler accused Gruber (and many others) of Communist sympathy, but it is now clear that she represented President Roosevelt on a mission to bring displaced Jewish refugees to the United States. Throughout the attacks on Gruber, there are no indications that Reid backed away from her support. Reid received many acknowledgments during her long life, including several from Jewish American organizations. One son went on to become ambassador to Israel during the Eisenhower administration. When she died, Reid received what the *New York Times* considered the penultimate encomium: She was "tiny, spirited, thoroughly feminine and every inch a newspaperman."

WOMEN AT WAR

Thanks to the work of Julia Edwards, Nancy Caldwell Sorel, Maurine H. Beasley, and others, as well as recognition at the Library of Congress, the story of female World War II correspondents is becoming complete. Out of some 1,600 American correspondents assigned to cover combat, nearly 100 were accredited women correspondents. Women in the theater of war included women photographers. Toni Frissell, who had been a fashion photographer, used her skills to photograph the Women's Army Corps to combat negative perceptions of women in uniform. Therese Bonney's photographic work made her a star at home as the heroine of a wartime comic book, "Photofighter." However, women reporters could only win overseas assignments by agreeing to cover the "women's angle," so they were barred from press briefings until late in the war and were not officially allowed to go to the front. Nonetheless, women did reach the war zones: Martha Gellhorn and Cowan of the AP; Dudley Harmon, United Press; Sigrid Schultz, *Chicago Tribune;* Helen Kirkpatrick, *Chicago Daily News;* McCormick, *New York Times;* Thompson, Higgins, Tomara, and Ann Stringer, all of the *Herald Tribune.* Mary Marvin Breckenridge was part of Edward R. Murrow's elite group "Murrow's Boys," reporting for CBS on radio. Other well-known names, including Bourke-White for *Time,* Robb of International News Service, and Iris Carpenter of the North Atlantic Newspaper Alliance, reported from the European Theater during World War II. The experienced Peggy Hull, again accredited, reported from the South Pacific for the Cleveland *Plain Dealer* and the North American Newspaper Alliance. In 1945, she was awarded a Navy commendation. And in what has generally been considered a footnote, if it is mentioned at all, Agnes Smedley covered the Japanese invasion of China for Great Britain's *Manchester Guardian,* a reporting history that later contributed to charges of spying by the Red-hunting *Counter Attack* and the *Chicago Tribune.*

As in World War I, the role of women correspondents in World War II did not clear the way for women in journalism. In the postwar world, women continued to flock into journalism schools, but upon graduation they found many of the same barriers that women had faced for 100 years. However, the stirrings for change finally emerged in what became the Second Wave of feminism, a time when women journalists began to connect their own status in the newsroom to women's status outside of it.

———————————◇———————————

NINE

THE SECOND WAVE

When Helen Rogers Reid died in 1970 and the *New York Times* remembered her as "tiny, spirited, thoroughly feminine and every inch a newspaperman," "thoroughly feminine" seemed to be the operative phrase, anchoring the editorial clearly in its time—the Second Wave of feminism. "Femininity" seemed to be under attack in ways that had not been seen before. From a 1950s culture that had appeared placid, there arrived—what seemed to men—a new shrieking sisterhood, angry young women, and, always, its handmaiden, the loss of femininity.

As a new consumerism and a conservative national ideology took over at the end of World War II, organized feminism disappeared from public consciousness. Nonetheless, the National Women's Party still operated, introducing the equal rights amendment (ERA) every year. The Business and Professional Women's (B&PW) organization agitated for equal opportunity in employment, as did women in federal government. And President John F. Kennedy established, although without giving it any power, a national Commission on the Status of Women. Mass media, for its part, resolutely proclaimed that American women already were the most spoiled in the world and certainly better off than women in Russia, who seemed to be most occupied mixing concrete and working on construction sites. Advertising, radio, television, magazine fiction, and "women's films" glorified separate spheres as much as ever.

Messages of empowerment still existed in the postwar years, however, by the example of women who were still in positions of authority and in understanding the overt texts of the culture in oppositional ways. By way of strong female leads—Joan Crawford and Bette Davis, for example—women's films overcame formulaic plots. Magazines were not simply the carrier of happy housewifery. As Joanne Meyerowitz has explored, magazines profiled independent women side by side with fiction that argued for women in the home. Meantime, an expanding mass media marketplace made television the center of the American home and provided if not equal, at least new opportunities for women and provided for the emergence of a new group of prominent women. Finally, feminism still existed, in perhaps its most radical form yet, in women who had been influenced by radical groups from the 1930s into the 1940s.

While women journalists made their way in the mainstream press, using what tools were at hand, issues of feminism were most discussed in educational and radical-politics circles that viewed women's oppression as part of the maintenance—the "hegemony," in the language of the time—that sustained the status quo of power and wealth. Some of these ideas came by way of discussions on the Left, particularly in the Communist Party. By the late 1930s, the party, having embraced the reforms of Franklin Delano Roosevelt, moved away from an emphasis on revolution and overthrow and attracted new members, increasingly women. Women's membership in the party increased to almost 50 percent by the end of the decade, largely because of the party's attention to female concerns. By 1943, women comprised half the membership of the American Communist Party, and by 1945, thanks to its women's councils, the party had begun to examine its position on women in ways that "laid important practical and theoretical groundwork for the women's liberation movements of the 1960s and 1970s." Intellectuals of the time were influenced by the ferment and sought to spread the word by publications that were available to an audience larger than fellow radicals. In 1940, Mary Inman published *In Woman's Defense,* which called for housework to be regarded as productive labor. Eleanor Flexner's benchmark *Century of Struggle* was written after the author had been influenced by left thinkers. Marxist language was not to be found in these publications, which were aimed for a broad audience, but the ideas had nonetheless been formed in the Left circles of the time.

One of the young women influenced by the foment of the 1930s and 1940s was Betty Goldstyn, later known by her married name, Betty Friedan. Although Friedan would insist she came to feminism by way of frustration with her role as an average American housewife, David Horowitz has made it clear she was a radical activist and labor journalist from 1941 to 1952. As documented in her papers, an FBI informant identified Friedan in 1941 for her friendships with Communists. She later went to work for the Left press, the Federated Press, and the United Electrical Workers (UEW). During her time with the UEW, she wrote an important pamphlet about working women, ideas that she would later massage for publication in the mass press.

Sometime during the mid-1950s, Friedan gave up her involvement with radical politics and turned to a career in mass media writing. Even without intention, many of the ideas from her radical past were repackaged for mass media articles—some not so successfully, as ever-vigilant editors red-penciled, for example, her references to a housing experiment that included African Americans. But it was from the pathway of recycling radical ideas into a mass media venue that she wrote *The Feminine Mystique,* the book that is credited as the starting point of the Second Wave of feminism. By that time, skilled in mass media feature writing and likely not so anxious to bring attention to her radical past at a time of Communist witch hunting, Friedan wrapped her ideas of feminism in the cloak of women's magazine writing. *The Feminine Mystique* ignored the connections between women's status and the allocation of the nation's power and wealth in preference for the individual step-by-step approach to salvation that the women's magazines favored. However, every indication from her early adulthood, beginning with her study at Smith College followed by her years as a labor journalist, is that by the time she wrote *The Feminine Mystique* Friedan herself was not the emerging, tentative feminist of, as she so famously put it, "the problem that has no name."

Her commitment to feminism at this time, however, may have been most connected to her own career as a freelance writer—the route of many 1930s radicals who emerged in the 1950s. She was planning her next book, which had nothing to do with feminism, when the success of *The Feminine Mystique* hurtled her into national celebrity. It was a mantle that she was most pleased to wear and, indeed, jealously guarded. But she was loathe to admit the radicalism that undergirded the book, and her insistence on presenting herself as an average American housewife in line with the mass media framing of the book alienated her from leadership of the emerging radical feminists while at the same time casting the National Organization for Women (NOW), which Friedan had originated, as a middle-class organization on a par with the abjured women's clubs. But the women who made NOW into a working organization were far from the stock figures of clubwomen. Indeed, they were women from the B&PW and women government workers, who had been familiar with employment discrimination and angered by the lack of governmental commitment to the national Commission on the Status of Women. Less philosophically attuned than their radically inspired sisters, the young women filling NOW chapters had come face to face with the discriminatory marketplace. As NOW chapters emerged across the nation (often spurred by Friedan on speaking tours for her book's publicity), they were filled with women for whom Friedan's basic ideas resonated, despite the mass media wrapping paper.

But it would be the young radical women of the 1960s who would be most publicly associated with the Second Wave. In the early 1970s, faith in mass media, particularly television, meant that feminism, as never before, would be argued in mass media venues. Decades later, the faith may seem misplaced, but at the time the women who sought change

were influenced by a culture in which the civil rights movement had seemed to gain its sympathy from its public actions—marches, sit-ins, the "freedom rides" through the
South and the violence they provoked—that dramatically illustrated the barriers to integration. The prestige press sent its
most ambitious reporters to the civil rights story—men who,
having missed World War II, covered civil rights with the
same intensity and hopes for fame. Television news, just coming into its own, provided pictures that riveted the nation,
while the still pictures of the large-format mass magazine
kept the images alive on the country's coffee tables.

As the anti–Vietnam War movement took hold, its
young male leadership adopted the strategies, they believed,
that had worked so well for civil rights. But in order to keep
and maintain the public eye, the young leaders, like any other
"content producers," found it necessary to come up with
larger and larger marches, more extreme events—flag-
burnings, rhetorical denouncements, medal-rejection ceremonies—all of which made good television. For the young
male leaders who absorbed the heady new attention, young
women who opposed the war played secondary roles, doing
the grunt work of social activism. As we know, the young
women finally had enough, and saw even in the radical Left
the same practices toward women that existed in other parts
of society. As women took to heart the radical imperative to
study their own oppression, they collided with the sexual
revolution and, as Sarah Evans maintains, the expectation that
the women adopted their male colleagues' "own more
promiscuous [sexual] standards."

As the young women formed women-only groups to
discuss feminism in the Marxist terms of the radical Left of

the time, they opted to mount their own publicity events or "agitprop"—the slang term for the Marxist concept of "agitation propaganda"—in the famous 1968 protest of the Miss America contest. The press flocked to the protest after Robin Morgan, one of the organizers, hinted at the possibility of a "bra burning," a phrase that was irresistibly euphonic to the headline writers of the time. At the same time, publicity-driven events were also being adopted by NOW to promote its agenda of equal employment and equal accommodations. Equal accommodations in particular could be demonstrated graphically, as when Friedan and a group of women sought to bring attention to the discrimination at the Plaza Hotel, which would not serve women in its Oak Room. Television cameras were quick to respond to the promise of well-dressed women challenging one of the most famous New York institutions (and helped fix NOW as a middle-class organization).

Although the Miss America and Plaza Hotel events emerged out of differing philosophies, what they had in common was not only the belief that mass media could change society, but some understandings of mass media craft traditions. Friedan was far from being the only feminist with mass media experience. A major similarity between the New York chapter of NOW and the small but influential radical organization, New York Radical Women, was that both memberships were composed of women who often had some connection to media. This was not so surprising, since New York was the center of media activity, the place where women as well as men arrived to build careers, and the place where women found barriers to employment, whereas men, at least most white men, did not. Women, of course, found barriers to employment everywhere, as they were still largely excluded from many professions and jobs. The upshot of the exclusion of women in media was that these women took their media savvy to the public stage by way of the media's center located in New York. Because of the intersection of belief in media and the existence of media professionals in an era when social protest was still able to get on the news agenda, much of the Second Wave of feminism seemed to be argued in the news programs of America.

However, these complicated issues were being compressed into the 90-second television news story. They were also events mounted by different wings of the movement for different purposes—the radicals attempting to illustrate the need for a cultural shift in the understanding of women (as in the Miss America protest, which sought to bring attention to how young women were turned into commodities) and the bread-and-butter issues of the NOW campaigns. But for news consumers, all protest looked the same, and the mass media—increasingly overwhelmed by protest movements of all kinds—were not so eager to treat the new wave of feminism in heroic terms. Thanks to the long history of feminism in America, mass media only had to adjust stereotypes, not invent them.

WOMEN JOURNALISTS AS ACTIVISTS

The 1960 U.S. Census reported that 37 percent of reporters and editors were women. Despite the numbers, however, women were clustered in small news operations, and as the Second Wave opened, women in news were not much better off than women reporters at the turn of the century. Indeed, they were perhaps less able to get the bylined story because there was no need of "front page" girls of the sensational press. Despite the 100-year record of women journalists, women still found most jobs in women's sections and on weeklies; schools of journalism were not leading the charge for change any more than they ever were; male editors were willing to accept only the occasional female reporter for general assignment reporting; women probably had less opportunity for editorial leadership as men took over most editorial positions in women's magazines; news organizations were still gender-segregated; women in broadcast news were less visible than they had been in the 1920s; the prohibitions against the female voice were stronger than ever. Salaries were openly discriminatory. For African Americans, the story was worse. In 1968, the Kerner Commission reported that fewer than 5 percent of editorial workers were African Americans. Another study indicated that in the nation's largest cities, African Americans comprised just 2.6 percent of news/ editorial staffs.

In response, women still clustered in professional organizations of their own. But, in contrast to previous times, a substantial number of women in journalism became activists in the larger world of feminism as well as activists within their own profession. In both radical and less radical women's groups, feminists trained in craft traditions helped get the story of feminism on the national agenda. Women in positions of journalistic authority helped move the story. And women in news organizations large and small risked their careers by participating in internal women's committees that agitated for change by all means necessary—from meetings with management to lawsuits. By the end of the decade, the face of journalism—and, indeed, the face of the nation—had changed.

NOW AND THE NEWS AGENDA

After several contentious years during which women in the Association of Women Broadcasters complained that the National Association of Broadcasters (NAB) ignored their concerns, NAB dropped the group. Stung and angry, the women started a new organization, the American Women in Radio and Television. Not surprisingly, Betty Friedan's talk to the New York chapter fell on receptive ears, none more so than Muriel Fox, the program chairman, who wrote Friedan an effusive letter of thanks: "For some time I've been fishing around for a Burning Cause in which to believe—the kind of cause one might perhaps someday espouse on a full-time basis. Your talk yesterday convinced me of the great need for a militant, intelligent organization devoted to women's rights."

Like many of the period's activists, Fox was a media professional as a vice president of the nation's major public relations firm, Carl Byoir. Fox had also experienced the discrimination of the day—rejected by NBC "because they already had a woman in the newsroom." But she was, indeed, to find her burning cause. Friedan turned to her in the initial planning for NOW. Fox became the organization's first public relations director with the skills to know how to put the organization—and Friedan, whom she always supported—on the national agenda. News releases went out in

appropriate news style, and press conferences were conducted in places where the press wanted to be—as in Friedan's apartment in New York's well-known Dakota apartment building. "Since Betty was a celebrity—with an interesting apartment in the Dakota—I knew it would help attract media. I especially wanted TV coverage at all our events." Fox provided a list of public relations achievements at the end of NOW's first year—a two-hour program devoted to women's civil rights on NBC's *Today,* a favorable article in the Sunday supplement *This Week,* major stories quoting Friedan. Her report noted that news was sometimes limited to the women's pages, but that "thanks to coverage by Associated Press, NOW has appeared on the front page of many leading American newspapers." As chapters grew and national campaigns began, Fox helped prepare chapter leaders in basic public relations techniques, as did another media professional, Karen DeCrow, who coordinated the first major NOW campaign to end gender discrimination in public accommodations. As DeCrow instructed one acolyte: "Stress the black analogy. Can you image a restaurant on Adams Street for whites only: A shocking thought. This is the same exact thing."

By choosing specific instances of discrimination in well-known companies—the men-only flights of United Airlines, for example—DeCrow, even with limited resources, was able to use the fame of the target to gain national attention. Not every campaign worked in terms of achieving favorable coverage; sometimes copydesk prejudices led to dismissive headlines and cutlines. Friedan's foray into the Plaza Hotel resulted in a news photograph of the group of women in fur coats sitting around the empty space left when the table was removed. This was hardly the tone of the lunch-counter sit-ins of the civil rights movement. But never before had women's rights been on the national agenda as consistently as provided by the launch of NOW.

AGITPROP

Robin Morgan was a child actress in early 1950s television, an antiwar radical who was influenced by the theatrical agit-prop demonstrations of the "Yippies" at the 1968 Democratic Convention in Chicago, which provided the model for the Miss America protest the following month. However, Lindsy Van Gelder's *New York Post* story the day before the demonstration hinted that women's brassieres would be set on fire in a burn barrel on the Atlantic City boardwalk, a lively promise that brought out the press contingent, including Charlotte Curtis from the *New York Times*. Gelder's phrase "bra burning" was not only euphonious, it seemed to be a playful and slightly lascivious version of the draft-card burnings of antiwar demonstrators. As it turned out, nothing was burned in the demonstration—no one was willing to risk breaking fire regulations. Bras were simply dropped into a barrel along with cosmetics, girdles, women's magazines, and other symbols of women's lives—but the phrase as applied to Second Wave feminism came to be indestructible.

Morgan established WITCH (the acronym was for a longer name that was never used but was invented simply for the initials it could supply) as an agitprop organization, again using small cohorts of women in ways that would attract attention. This included setting white mice free in a bridal gown exhibition at Madison Square Garden and casting a "hex" on Wall Street. Other radical women mounted similar kinds of actions such as the "ogle-in" (gawking at men to illustrate the kind of unwelcome attention that women received) and the disruption of legislative hearings of women's issues at a federal hearing on population control. The African American activist Florynce Kennedy, who had long opposed racism in media, set up actions such as a "pee-in" at Harvard University and, in Los Angeles, the "Hollywood Toilet Bowl," so named, according to Ellen Frankfort, a *Village Voice* writer, to connect bodily waste to the "stench of the body politic."

Outside of the liberal press, such connections were not so easily made. More easily understood by mainstream media were simple protests and picketing attached to clearly understood disparities. So while picket lines outside Colgate-Palmolive headquarters in New York aimed to bring attention to female consumerism, it was interpreted as a call to boycott by the craft traditions of the press. NOW actions, unlike those of the radical left, were more attached to particular campaigns NOW's picket line outside the *New York Times* was to illustrate the paper's refusal to desegregate its help wanted advertisements, part of NOW's public accommodations campaign. But the lines between radicals and NOW in New York often blurred, and actions were mounted by women who came from different philosophies.

That mixture of philosophies was particularly evident in the eleven-hour "sit-in" at *Ladies' Home Journal*. For radicals, women's magazines conveyed repressive ideas, but for women journalists, women's magazines were a source of jobs. The professional journalist Susan Brownmiller, representing the professional women's organization Media

Women, originated the idea of the confrontation with *Journal* editor John Mack Carter. However, in the permeable world of New York feminism, the sit-in was joined by women radicals Shulamith Firestone, Anne Koedt, Karla Jay, Minda Baxman, and Ros Baxandal. As some 200 women swept into Carter's office, the alerted media were on the scene. The women proposed new articles: "Prostitutes and the Law," "Can Marriage Survive Women's Liberation," and a column on "How to Have an Orgasm." Proposed cover art included a pregnant woman holding a sign that said "Unpaid Labor." Carter demurred. Firestone leapt toward his desk. There was concern he would be toppled through the plate glass window of his grand office. In the end, the *Journal* agreed to have a one-time-only pullout section, to the disappointment of some radicals, who thought the action was to result in a real takeover of the magazine.

A less noted upshot was that in the course of preparing the insert, Lenore Hershey, Carter's second in command, became a convert: "For the first time in my life, I got the feeling of what it was like to have control of a situation, to be in charge." When Carter was forced from the job, Hershey applied and gained the position. "I could either wait for another male to whom I could genuflect: Or I could strike out for the job myself."

SPREADING THE WORD: WOMEN IN JOURNALISM

Hershey's epiphany was not so unusual in the Second Wave; it was experienced by women in journalism as much as by any other women who had been kept out of jobs or had been paid less because of gender. Radicals pioneered "consciousness raising" (CR) as way for women to understand the institutional prejudices against women. In NOW's CR groups, that understanding was connected to women's own experiences, especially on the job, and it helps account for NOW's emphasis on equal employment opportunities.

Whether instigated by formal group meetings or not, many of the women in journalism took a new consciousness to their workplaces. Women in journalism of the Second Wave used the power they exercised as gatekeepers to put feminism on the news agenda. Second, women in journalism increasingly demanded equity on the job and were willing to use lawsuits and new federal broadcasting regulations to achieve their ends. In their demand for job equity, women in journalism were joined by women in the feminist community, many of them attorneys working for little or no money. The advancement of women in journalism was considered necessary if women's issues were going to be portrayed accurately in the mass media.

One of the characteristics of the Second Wave was its acceptance by women—although not all women—who had already achieved some success. This acceptance may not have been in the rhetoric of Marxism, but few successful women could ignore their own difficult climb. In journalism, this acceptance could result in an avenue for the entry of feminist ideas to a national audience. ABC anchor and documentary producer Marlene Sanders, an early member of NOW, was on hand to cover the *Journal* sit-in and was sympathetic to feminism after a difficult career at ABC. Barbara Walters produced an early half-hour documentary on the women's movement. Ellen Goodman provided movement-friendly stories in her column at the *Boston Globe*. On the day-by-day level, the story of feminism was also advanced by women in their traditional roles as women's editors. The original NOW story, for example, had been funneled to Joyce Miller, women's editor of the Associated Press. Miller sent out the story with little change. Women's editors ran the story in their sections because it was considered of no interest to the news sections. Indeed, it may have been a women's newspaper editor who shortened "women's liberation" to "women's lib" and thus gave the Marxist term an acceptable, slangy American slant (as well as making it possible for the term to fit into a one-column headline). Moreover, women's editors published Second Wave stories at a time when some women reporters chose to ignore women's issues lest their own careers be frozen in the purdah of "women's news." Liz Trotta, for example, seeking a career in broadcast news, refused to cover the weddings of President Lyndon Johnson's daughters in fear that she would never go beyond that kind of assignment. Other women—such as Lesley Stahl at CBS—found nothing to be gained for their own careers by connection to the women's movement.

The most important women's editor to advance the story was Charlotte Curtis, who was head of what had been the old society section at the *New York Times*. She kept her distance from organized feminism (including participation in the women's lawsuit at the *Times* itself) but found a place in her section for feminist news. This did not always please Fox, who would have preferred NOW to be in news

columns, but Curtis provided a congenial place for feminism, and sometimes beyond, thanks to the company's syndication service. Curtis also permitted her writers to cover
feminism in long articles, as her section was changing to a
"lifestyle" approach. No *Times* writer was more important
than Judy Klemesrud, who covered feminist activities to
such an extent that at her funeral Friedan called her "one of
our own." As the nation's agenda setter, the work of Klemesrud and other female writers on the *Times* enlarged the feminist forum.

Curtis was able to take advantage of changes already
under way in women's sections. Before the Second Wave,
pioneers were bringing new content to the women's sections under the "lifestyle" rubric: Dorothy Brant Brazier at
the *Seattle Times;* Dorothy Misener at the *Miami Herald,* the
Detroit Free Press, and the *Philadelphia Inquirer;* Vivian Castleberry at the *Dallas Times Herald;* Marie Anderson at the
Miami News; Dorothy Jurney at the *Detroit Free Press.* As
Marie Manning had done at the turn of the century, the
women introduced new subjects strategically. As Castleberry
has described it: "I would take my little canoe out in the
waters to see how far I could get it from the shore. If the
waves got too high, I would take it back into the shoreline."
Jurney offered to "help out" the news editors when she
identified a story that she wanted for her section, which included, in 1959, a story on birth control, a breakthrough for
the time. Castleberry promoted local angles on national
stories, published new material when the boss was out of
town, and, after facing down management, was able to break
prohibitions on the coverage of African Americans. In 1968,

the publisher of the *Dallas Times Herald* finally agreed to allow an African American bride to appear in the paper, the first step for increased coverage of African Americans in general. Whenever the women broke traditions they were, as Marie Anderson remembered, called "rabble rouser" or "pinko." Castleberry bosses hired managers specifically to "handle her."

These changes made by individual editors began to influence newspapers nationally as the University of Missouri developed an awards program for women's sections, and conferences brought women together from across the country. But changes came with difficulty. Castleberry told one of her numerous bosses: "You can do things to me, you can bend me to the ground. But I will be just like a tree with a taproot that is extremely deep. I will stand up tomorrow and I will still be there fighting for what I believe."

While the changes to women's sections sometimes could provide opportunities for professional writers, they were probably most useful to the Second Wave in making acceptable subjects that had been considered off limits for family newspapers. Eager to prove their competitiveness, magazines and newspaper magazine sections were open to "in-depth" stories behind the television pictures, and the large cohort of female freelance writers in New York were eager to supply them, even to the point where radicals attacked such writers for using the movement to advance their own careers. Professional women writers who were members of the movement were not so shy about using that knowledge in the mainstream, such as Susan Brownmiller. The *New York Times* opened up the pages of its weekly magazine to publish her personal account of the Second Wave, "Sisterhood Is Powerful: A Member of the Women's Liberation Movement Explains What It's All About."

FIGHTING FOR PARITY

As women editors and journalists were putting the movement on the public agenda, they were also fighting to improve the role of female journalists as a class. These efforts could involve confrontational meetings with management, the threat and the actuality of lawsuits, expense, and personal risk. The *New York Times,* which had avoided hiring women unless as a "special" and which had continued to demonstrate a subsequent record of employment and salary discrimination, was involved in negotiation with its women employees until the 1980s. Lawsuits were launched at *Time* and *Newsweek,* newsweeklies that had long declared that women could only work as researchers but not as reporters. Thanks to an activist Federal Communication Commission, which demanded that local broadcasters reflect diversity in their hiring and programming, NOW was active in assisting its local chapters in challenging the licenses of broadcasters who did not hire women. Oprah Winfrey in Tennessee and Jessica Savitch in Texas were hired in part because of local television's sudden attention to equal opportunity hiring that federal licensing required. But Winfrey and Savitch also represented an unexpected bonanza in hiring women: Not only did women reporters open up new areas of content, women in the co-anchor chair helped ratings in major ways. As it turned out, viewers and listeners did not have the objections to the female voice that some male broadcasters were still claiming in the period.

At the networks, which were under a different set of regulations than local broadcasters, nationally known on-air women took the lead in challenging gender discrimination. At ABC, Carole Simpson, familiar with discrimination as an African American, could only reach the ABC news chief Roone Arledge by mounting a public challenge at a luncheon. After her presentation, "You could have heard a pin drop." Sylvia Chase led a challenge at CBS. NBC was the most difficult of all. The lawsuits and challenges consumed the 1970s and reappeared in the 1980s, when many hiring goals had not been met. The women who were most active generally found their careers constrained in an industry whose management was closely connected and shared similar outlooks.

CHANGES IN CONTENT

By the 1970s, the Second Wave was reaching a high point. Given that shelter magazines traditionally had most inculcated the idea of female domesticity, the women's magazines of the time all found a place, in varying degrees, to address the movement. *Redbook,* whose editor Sey Chassler was on NOW's board of directors, provided to its four million readers articles that had been opened up by radical discussion: lesbianism, rape, and—in acknowledgment of new range of women's interest—a "Guide to Backpacking." Anne Koedt's short article in the left press, "The Myth of the Vaginal Orgasm," introduced discussions of orgasm into the mass press, even in *Ladies' Home Journal,* which assured readers that "a woman can adjust herself to have an orgasm in a very short time." The book business flourished with movement-friendly best sellers in the early 1970s thanks to the demand for new content; this was soon followed by yet another flurry, when even newer content became available from those who opposed the movement. This, indeed, marked the decline of the Second Wave. But although the mass press was pleased to encompass much of the new content, one topic was left alone—abortion. Except for one publication.

MS. MAGAZINE

The media product next to *The Feminine Mystique* that remains most associated with the Second Wave is *Ms.* magazine, founded in 1972. To radicals, *Ms.* would become the example of the success of "liberal feminism," and they deplored its emphasis on personal awareness rather than on the levers of institutional change. Gloria Steinem, most associated with the magazine, was abjured by the radicals because she was seen to have achieved mass media fame on the basis of the media demand for beauty alone.

Steinem called herself a "revolutionary" (as opposed to Friedan, whom she called a "reformer"), but she had not been associated with radical groups as they emerged from the antiwar movement, she did not take part in any of the early actions, and she held no formal leadership positions. She had been a successful freelance writer in the 1950s and 1960s, already the subject of media attention because of her classic good looks and her management of her career. An early article in *Look* magazine, for example, used photographs of her to represent pieces on a game board—not the usual authorial presentation in a freelance article. But she was drawn to the public discussion of radicals such as the Redstockings when she covered them as a columnist for *New York* magazine, and she soon became an articulate speaker on feminist issues, sought out by television interview programs.

Clearly, Steinem did receive media attention because of her looks, in much the same way that Inez Milholland had become the focus of the First Wave. At that time, William Randolph Hearst asked his star reporter Adela Rogers St. Johns to find a suffragist who would "make suffrage look attractive to the young." As St. Johns recalled, she found Milholland, "in her puffed-sleeved shirtwaist and Merry Widow sailors she was beautiful enough even for the flashlight cameras of that day." In the same way, Steinem fit the technology of her day, representing characteristics that were attuned to television. From the clear demarcation of her simple tops and well-fitted jeans to the smooth lines of her cascading hair and the flat accent of her speaking style that was humorous but still cool, Steinem projected calmness and coolness, a contrast to the discomfort promoted by the voluble and confusing Friedan and other activists.

Steinem's national recognition gave her the cachet to start a national magazine and Katharine Graham, publisher of the *Washington Post,* provided seed money. The concept of a magazine serving women drawn to feminism was in tune with a shift in the magazine industry as it moved from large general-interest magazines to specialized publications. Moreover, the women Steinem drew around her to mount the magazine came from the pool of the nation's most talented magazine journalists, including Patricia Carbine, who had returned *McCall's* magazine to profitability before giving up her vice presidency to take the helm of *Ms*. Finally, Steinem's years in the business had sensitized her to the need for "launch," and among the founders was Letty Pogrebin, former publicist for Bernard Geis Associates, a book publishing firm that specialized in books by celebrity authors and in subject matter that otherwise lent itself to promotion. (Geis published Helen Gurley Brown's famous *Sex and the Single Girl*.) Under Pogrebin's influence and with a publicity director as one of the first hires, *Ms*. always found ways to connect itself to the national scene, as when the astronaut Sally Ride took the magazine into space and made it part of the Smithsonian collection.

But in the end, it would be the editorial message that would prove itself suited to a national audience. From the beginning, Steinem promoted a view of feminism as inclusive. *Ms*. was conceived as a national publication with an appeal to women across lines of color, class, sexual orientation, political views, and ethnicity in the belief that shared womanhood provided sufficient commonalities that made other differences not so important. While traditional service magazines set out domesticity as the shared characteristic of women, *Ms*. saw gender alone as the commonality that united differences. Under that philosophy, *Ms*. celebrated difference as branches emerging from the central trunk of female gender. Under that mantle, *Ms*. regularly introduced subject matter that was hardly the stock in trade of general-interest magazines, including the subject of abortion. While the new content was in some sense mitigated or normalized by the use of comforting craft traditions of magazines—glossy paper, use of color, celebrity covers, "sell lines," and editorial "departments"—support of abortion was the magazine's unwavering bottom line. Eventually, it was the magazine's support of abortion that was most responsible for its final inability to make *Ms.* a viable commercial project supported by advertising.

Through the magazine's complicated ownership history (it is now published by the nonprofit Feminist Majority), Steinem remained (and remains) its stable figurehead, helping *Ms.* to become a brand name as much as *Ladies' Home Journal.*

THE FIFTIETH ANNIVERSARY MARCH

Both the radical and the NOW wings of the Second Wave agreed on the importance of public actions, albeit for different ends. To many activists of the period, however, the most effective and remembered public action was the massive march sponsored by NOW (and many other aligned groups) to celebrate the fiftieth anniversary of the final ratification of the Nineteenth Amendment—August 26, 1970. It was also a way to replay Alice Paul's suffrage march in 1913, which was credited with changing the perception of suffrage in media.

Unlike the 1913 march, however, the political motivation for the 1970 march was unclear. Even though the U.S. House of Representatives had given approval to the equal rights amendment earlier in the month and the amendment was being readied to face the formidable opposition in the U.S. Senate, the march did not include passage of the ERA in its list of three demands, which were instead abortion on demand, 24-hour-a-day child care, and, in a general clumping, equal opportunity for women in education and employment. Moreover, U.S. Rep. Martha Griffiths (D-Mich.), who was most responsible for managing the House success, was not included in the march. Indeed, Griffiths was never embraced by the movement and probably was distanced even further after the House passage chose to characterize her in ways that pointed up that she was different from what was considered the usual feminist. She was lauded for "disdaining the militant overkill of many leaders of the women's liberation movement"; "no man hater"; even a "graceful feminist." Griffiths herself never characterized herself in these ways, but clearly this kind of media approval could only serve to challenge a leadership position.

The march as it was finally accomplished was far different from the national work stoppage or "strike day" that Betty Friedan, true to her labor past, had proposed as part of her final address as president of NOW. However, her concept of a labor strike did not comport so well with NOW's campaign seeking access to the workplace while radical women claimed a work stoppage would only jeopardize working women's jobs. Moreover, confusion swirled about what "strike day" meant. Did work stoppage mean housewives should not cook dinner, that women should withhold sex from partners? Should women risk their jobs and the support of families? At the same time, Friedan had no support in much of the feminist community, and NOW organizers faced the likelihood that a "strike day" would end up representing the divisions of the movement in a public way.

Although confusion existed until the anniversary day (and provided much fodder for the media), organizers shifted focus from a *national* strike day to a celebration of women's empowerment to be illustrated by the New York City march. Jacqui Ceballos, president of New York NOW, realized that the decision to mount a march meant that its organizers, like those of antiwar demonstrations, had to deliver enough marchers to attract media coverage. "The 1,500 or so card-carrying feminists would show, but how could we attract others? A poor showing would increase the ridicule we were constantly subject to, and hurt the movement." Ceballos's own concern with the ERA was mounted as a separate pre-march promotion when a group of feminists "invaded" the Statue of Liberty to hang two banners, one promoting the ERA and one the march.

The coverage of the earlier event by network news hel-icopters (new in the television business) and the other pre-march activities helped make the New York march one of the remembered successes of the Second Wave. Fifty thousand women were said to have participated. The *New York Times* provided a banner headline and a four-column picture of ex-uberant women arm in arm, marching down Fifth Avenue, reminiscent of coverage of the suffrage parades. Friedan re-members the march as the "high point" of her political ca-reer. To the thousands of women who participated in the march or who followed the New York coverage, the march represented what seemed at the time an undiminished future for feminism. The march prompted *Life* magazine to give the movement its cover the following week—"the revolution that will affect everyone."

In the frenzy of the moment, just a few observers noticed the sarcasm by television commentators, the use of images of stridency in television and photographic coverage, the absence of coverage in the African American press, or the negative reaction to events mounted in other parts of the country. Marches in cities that did not bring thousands to the cause were negatively noticed by local newspapers. "Strike

Gains Very Little Momentum," the *Milwaukee Journal* in-toned. The *Chicago Tribune,* interpreting the strike in terms of the original purpose, headlined its story, "Strike Flops Women in City Keep Working." A copyeditor for the *San Francisco Examiner* captioned a wire photo of the Washington march "[A]ngry-looking young women militants grimly march up Connecticut Avenue in Washington," although there was nothing particularly grim about the women photographed.

What such press coverage represented was the depth of antifeminist attitudes that were never far from the surface, even as the movement appeared to go from one success to the other. By the time NOW, the League of Women Voters, the Association of University Women, and many of the or-ganizations finally put their efforts into the passage of the ERA in the 1970s and into the 1980s, antifeminist forces had gathered strength enough to counter the feminist impulse. The abortion controversy alone helped bring together the resources of the nation's Catholic bishops with the emerging power of the fundamentalist right.

Their forces gathered at a time when mass media was losing the influence in which feminists had put so much faith. From easily prepared, low-tech newsletters—Phyllis Schlafly's technique—to early adoption of cable and com-puters and the use of zip codes and 800 numbers, antifemi-nist forces constructed a media countermovement. In 1993, Steinem, always prescient in such matters, noted that by such techniques antifeminists had created their own media. "Meanwhile, we goody two-shoes here have been trying to influence the mainstream media."

However, by the mid–1970s, the Second Wave's media

moment was receding, as mass media moved to new subjects and a conservative Federal Communications Commission rescinded many of the regulations that had demanded change.

JOURNALISM EDUCATION

The complaints Ruby Black made against journalism schools in 1924 could have been repeated a half century later with little change, even though many more teaching positions had come into being in the 1950s and 1960s. Women students comprised 41 percent of journalism school enrollments in 1968, but just seventy-six women were employed in the nation's fifty-five journalism schools. Despite increasing numbers of women students, women faculty had trouble even hearing about openings, because word-of-mouth tips left women out of the network. Two of the women who did hold academic positions (they were also among the few who held PhDs in the field), Ramona Rush and Carol Oukrop, prepared a report for the accrediting body clearly indicating that fewer women were hired and that women were paid less and promoted less than their male counterparts. Just three African American women were members of the national professional organization—Lillian E. Bell, Jewell P. Ross, and Biswananth Shaw—out of an estimated eighteen women of color teaching in journalism programs nationwide. Marion Marzolf remarked, "[E]ven the men seemed shocked." Hazel Dicken-Garcia was the first person to file a discrimination lawsuit against a journalism program, charging salary discrimination at the University of Massachusetts. In 1982, four years after the filing, the Equal Employment Opportunity Commission (EEOC) upheld the charge.

However, by 1982, the campaign for the equal rights amendment, which had taken years of energy and resources by its proponents, was finally abandoned. A new political ideology reified domestic messages, although not in ways that assisted women dealing with family and work. A rising generation of young women was able to take advantage of new opportunities, but resisted connections—or were unaware that connections existed—with women who had made them possible.

Sixty years earlier, journalist Marie Manning, fearing that memories of the First Wave were disappearing, asked despairingly, "Does history have to be written in blood to be remembered?" The question seemed ready to be asked again.

TEN

MAKING A DIFFERENCE

When Terry Gross, the long-time host of National Public Radio's "Fresh Air," entered radio, it was thanks to a training program mounted by women volunteers. "It didn't matter that I had no radio experience," Gross said. "The producers were almost as committed to training other women as they were to getting the program on the air. They were convinced that the mass media would continue to ignore or misinterpret the women's movement until women were in a position to make editorial decisions and report the stories."

Activists still seek hiring of women in journalism not only to ensure equal job opportunity but also in the belief that the presence of women in media will lead to increased coverage of women's issues. In related concerns, the depictions of women in media—another legacy of the Second Wave—continue to be followed, although now from the Right as much as the Left, in the shared belief that those depictions can shape larger attitudes. Depictions may be traced from the roles women are given in entertainment products to counting the number of times women are quoted in significant, front-page stories. Research that has suggested teenage girls, for example, model themselves in terms of class, race, and gender from media images has prompted the growth of the media literacy field.

Not everyone agrees that mass media have such power to shape attitudes and society. Some scholars believe that audiences take their own meanings from the content of mass media, even ones that can be quite opposite of overt messages. In other words, audiences understand content by the context they bring to it. This is true for a new group of feminists, the Third Wave, who do not necessarily reject the same mass media images that offended a previous generation. Who is to determine what are detrimental messages? They contend that women's power is in not aping the male model.

These varying interpretations of the power of media have not made it any easier for female media practitioners, who must consider their own roles in the promulgation of images that may, or may not, be influential. In the spring of 2005, the issue of female influence in media came to national attention for a short and heated time. Susan Estrich, a law professor at the University of Southern California and news commentator (as well as former manager of the 1988 Democratic presidential campaign of Governor Michael Dukakis), charged that women columnists were dramatically underrepresented on the nation's opinion pages, particularly at the *Los Angeles Times.* Her strongly worded e-mail to the paper's opinion editor, Michael Kinsey, included the suggestion that Kinsey's decision-making abilities had been impaired by his illness, Parkinson's Disease——an attack that opened her to personal characterizations that centered on female hysteria, as Myrna Blyth put it, "an over-the-top hissy fit." Although

Editor and Publisher magazine also noted that just one of four editorial columnists nationwide were women and the record of the nation's major newspapers was substantially worse, the female professional community was divided. For conservatives, Estrich was simply trying to enlarge voices on the Left, including her own. For Lakshmi Chaudhry, a writer for the Left-leaning online journal *AlterNet,* the *number* of women in journalism was not so important, since even women reporters and women managers were likely to "confirm conventional wisdom rather than challenge it."

Underneath the political rhetoric, however, old issues remained. Anne Applebaum, the only regular female columnist at the *Washington Post* (out of nineteen), claimed Estrich had "launched a conversation that is seriously bad for female columnists and writers. None of the ones I know—and, yes, I conducted an informal survey—want to think of themselves as beans to be counted, or as 'female journalists' with a special obligation to write about 'women's issues.'" The experienced foreign correspondent Georgie Ann Geyer thought that Estrich's demand was oddly "old-fashioned." "She wants more columns by women, but she only wants their 'women's voices.'" Chaudhry, however, represents a new attention to ownership issues that goes beyond hiring. "For decades, liberals have pushed numerical strength as a means to censure representation of those marginalized either by race or gender." She cautions, "Simply changing the demographics of newsroom[s] won't change the product, especially in a period of media consolidation."

Thus, even in a period of enlarging opportunities for women, old questions still face women in journalism. Do they have an obligation to cover women's issues? Can women's issues be separated from institutional issues? Do women bring to their work outlooks and experiences that otherwise would not be noticed? Is there a role for women's sections? Indeed, is there a role for a *woman* journalism, or is it simply an unnecessary descriptive. Do women in journalism make a difference?

DO WOMEN JOURNALISTS MAKE A DIFFERENCE?

Despite the generally dismal job opportunities in newspaper work, a recent survey records a slight increase in the employment of women, up to 37 percent in the newsroom. Among supervisors, 34 percent were female and 40 percent were reporters. However, the Annenberg Public Policy Center found little change in the "glass ceiling" for women in leadership positions of communication companies across all communication crafts—women comprised just 15 percent of executives and 12 percent of board members. Moreover, although women in leadership positions have been on the increase, research finds that women continue to be mentioned an average of 24 percent in front page stories in the past two decades. In recent localized research of two Minneapolis dailies, that percentage is down slightly, to 22 percent. In results that might be thought fairly typical, the Minnesota survey found that over a ten-year period, coverage of women had increased in metro, sports, variety, and opinion sections. Sports coverage of women had doubled, from 7 percent to 14 percent, while coverage had decreased in business.

Less easy to quantify is the impact women's employment has had on media products. One examination of the editorial changes at women's magazines in the 1965–1985 period found that the increase in the number of women executives initially coincided with an increase in positive portrayals of women. But in the second period, fewer articles appeared that described women as in charge of their environment, while more were published that represented women as passive dependents and as family servants. Researchers concluded that the content of the magazines was more likely to represent the cultural climate of the times than the presence of female executives.

Other research upholds the conclusion. A 1999 study found that women's magazines covered breast cancer in terms of "coping" stories—the traditional approach. Other health care scholars concluded that the increasing prominence in health care given to women in the 1990s was in ways most helpful to the health care industry. Barbara Seaman warned as early as 1997 that the mainstream media was failing to report the dangers of estrogen therapy for women. Negative results did not get widely reported for five more years; but women as reporters or executives did not seem to play a role in seeking an earlier release of such information.

At one time, such health subjects might have been found in the strengthened women's sections. But the efforts of Vivian Castleberry and the other women's section editors were already fading by the mid-1970s as the move to lifestyle sections resulted in expanded entertainment coverage rather than serious reporting. Although the revamped sections offered an entry place for young female reporters who could write in the lively style that younger readers were thought to want, the move to lighter fare neither staunched the outflow of those readers nor held traditional readers.

In 1991, the *Chicago Tribune* sought to bring back traditional readers and offer a viable product to advertisers by introducing "Womannews," a place where important issues could be discussed in a woman-controlled setting. This sense of separateness was encouraged by setting out "Womannews" as a newspaper within a newspaper, a tactic not so different from the old department store advertisement that enclosed its space as to represent women's own realm. There was concern. Was "Womannews" an update of the old women's sections that so many Second Wave and earlier feminists disliked?

Therese Lueck, however, places "Womannews" in the frame of "cultural feminism," one of the longstanding threads of American feminism. Cultural feminism claims that gender differences exist and, in the face of a male society that has downgraded female-associated characteristics, seeks to imbue them with positive values. As Alice Echols describes it, cultural feminism "equated women's liberation with the nurturance of a female counterculture, which it hoped will supersede the dominant culture." These ideas were not so far from notions of women's moral culture of the nineteenth and early twentieth centuries that sought suffrage under a rationale that women could purify society, ideas that blurred into Second Wave thinking, as when Gloria Steinem predicted a kinder, gentler world in articles she wrote for *Look* ("Why We Need a Woman President in 1976") and for *Time* ("What It Would Be Like If Women Win").

Carol Gilligan's 1981 book *In A Different Voice* was particularly influential in proselytizing the idea that women were essentially different from men and describing the difficulties that came with integrating female sensibilities into the hierarchal model of the male world. For many women, what kept women in subservient positions was that their sensibilities did not fit with the male model; hence, the male model should be made more accommodating.

However, as "Womannews" illustrated, cultural feminism as it evolved in the mass media world had less to do with influence on the dominant culture than in finding a place within the dominant culture. While mass media in this form can function as a useful tool and can increase female self-worthiness (so much a theme of media products aimed at women), that does not necessarily lead to an appreciation of woman's culture in the wider world, and it does not necessarily lead to systemic change.

Indeed, despite the explosion of new media products aimed at women—special sections, magazines, cable channels, and Internet sites—media-instigated discussion of women has remained in time-honored terms of coping by way of individual solutions. Even *Oprah,* in the long tradition of women's magazines, focuses on self-empowerment and improvement rather than wider change.

The interest in women as markets did not translate into women as a class, even in a news frame. In a female context, the old organizing traditions aimed at garnering media attention no longer worked. The March for Women in April 2004 drew, at its most conservative estimate, a half million marchers, but no matter how many women reporters and managers existed at the time, the march still received just scattered coverage—in contrast to the coverage given to the smaller march of the Promise Keepers, a men's organization that encourages a hierarchal structure in the home.

Whether on the Left or Right, interest in women has

come to be subsumed under respective ideologies. On the Right, commentators call for reform of women in media images as part of their overall policy concerns that view media as weakening values they hold. On the Left, issues of women in media, in both hiring or image, are connected to reform activities linked to media ownership.

MEDIA LANDSCAPE

The doorway to women's successes was opened by Second Wave reforms that achieved access by means of legislative and legal decisions in which industry hiring practices of the time were found to be incompatible with national standards of equity. The great irony of the journalistic reforms achieved in the Second Wave is that they arrived at a time when the mass media were about to undergo their greatest change in 100 years. Because of the growth of cable and Internet sources, the Federal Communications Commission abolished policies that demanded inclusiveness, claiming that the new avenues of news and information provided a sufficiently diverse media marketplace to serve the nation. Ownership caps on broadcast properties were lifted under the new rationale and, with them, the obligation for broadcasters to serve local populations. These new freedoms allowed the broadcasting industry to return to the roots of entertainment that had undergirded its beginnings and—except for the interlude of 1970s news—had been the major way to maximize its profits.

Moreover, in the new ownership world, media products owned by one part of the corporation are used for the benefit of the profit line for all, and owners see logic in using one arm of their operation to massage another. Most recognizably, entertainment products are routinely promoted in news programs on outlets owned by the same company; news commentators move easily from one media arm of the corporation to another; news programs promote Web pages and their additional advertising support; information assembled just once is amortized over multiple outlets with slight changes in form but not content. The emphasis on profit has removed boundaries separating news, entertainment, and advertising. Product placement is endemic. Guests on talk shows cannot be imagined unless they are promoting another product, a practice once condemned as "plugola." All media outlets seek "partners" of one sort or another, and partners exact payment. "The dilemma facing women journalists," according to a recent discussion, "is that they are being deployed to pander to women audiences' status as consumers."

STEREOTYPES AND CONSUMERISM

Female consumerism along the lines of homemaking remains as important as ever, as are fashion and accoutrements. However, what is particularly interesting about this period is that much of female consumerism is connected to female appearance. The current emphasis is not simply a matter of fashion, but conforming all aspects of the body to a predetermined physical look. A participant in a cosmetic surgery program taps her new nose and marvels how "it" looks—as if the body part is attached but not a real part of the individual. Women models change in hue but not in bone structure. As they did 100 years ago, such models can invoke familiar feelings of angst, even unworthiness, perhaps a happy place for the advertisers, although not useful for a demographically changed nation.

No woman can escape the judgment of the physical. *Time* magazine's coverage of the death of Susan Sontag was as "The Sensuous Intellectual." Her intellect was one thing, but "it didn't hurt that she also possessed a dark, slightly exotic beauty, the kind that could make her seem like the star of her own foreign film." *Time* has a long history of representing women in less than empowered ways, for example its 1997 story, "Reporting on the Birth and Death of Feminism." The cover consisted of the unattached, floating heads of Susan Anthony, Betty Freidan, Gloria Steinem, and actress Calista Flockhart. At Steinem's marriage in 2001, *Time*'s headline was "Finally Real"—an intimation that something was missing in her premarriage days. Steinem has long met marketplace standards of beauty, but beauty, apparently, must be accompanied by other standards for the *Time* imprimatur.

Although media products such as *Time* will only grudgingly admit to new standards in the culture, advertisers are more likely to pick up on trends, including changes in the status of women, if they can be interpreted in ways that sell goods. In the first part of the century, independence for women was connected to the freedom to smoke cigarettes— "torches of freedom," as the publicist Edward Bernays was to call them. In the 1920s, independence came to be represented by a famous automobile advertisement featuring young women with bobbed hair on the "road to Laramie." In the Second Wave, "Charlie" perfume was positioned to suggest its scent represented liberation; Peter Pan Company introduced a bra that did not do anything; and jeans, rather than being a statement of working-class alignment, came to be fashionable.

Mass media stand at the ready to accommodate Third Wave feminism along lines long established. The challenge for Third Wave feminism is to find ways that its interpretations of the feminine do not disappear into a mass media marketplace that seeks to promote definitions that reify old ones or promote advertising. Women journalists face the problem they have always faced: how to avoid collaboration in the promotion of ideology that is not useful, and may be detrimental, to the readers they serve.

THE THIRD WAVE AND MEDIA

In the United States, Naomi Wolf's 1991 *The Beauty Myth* identified the Clarence Thomas hearings as the beginning of a time when gender issues were driven back into the public eye by a series of media events and politics—the rape trials of William Kennedy Smith and Mike Tyson, the contentious place of Hillary Clinton in the Clinton presidential campaign, and the strength of the religious right in putting abortion and homosexuality at the center of political discourse. Writers and editors of essay collections, including Rebecca Walker and Barbara Findlen, Leslie Heywood and Jennifer Drake, Rory Dicker and Alison Piepmeier, Daisy Hernandez and Bushra Rehman, and Ophira Edut, have similarly established a place for young women to discuss how they differ from a previous generation. The first extended exploration was in the 2000 *Manifesta: Young Women, Feminism, and the Future* by Jennifer Baumgardner and Amy Richards. They identify how a new generation of women emerged from influences in popular culture—Madonna; a new glossy magazine; Wolf's book; the punk-rock band Riot Grrls; and articles in *Bust* and other zines that introduced "girl culture." "All this Girlie Culture, from Madonna to *Bust,* is different from the cultural feminism of the Seventies," they write. "We, and others, call this intersection of culture and feminism 'Girlie.' Girlie says we're not broken, and our desires aren't simply booby traps set up by the patriarchy. Girlie encompasses the tabooed symbols of women's feminine enculturation—Barbie dolls, makeup, fashion magazines, high heels—and says using them isn't shorthand for 'we been duped.'"

Young women who embrace the "girlie" often reject Second Wave feminism for its perceived grimness vis-à-vis fashion and appearance. At one point, the home page for the Third Wave magazine *Bitch* connected unshaven legs to Second Wave feminists. In Third Wave culture, women who refuse to shave leg hair are not necessarily rejecting mass-mediated standards of beauty—which was the belief of earlier feminists—as much as they are rejecting personal choice to take on a kind of feminist uniform. To quote Baumgardner and Richards: "The point is that the cultural and social weapons that had been identified (rightly so) in the Second Wave as instruments of oppression—as sex objects, fascist fashion, pornographic materials—are no longer being exclusively wielded against women and are sometimes wielded by women."

The most generally accepted understanding of Third Wave feminism is that it rejects the idea that there are clear characteristics for each gender. Rather, the Third Wave sees an essential equality between the sexes because differences cross gender. Girliness is just one of the differences on a continuum of differences, and women drawn to girliness can be as powerful as anyone else; indeed, expressions of girliness can be expressions of power. Moreover, being both girlie and powerful (as is the lead character of "Buffy the Vampire Slayer") offers a reinterpretation of "femininity." Femininity does not have to be regarded in the stereotypical terms of passivity but can represent independence.

Third Wave approaches have support from academic researchers who find that Second Wave interpretations of essential difference lack scientific evidence. Rosalind C. Barnett and Caryl Rivers argue that research that seemed to support female essential difference was flawed—particularly Gilligan's study of female psychology, as well as a famous survey from the American Association of University Women that suggested adolescent girls had less self-esteem than boys. They argue that no data support gender-only difference and that gender difference has come to be a "bandwagon" now so widely accepted that its concepts have been taken into higher education and are found in courses across curricula. The authors warn, "The essentialist perspective has so colored the dialogue about the sexes that there is scant room for any narrative other than difference." That statement seemed to be further supported when Harvard University president Lawrence Summers in 2005 raised the issue that women may not do well at math and science for inborn reasons.

The Third Wave is already on the media agenda because it provides irresistible content—sexiness and independence—that (again) can be framed as the freedom to buy. Moreover, femininity has long been defined in terms of how well it "works" in terms of attracting the male gender. Femininity as essentially a female expression of personality that may (or may not) be connected with sexual partnering is hard for Western culture to concede and may pose the largest problem for new feminists seeking to articulate power as outside of male attraction.

At the crux of new explorations of feminism are incoming women journalists, now representing the substantial new majority of journalism programs. While women journalists may be happy to know they have the choice of accepting the new "liberatory" feminine in their personal lives, their choices may contend, for example, with television jobs in which female reporters, not just anchors, have to give so much attention to hair and dress as to be themselves dispersal mechanisms for consumer culture. Moreover, while media content finds the feminine and the independent a seductive combination, it is not so easy to accept the rest of the package of difference that the Third Wave purports. For media purposes, the continuum has seemed stopped at the first level, which can be accommodated without much difficulty. Indeed, the feminine and the independent have long been part of "feisty," a definition that has particular relevance for women journalists.

GENDERED WRITING REDUX

There is a kind of desperation in play as daily journalism seeks to attract the eyes of the demographically desirable to serve today's advertisers. Eager to find techniques to attract younger readers, newspapers have taken their cues from other platforms. One technique is the adoption of the casual, anecdotal style of writing not so different from blog contributors or television and radio talk show conversations. The style has been most represented by Candace Bushnell, whose newspaper column translated into the television program "Sex in the City," and Helen Fielding, whose "Bridget Jones's Diary" for a British newspaper was translated to film. Although casual writing is found throughout mass media today in a move to accessible "softer journalism," first-person writing is particularly connected to female writers, whose writing is expected to be either personal and revealing or, increasingly, angry and ranting—the colonial "scold" brought back to life. Journalist Zoe Heller describes the process of gendered writing:"When a woman journalist is invited to use the first person to inject some more 'attitude' into a piece, it is often a coded entreaty to beef up a specifically female perspective." Observing this "new girl writing," Chambers, Steiner, and Fleming call the style "covertly antifeminist."

Female writers who are so willing to write about their personal lives are reifying the old cultural values that expect women to be open about private affairs as much as men are expected to guard theirs. We might note that coverage of breast cancer peaks whenever a female celebrity reveals she has the disease, suggesting that society's receptivity to women as victims is heightened when it also serves as a leveling tool for powerful women. It is questionable whether male celebrities find public admissions of diseases or frailties helpful to their careers. Yet women who reveal, either as writers or as victims, cannot depend on automatic approval. With power in the hands of the audience, women must work harder to make sure of a favorable reception—breast cancer survivors must be compelling and women columnists more

deadly and extreme in their aim than their male counterparts, one of the hallmarks of the *New York Times* female
opinion columnist, liberal Maureen Dowd, as much as conservative female writers such as Ann Coulter.

A second aspect of gendered writing is the use of
women columnists as attackers on other women—the
Estrich incident being one example. The British journalist Janet Street-Porter has spoken out on the role of the
female "ranter," the popular columnist who specializes in
criticism of other women at the behest of largely male editors looking for popular content. "I want people to think
about the fact that every time they buy one of the tabloids
that pay a woman to belittle other women in print, they are
prolonging the time in which this sort of behavior is considered to be accepted and normal behavior, for money and
profile that the only way we could feed our egos was by
betraying our sex."

Sob-sister journalism is no longer in vogue, but pres-
sures still exist for women to write according to a perceived
type, a logical demand from an industry that finds profit in
dipping into the culture's easy stereotypes. Still, as in sob-
sister journalism, the rewards for the new style of female
columnist can be substantial—wealth and fame nationally
and some reduced form of that on a local level. But as Heller
warns, "The request may seem innocuous enough, but in
taking such an invitation a woman takes her first step away
from the neutrality and freedom of being simply a writer
toward the ghetto of writing 'as a woman.'"

The caution for women journalists to distance themselves from "writing like a woman" echoes the dissatisfaction

of the professional women writers of the nineteenth century who wrote sentimental fiction because that was the editorial demand. A Third Wave feminist would point out that "writing like a woman" is not a naturally occurring phenomenon, but simply a male, shorthand way of calling for a kind of writing that sells in the culture of the moment. It is to be considered that Judith Sargent Murray, Margaret Fuller, Anne O'Hare McCormick, and legions more also "wrote like a woman."

"Women's history" is a complicated business, hardly a story to be told in terms of winners and losers, great men, or progress forward, as in a woman's context all the usual benchmarks may have differing and contested definitions. This is certainly true in telling the story of women in the profession of journalism. At its most basic, the "struggle for equality" for women in journalism has been the struggle to receive the same education, the same opportunities for employment, and the same opportunities to rise in the ranks as men. These ambitions have been complicated by the terms of the craft imperatives to maintain the very standards that have not served to advance women in general. Thus, part of the history of women in journalism is the story of how women have accommodated identities of themselves as the price of admission.

Many of the shut doors are now open. But if there is hesitancy in proclaiming victory, it is not so much because of issues of glass ceilings as the fear that winning equality may turn out to be a pyrrhic victory. Women as much as men have entered journalism because, at bottom, it was considered a noble and influential profession. Its nobility may have been patchy, and its influence is surely on the wane. Yet small and large successes have served to keep alive the vision embodied in the First Amendment and to give reason for the various strategies that women have employed to find a place at the table. At this writing, *New York Times'* reporter Judith Miller remains in jail to protect one of the profession's most valued principles. We may consider that any one of the women who preceded her would have willingly gone in her stead, and the same can be said for the many more women who now follow.

NOTES

CHAPTER ONE

1 *The Daughters of: Boston Post-Boy,* August 20, 1773.

As the male: Abigail Adams to John Adams, March 31, 1776; John Adams to Abigail Adams, April 14, 1776; in L. H. Butterfield, Wendell D. Garrett, and Marjorie E. Sprague, eds., *Adams Family Correspondence,* 6 vols. (Cambridge, Mass.: Belknap Press of Harvard University Press, 1963–65) 1:369–70, 382.

2 *As Sara Evans:* Sara M. Evans, *Born for Liberty: A History of Women in America* (New York: Free Press, 1989), 47.

A character in: Charles Brockden Brown, *Alcuin: A Dialogue* (1798; repr. New York: Grossman Publishers, 1971), 29.

Between 1740: Patricia Cleary, "'She Will Be in the Shop': Women's Sphere of Trade in Eighteenth-Century Philadelphia and New York," *Pennsylvania Magazine of History and Biography* 119, no. 3 (July 1995): 181–202; Claudia Goldin, "Women's Economic Status," *Journal of Interdisciplinary History* 26, no. 3 (Winter 1986): 402.

To take as example: Numerous scholarly accounts exist of female colonial printers: Susan Henry, "Exception to the Female Model: Colonial Printer Mary Crouch," *Journalism Quarterly* 62, no. 185 (1985), 649, 725–33; Susan Henry, "Colonial Women Printers as Prototype: Toward a Model for the Study of Minorities," *Journalism Quarterly* 63 (1976); Susan Henry, "Sarah Goddard, Gentlewoman Printer," *Journalism Quarterly* 57 (1998): 23–30; Ira L. Baker, "Elizabeth Timothy: America's First Woman Editor," *Journalism Quarterly* 54 (1977): 80–85. *See also,* Maurine H. Beasley and Sheila Gibbons, *Taking Their Place: A Documentary History of*

Women in Journalism (Lantham, Md.: University Press of America, 1993).

3   *Elite homes:* For Elizabeth Magawley, Elizabeth Graeme, and the "female wits" of the colonial period, see David S. Shields, *Civil Tongues and Polite Letters in British America* (Chapel Hill: University of North Carolina Press for the Institute of Early American History and Culture, Williamsburg, Va., 1997), 130–40. For Phillis Wheatley, Elizabeth Drinker, Mercy Otis Warren, and Judith Sargent Murray, see Linda K. Kerber, *Women of the Republic: Intellect and Ideology in Revolutionary America* (Chapel Hill: University of North Carolina Press for the Institute of Early American History and Culture, Williamsburg, Va., 1980).

The role of women: Cleary, "She will be in the shop," 182.

4   *Woman scolds:* Jane Kamensky, "The Colonial Mosaic: 1600–1760," in Nancy F. Cott, ed., *No Small Courage: A History of Women in the United States* (New York: Oxford University Press, 2000), 51–108.

Philadelphia's Elizabeth: American Weekly Mercury, August 13, 1730.

As in your sex: American Weekly Mercury, January 5, 1730.

She as a: American Weekly Mercury, January 3, 1739–40. Quoted in David Copeland, "Virtuous and Vicious: The Dual Portrayal of Women in Colonial Newspapers" (paper presented at the annual meeting of the Association for Education in Journalism and Mass Communication, August 1994).

Wives should: Pennsylvania Gazette, October 8, 1730.

Women were: American Weekly Mercury, November 17, 1735; *Pennsylvania Gazette,* September 18, 1735; *Boston Evening-Post,* March 24, 1740; *Boston Evening-Post,* December 17, 1750. Quoted in Copeland, "Virtuous and Vicious."

Most of all: Maryland Gazette, December 24, 1745; *New-York Journal,* August 7, 1770; *Providence Gazette and Country Journal,* February 16, 1765. Quoted in Copeland, "Virtuous and Vicious."

5   *Women should:* "The Mental and Personal Qualifications of a Wife," *Hutchin's Improved: Being an Almanack for the Year of Our Lord, 1771* (New York: Hugh Gaines, n.d.).

One newspaper contributor: Boston Post-Boy, August 20, 1770.

The Pennsylvania Magazine: "One Cause of Uneasiness in the Married State," *Supplement to Pennsylvania Magazine, or, American Monthly Museum* (December 1775), 602.

As a Boston: Quoted in Linda K. Kerber, *Toward an Intellectual History of Women* (Chapel Hill: University of North Carolina Press, 1997), 33.

An intelligent woman: Kerber, *Toward an Intellectual History of Women,* 32.

The advice rolled: Frank Luther Mott, *A History of American Magazines 1741–1850,* vol. 1 (Cambridge, Mass.: Harvard University Press, 1957), 65.

Early on. Quoted in Kerber, *Toward an Intellectual History of Women,* 54.

Benjamin Rush: Ibid., 24, 25.

6   *Writing in a:* "An Occasional Letter on the Female Sex," *Pennsylvania Magazine, or, American Monthly Museum,* August 1775, 363. Unsigned, attributed to Thomas Paine.

When General George Washington: Evans, *Born for Liberty,* 50.

7   *In the 1780:* Esther DeBerdt Reed, "The Sentiments of an American Woman," *Pennsylvania Gazette,* June 21, 1780, quoted in Mary Beth Norton, *Liberty's Daughters: The Revolutionary Experience of American Women, 1750–1800* (Boston: Little, Brown, 1980), 178–90.

It is significant: Boston Post-Boy, August 18, 1773.

The graphic images: Joan D. Dolmetsch, *Rebellion and Reconciliation: Satirical Prints on the Revolution at Williamsburg* (Williamsburg, Va.: Colonial Williamsburg Foundation, 1977), 4, 7.

[T]he frontispiece: Kerber, *Women of the Republic,* 234.

8   *Petitions for divorces:* Nancy F. Cott, *The Bonds of Womanhood: "Women's Sphere" in New England, 1780–1835* (New Haven, Conn.: Yale University Press, 1977).

8 *Colonial newspapers:* Patricia Bradley, *Slavery, Propaganda and the American Revolution* (Jackson: University Press of Mississippi, 1998), 16–17.

9 *In a private letter:* Benjamin Franklin, "Advice to a Friend on Choosing a Mistress," *The Autobiography and Other Writings* (New York: Penguin Books USA, 1986), 207–09.

The revolutionary press: Bradley, *Slavery, Propaganda and the American Revolution,* 1–24.

Hovering just: Winthrop Jordan, *White Over Black: Attitudes Toward the Negro, 1550–1812* (Chapel Hill: University of North Carolina Press, 1968).

Four years later: Bradley, *Slavery, Propaganda and the American Revolution,* 19.

Not the usual: Richard Slotkin, "Narratives of Negro Crime in New England 1675–1800," *American Quarterly* 25 (March 1973): 3–29.

10 *Although the history:* Pauline Schloesser, *The Fair Sex: White Women and the Racial Patriarchy in the Early American Republic* (New York: New York University Press, 2002).

Women were not to: Joan Huff Wilson, "The Illusion of Change: Women and the American Revolution," in Alfred F. Young, ed., *The American Revolution: Explorations in the History of American Radicalism* (DeKalb: University of Northern Illinois Press, 1976), 385.

11 *Rosemarie Zagarri:* Rosemarie Zagarri, "The Rights of Man and Woman in Post-Revolutionary America," *William and Mary Quarterly* 55, no. 2 (3rd ser., 1998): 229.

A republican mother: Kerber, *Toward an Intellectual History of Women,* 58.

12 *In 1785:* "Humanus: In Behalf of the Fair," *Massachusetts Centinel* (Boston), February 19, 1785, quoted in Carol Sue Humphrey, *The Revolutionary Era: Primary Documents on Events from 1776 to 1800* (Westport, Conn.: Greenwood Press, 2003), 193–94.

13 *But, finally:* Judith Sargent Murray, "On the Equality of the Sexes," *Massachusetts Magazine, or American Monthly Mu-*

seum, March 1790, 132, in Sharon M. Harris, ed., *American Women Writers to 1800* (New York: Oxford University Press, 1996), 55.

13   *Later, Murray:* Judith Sargent Murray [Constantia], *The Gleaner: A Miscellaneous Production* (1798, repr. Schenectady, N.Y.: Union College Press, 1992).

 By 1795: David Lundberg and Herbert May, "The Enlightened Reader in America," *American Quarterly* 28 (Summer 1976): 262–93.

14   *Wollstonecraft claimed:* Quoted in Zagarri, "The Rights of Man and Woman in Post-Revolutionary America," 208.

15   *As early as 1784:* Frank Luther Mott, *A History of American Magazines 1741–1850,* 5 vols. (Cambridge, Mass.: Belknap Press of Harvard University Press, 1938–1968), 1:29.

 In 1787: Mott, *A History of American Magazines,* 1:65.

 Thomas's Federalist: Ibid.

 Although the names: Ibid., 1:66.

16   *In a 1795 satire:* "Sensible Women the Best Wives," *New-York Weekly Magazine,* October 28, 1795, 134.

 In the same year: "The Matrimonial Creed," *Philadelphia Minerva,* May 14, 1795, 2.

 In 1802: "Plans for the Emancipation of the Fair Sex," *Lady's Magazine and Musical Repository,* January 1802, 43.

17   *In 1812:* "On Women," *New-York Weekly Museum,* August 15, 1812, 58.

 Some months later: "Morality on the Equality of the Sexes," *New-York Weekly Museum,* October 16, 1813, 96.

18   *All despotism subsists:* Brown, *Alcuin: A Dialogue,* 59.

 Education for women: Thomas Jefferson to Nathaniel Burwell, March 14, 1818, *The Writings of Thomas Jefferson,* 10 vols. (Washington, D.C.: Thomas Jefferson Memorial Association of the United States, 1903–04), 10:104–06.

CHAPTER TWO

20   *So affected were readers:* "New-York City Trinity Church-Yard," *New York Daily Times,* August 14, 1855, 3.

21   *The formulaic plots:* Barbara Welter, "The Culture of True Womanhood: 1920–1860," *American Quarterly* 18, no. 2 (Summer 1966): 151–74.

22   *But it is not all:* Janice Radway, *Reading the Romance: Women, Patriarchy, and Popular Literature* (Chapel Hill: University of North Carolina Press, 1984).

      Joanne Dobson finds: Joanne Dobson, "The Hidden Hand: Subversion of Cultural Ideology in Three Mid-Nineteenth-Century American Women's Novels," *American Quarterly* 38, no. 2 (Summer 1986): 226, 228.

23   *So many existed:* Caroline Ticknor, *Hawthorne and His Publisher* (Boston: Houghton Mifflin, 1913), 141–43.

24   *At its most typical:* Herbert Ross Brown, *The Sentimental Novel in America 1778–1860* (Durham, N.C.: Duke University Press, 1940), 156.

25   *Early in the new century: The Port Folio* 2, no. 50, December 18, 1803, 393.

26   *The* New-York Mirror: Frank Luther Mott, *A History of American Magazines, 1741–1850,* 5 vols. (Cambridge, Mass.: Harvard University Press, 1938–1968), 1:322.

      Carolyn H. Gilman: Maurine H. Beasley, "Caroline H. Gilman," *American Magazine Journalists, 1741–1850,* vol. 73 of Sam G. Riley, ed., *Dictionary of Literary Biography* (Detroit, Mich.: Gale Research, 1988), 138.

      Upon the strength: Mott, *History of American Magazines,* 1:713–14.

      Other women writers: Ibid.

27   *In 1837:* Mott, *American Journalism: A History,* 1:591.

28   *As one scholar noted:* Dorothy A. Bowles, "Linda H. Sigourney," *American Magazine Journalists, 1741–1850,* in Riley, ed., *Dictionary of Literary Biography,* 73:207–16.

      Her resulting fame: Ibid., 269.

29   *Women, she wrote:* Sam G. Riley, "Ann Sophia Stephens," *American Magazine Journalists, 1741–1850,* in *Dictionary of Literary Biography,* 73:305.

30 *In 1850:* Donna Born, "Sara Jane Clarke Lippincott (Grace Greenwood)," *American Newspaper Journalists, 1690–1872,* vol. 43 of Perry J. Ashley, ed., *Dictionary of Literary Biography* (Detroit, Mich.: Gale Research, 1985), 307.

Hale was: Mott, *American Journalism: A History,* 1:592.

Although Hale's name: Patricia Okker, *Our Sister Editors: Sarah J. Hale and the Tradition of Nineteenth-Century American Women Editors* (Athens: University of Georgia Press, 1995), 45.

31 *And although:* Editor, "Rights of Married Women," *Lady's Book,* May 1837, 212.

It is likely: "Mary Wollstonecraft," *Casket* (June 1830), 14–17.

32 *Thus, even Hale's:* Okker, *Our Sister Editors,* 81.

As the foremost: Fred Lewis Pattee, *The Development of the American Short Story* (New York: Harper and Brothers, 1923), 71.

33 *Although the sentimental:* Pattee, *The Development of the American Short Story,* 83.

Nine-tenths of the: Ada Van Gastel, "Caroline M. Kirkland," *American Magazine Journalists, 1741–1850,* in Riley, ed., *Dictionary of Literary Biography,* 73:211–12.

34 *Authors who submitted:* Joseph Satterwite, "The Tremulous Formula: Form and Technique in *Godey's* Fiction," *American Quarterly* 8, no. 2 (Summer 1956): 211–12.

Despite what they said: Ann D. Wood, "The 'Scribbling Women' and Fanny Fern: Why Women Wrote," *American Quarterly* 23, no. 1 (Spring 1971): 3–24.

35 *By the Civil War:* Donna Rose Casella Kern, "Sentimental Short Fiction by Women Writers in *Leslie's Popular Monthly,*" *Journal of American Culture* 3, no. 1 (Spring 1980): 113–22.

Fern was probably: Carolyn Kitch, "'The Courage to Call Things by Their Right Names': Fanny Fern, Feminine Sympathy, and Feminist Issues in Nineteenth Century American Journalism," *American Journalism* 13, no. 3 (Summer 1996): 296.

36   *Altogether:* Ibid.

37   *Accounts of her managerial:* Quoted in Frank Luther Mott, *American Journalism: A History, 1690–1960,* 3rd ed. (New York, Macmillan, 1962), 217.

Cornelia W. Walter: "Woman: Naturally Intellectual," *Sargent's New Monthly Magazine of Literature, Fashion, and the Fine Arts* 1, no. 6 (June 1864): 260–62.

38   *They crouched:* Quoted in Paula Blanchard, *Margaret Fuller: From Transcendentalism to Revolution* (New York: Dell, 1978), 231.

39   *Poe, one:* Ibid., 131–32.

As Mason Wade wrote: Mason Wade, *Margaret Fuller: Whetstone of Genius* (New York: Viking, 1940); Sandra M. Gustafson, "Choosing a Medium: Margaret Fuller and the Forms of Sentiment," *American Quarterly* 47, no. 1 (March 1995): 34–65.

CHAPTER THREE

41   *In 1857:* Quoted in Ellen Carol DuBois, ed., *Elizabeth Cady Stanton Susan B. Anthony Correspondence, Writings, Speeches* (New York: Schocken Books, 1981), 76.

42   *When we consider:* "Friend to the Fair Sex," *American Mechanics' Magazine: Containing Useful Original Matter,* April 2, 1825, 144.

She was soon abhorred: Quoted in Lori D. Ginzberg, "'The Hearts of Your Readers Will Shudder': Fanny Wright, Infidelity, and American Freethought," *American Quarterly* 46, no. 2 (June 1994): 195.

She was ridiculed: Phillip Lapsansky, "Graphic Discord: Abolitionist and Antiabolitionist Images," in *The Abolitionist Sisterhood: Women's Political Culture in Antebellum America,* Jean Fagan Yellin and John C. Van Horne, eds. (Ithaca, N.Y.: Cornell University Press with Library Company of Philadelphia, 1994), 226.

43   *Her reward:* "Ernestine L. Rose: Speech to the National Women's Rights Convention, 1858," in Elizabeth Cady

Stanton, Susan B. Anthony, and Matilda Joselyn Gage, eds., *History of Woman Suffrage,* 6 vols. (1892; repr. New York: Arno Press, 1969), 1:692.

44   *Despite a public opinion:* Quoted in Carroll Smith Rosenberg, "Beauty, the Beast and the Militant Woman: A Case Study in Sex Roles and Social Stress in Jacksonian America," *American Quarterly* 23, no. 4 (October 1971): 564, 572, 581.

   However, Therese Lueck: Therese L. Lueck, "Women's Moral Reform Periodicals of the 19th Century: A Cultural Feminist Analysis of *The Advocate," American Journalism* 16, no. 3 (Summer 1999): 37–52.

45   *Under Stanton's influence:* DuBois, *Stanton Anthony Correspondence,* 15.

46   *Reform periodicals:* Bertha-Monica Stearns, "Reform Periodicals and Female Reformers, 1830–1860," *American Historical Review* 37, no. 4 (July 1932): 678–99.

48   *William Lloyd Garrison:* Julie Winch, "'You Have Talents— Only Cultivate Them': Philadelphia's Black Female Literary Societies and the Abolitionist Crusade," in *The Abolitionist Sisterhood,* Jean Fagan Yellin and John C. Van Horne, eds., 105.

49   *When Lydia Maria Child:* Leonard Ray Teel, "Abolitionism at the Crossroads: Lydia Maria Child and the *National Anti-Slavery Standard,"* in *The Civil War and the Press,* David B. Sachsman, S. Kittrell Rushing, and Debra Redding van Tuyll, eds. (New Brunswick, N.J.: Transaction, 2000), 76.

50   *As she later wrote:* Quoted in Mary Kelley, *Private Woman, Public State: Literary Domesticity in Nineteenth-Century America* (New York: Oxford University Press, 1984), 169.

51   *Stowe was a member:* Joan D. Hedrick, *Harriet Beecher Stowe: A Life* (New York: Oxford University Press, 1994).

   They included: Forrest Wilson, *Crusader in Crinoline: The Life of Harriet Beecher Stowe* (Philadelphia: Lippincott, 1941), 232.

52   *Down goes the hammer:* Joan D. Hedrick, ed., *The Oxford Harriet Beecher Stowe Reader* (New York: Oxford University Press, 1991), 323.

53 *As one Stowe scholar:* Ibid., 406.

54 *By 1846:* Quoted in Jean Soderland, "Priorities and Power: The Philadelphia Female Anti-Slavery Society," in *The Abolitionist Sisterhood,* Jean Fagan Yellin and John C. Van Horne, eds., 81.

Why this shift: Ibid.

Sewing circles: Quoted in Soderland, "Priorities and Power," 82.

55 *Henry brought me:* DuBois, *Stanton Anthony Correspondence,* 63.

56 *Woman's Rights Convention:* Nancy F. Cott, *No Small Courage: A History of Women in the United States* (New York: Oxford University Press, 2000), 235.

57 *Eleanor Flexner:* Eleanor Flexner, *A Century of Struggle: The Woman's Rights Movement in the United States* (1959; repr. Cambridge, Mass.: Belknap Press of Harvard University Press, 1975), 74.

58 *As Miriam Gurko finds:* Miriam Gurko, *The Ladies of Seneca Falls: The Birth of the Woman's Rights Movement* (New York: Schocken Books, 1976), 103–04.

In an early: Stanton, Anthony, and Gage, eds., *History of Woman Suffrage,* 2:264.

59 *Three years later:* Ibid., 2:42–44.

60 *In the 1906:* Ibid., 5:175.

61 *She mounted a:* Elizabeth J. Clapp, "'A Virago-Errant in Enchanted Armor?': Anne Royall's 1828 Trial as a Common Scold," *Journal of the Early Republic* 21 (Summer 2003): 208–32. *See also,* Maurine Beasley, "The Curious Career of Anne Royall," *Journalism History* 3 (Winter 1976–1977):1–46, 98–102.

Journalism historian: Frank Luther Mott, *American Journalism: A History, 1690–1960* (New York: MacMillan, 1962), 312.

Let men: "Women in Pantaloons," *National Era,* October 4, 1849, 160.

62 *The* Washington Star: Quoted in Sarah Harvey Porter, *The Life and Times of Ann Royall* (Cedar Rapids, Iowa: Torch Press Book, 1909), 226.

63 *In 1850:* Quoted in Kathleen Endres, "Jane Grey Swisshelm: Nineteenth Century Journalist and Feminist," *Journalism History* 2 (Winter 1975–1976): 431.

64 *Writing in her autobiography:* Jane Swisshelm, *Half A Century,* 2nd ed. (Chicago: Jansen, McClurg, 1880).

She clearly exasperated: Pittsburgh Saturday Visiter, July 12, 1851.

It speaks to the strength: Patricia L. Dooley, "Mary Clemmer Ames (1831–1884)," in Nancy Signoreilli, ed., *Women in Communication: A Biographical Sourcebook* (Westport, Conn.: Greenwood Press, 1996), 1–19.

CHAPTER FOUR

67 *As Martha Solomon:* Martha Solomon, "The Role of the Suffrage Press in the Woman's Rights Movement," in Martha M. Solomon, ed., *A Voice of Their Own* (Tuscaloosa: University of Alabama Press, 1991), 13.

68 *Linda Steiner finds:* Linda Steiner, "Finding Community in Nineteenth Century Suffrage Periodicals," *American Journalism* 1, no.1 (Summer 1983): 1–15.

70 *Knowing, then:* Quoted by Wendy Hamand Venet, "The Emergence of a Suffragist: Mary Livermore, Civil War Activism, and the Moral Power of Women," *Civil War History* 48, no. 2 (2002): 143–64.

Two researchers: Hazel Dicken-Garcia and Janet Cramer, "Images of Women in Civil War Newspapers: Leave the 'Proper Sphere,'" in *The Civil War and the Press,* David B. Sachsman, S. Kittrell Rushing, and Debra Redding van Tuyll, eds. (New Brunswick, N.J.: Transaction, 2000), 265.

Also to be considered: Hazel Dicken-Garcia, "Visibility of Women in Newspapers: Advertisements during the Civil War," in Sachsman, Rushing, and van Tuyll, eds., *The Civil War and the Press,* 349–71.

While a number: Martha M. Solomon, "The Role of the Suffrage Press in the Woman's Rights Movement," in Solomon, ed., *A Voice of Their Own,* 1–16.

71   *Amelia Bloomer's:* Edward A. Hinck, "*The Lily,* 1849–1856: From Temperance to Woman's Rights," in Solomon, ed., *A Voice of Their Own,* 30–47.

The Una: Mari Boor Tonn, "The *Una,* 1853–1855: The Premiere of the Woman's Rights Press," in Solomon, ed., *A Voice of Their Own,* 48–70.

The fact is: Quoted in Janet Cramer, "For Women and the War: A Cultural Analysis of the *Mayflower,* 1861–1864," in Sachsman, Rushing, and van Tuyll, eds., *The Civil War and the Press,* 222.

Postwar editors: Lynne Masel-Walters, "To Hustle with the Rowdies: The Organization and Functions of the American Woman Suffrage Press," *Journal of American Culture* 3, no. 1 (Spring 1980): 168.

When Susan B.: "Susan B. Anthony's Vote," *Harper's Weekly,* July 5, 1873, 581; "The Strenuous Life of A Woman Reformer," *Current Literature* 11, no. 5 (May 1906): 493.

73   *Stanton could:* Elizabeth Cody Stanton, "Manhood Suffrage," *The Revolution,* December 26, 1868, 392.

Although those: The Revolution, January 14, 1869, 24–25.

74   *The prejudice against:* Elizabeth Cady Stanton, Susan B. Anthony, Matilda Josyln Gage, eds., *History of Woman Suffrage* 6 vols. (1881–1922, repr. New York: Arno Press, 1969), 1:68–81.

While we would: The Revolution, December 6, 1869, 360.

75   *As Bonnie J. Dow:* Bonnie J. Dow, "*The Revolution,* 1868–1870: Expanding the Woman Suffrage Agenda," in Solomon, ed., *A Voice of Their Own,* 71–109.

These were approaches: Steiner, "Finding Community in Nineteenth Century Suffrage Periodicals," 10.

76   *The* Woman's Journal: *Harper's Weekly,* January 29, 1870, 67.

The new paper: Lynne Masel-Walters, "A Burning Cloud by Day: The History and Content of the *Woman's Journal,*" *Journalism History* 3, no. 4 (Winter 1976–77): 103–10.

Its main goal: Masel-Walters, "A Burning Cloud by Day," 105.

77   *The postmaster's son:* Ruth Barnes Moynihan, *Rebel for Rights: Abigail Scott Duniway* (New Haven, Conn.:Yale University Press, 1983), 180.

78   *Duniway also:* Masel-Walters, "To Hustle with the Rowdies," 171.

Duniway referred to: Quoted in Moynihan, *Rebel for Rights,* 211.

79   *You must realize:* Quoted in E. Claire Jerry, "Clara Bewick Colby and the *Woman's Tribune,* 1883–1909," in Solomon, ed., *A Voice of Their Own,* 118.

80   *The new firm:* Quoted by Louis Beachy Underhill, *The Woman Who Ran for President* (New York: Penguin Books, 1995), 67–68.

81   *Frederick Hudson:* Quoted in ibid., 91.

82   *The* Herald *and the* Tribune: Quoted in ibid., 112.

We have waited: Quoted in ibid., 113.

83   *She seems to be:* Quoted in ibid., 115.

Women have crucified: Quoted in ibid., 119–20.

84   *We mean treason:* Quoted in ibid., 126.

86   *The* Weekly *responded:* Quoted in ibid., 246.

I do not feel: Quoted in Ellen Carol DuBois, ed., *Elizabeth Cady Stanton Susan B. Anthony Correspondence, Writings, Speeches* (New York: Schocken Books, 1981), 107.

87   *She could:* Quoted in Underhill, *The Woman Who Ran,* 271.

88   *Then . . . Mrs. Stanton and:* Quoted in "Victoria Woodhull," Spartacus Educational, USA Journalists, http://www .spartacus.schoolnet.co.uk/USAWwoodhullV.htm (accessed May 17, 2005).

CHAPTER FIVE

90   *It is here in the home:* Ellen Carol DuBois, ed., *Elizabeth Cady Stanton Susan B. Anthony Correspondence, Writings, Speeches* (New York: Schocken Books, 1981), 71.

Public opinion: [Philadelphia] *North American,* December 1, 1876, 4.

90   *Stanton's lectures:* Dubois, *Stanton Anthony Correspondence,* 138.

91   *The German radical:* Quoted in Mari Jo Buhle, *Women and American Socialism, 1870–1920* (Urbana: University of Illinois Press, 1981), 27.

The women's page: Jon Bekken, "Dusting with a Ballot: The Portrayal of Women in the *Milwaukee Leader*" (paper presented at the annual meeting of the Association for Education in Journalism and Mass Communication, August, 1995). Available at http://list.msu.edu/archives.

92   *Josephine St. Pierre Ruffin:* Rodger Streitmatter, *Raising Her Voice: African-American Women Journalists Who Changed History* (Lexington: University Press of Kentucky, 1994), 62.

Reform activity: Anne Ruggles Gere, *Intimate Practices: Literary and Cultural Work in U.S. Women's Clubs, 1880–1920* (Urbana: University of Illinois Press, 1997), 258–59.

93   *He could also:* Quoted in Jennifer Scanlon, *Inarticulate Longings: The Ladies' Home Journal, Gender and the Promises of Consumer Culture* (New York: Routledge, 1995), 200.

The home gained: Colleen McDannell, *The Christian Home in Victorian America, 1840–1900* (Bloomington: University of Indiana Press, 1986), 47.

95   *Scholars of American consumption:* Stuart Ewen and Elizabeth Ewen, *Channels of Desire: Mass Images and the Shaping of American Consciousness* (Minneapolis: University of Minnesota Press, 1992).

Or, as William Leach: William R. Leach, "Transformation in a Culture of Transformation: Women and Department Stores," *Journal of American History* 71 (September 1984): 329–42.

97   *[T]he added value:* Patricia Bradley, "John Wanamaker's 'Temple of Patriotism' Defines Early Twentieth Century Advertising and Brochures," *American Journalism* 15, no. 2 (Spring 1998): 15–35; Herbert Ershkowitz, *John Wanamaker: Philadelphia Merchant* (Conshohocken, Pa.: Combined Publishing, 1999).

98 *Instead, canned milk:* Thomas Hine, *The Total Package: The Evolution and Secret Meanings of Boxes, Bottles, Cans, and Tubes* (Boston: Little, Brown, 1996), 70.

99 *One Pear's Soap:* Frank Luther Mott, *A History of American Magazines, 1885–1905* (Cambridge, Mass.: Belknap Press of Harvard University Press, 1957), 4:26.

100 *The major shelter:* Ibid., 359–68.

101 *Croly was:* Smith, Henry Ladd, "The Beauteous Jennie June: Pioneer Woman Journalist," *Journalism Quarterly* 40, no. 1 (Spring 1963): 169–74.

    In the same period: Elizabeth V. Burt, "Pioneering Women Journalists: Sallie Joy White, 1870–1909" (paper presented at the annual meeting of the Association for Education in Journalism and Mass Communication, August, 1998).

102 *Arthur Brisbane:* Ishbel Ross, *Ladies of the Press* (1936; repr. New York: Arno Press, 1974), 38–45.

103 *What a certain:* Quoted in Barbara Ehrenreich and Deirdre English, *For Her Own Good: 150 Years of the Experts' Advice to Women* (Garden City: Anchor Press, 1978), 135.

    In what Charles Ponce de Leon: Charles Ponce de Leon, *Self-Exposure: Human Interest Journalism and the Emergence of Celebrity in America, 1890–1940* (Chapel Hill: University of North Carolina Press, 2002).

104 *The* Munsey's *profile: Munsey's Magazine,* January 1892, 408.
    Later: Munsey's Magazine, February 1907, 588–92.
    The families of few: "The President—His Mother, His Wife and His Children," *Ladies' Home Journal,* April 1902, 3.
    When Pulitzer reporter: Mott, *A History of American Magazines,* 4:523.

105 *Thus,* Ladies' Home: "Ethel Barrymore at Home and Play," *Ladies' Home Journal,* June 1903, 3.
    For the unbelieving: Gertrude Vivian, "Actresses as Housekeepers," *Ladies' Home Journal,* November 1906, 50–51.
    Actress or not: Gustav Kobbe. "The Girlishness of Ethel Barrymore," *Ladies' Home Journal,* June 1903, 4.

105 *Sweet, unaffected:* "Annie Russell Out-of-Doors," *Ladies' Home Journal,* May 1903, 6.

106 *In the general condemnation:* "Points on Journalism," *New York Times,* April 16, 1898, 12.

It is a very fine: Carolyn Kitch, "The American Woman Series: Gender and Class in *The Ladies' Home Journal,* 1897," *Journalism and Mass Communication Quarterly* 75, no. 2 (Summer 1998): 243–62.

107 *Our rule is:* Quoted in Matthew Schneirov, *The Dream of a New Social Order: Popular Magazines in America 1893–1914* (New York: Columbia University Press, 1994), 53.

108 *In the home:* "Scientific Soap Bubbles," *New York Times,* December 31, 1893, 10.

A study of the Army: "A Study of the Army Woman," *New York Times,* September 17, 1893, 11.

109 Good Housekeeping *warned:* Margaret Marsh and Wanda Ronner, *The Empty Cradle: Infertility in America from Colonial Times to the Present* (Baltimore, Md.: Johns Hopkins University Press, 1996), 120.

The use of the word: Lyman Abbott, "Is the Vote Injurious to Women?" *Ladies' Home Journal,* February 1910, 21–22.

The great uterine manifesto: Ehrenreich and English, *For Her Own Good,* 115.

110 *So, too, was the woman:* Ellen Garvey, *The Adman in the Parlor: Magazines and the Gendering of Consumer Culture, 1880s to 1910s* (New York: Oxford University Press, 1996), 106–34.

111 *These included:* "Chronicle and Comment," *The Bookman: A Review of Books and Life,* September 1896, 20.

But Gilder was: Ida M. Tarbell, *All in the Day's Work* (1939; repr. Boston: G. K. Hall, 1985), 265.

112 *The image was so:* Quoted in Carolyn Kitch, *The Girl on the Magazine Cover: The Origins of Visual Stereotypes in American Mass Media* (Chapel Hill: University of North Carolina Press, 2001), 39.

Though the Gibson Girl: Carolyn Kitch, "Destructive Women and Little Men: Masculinity, the New Woman, and Power in the 1910s Popular Media," *Journal of Magazine and New Media Research* 1, no. 1 (Spring 1999): 2, 4. *See also,* Kitch, *The Girl on the Magazine Cover,* 36–45.

113 *The headline of:* "Will Women Grow More Masculine? A Woman Physician Discusses Dr. Shrady's Proposition to the Effect That They Will Do So," *New York World,* January 11, 1894, 4.

There are babies: Quoted in Mariea Caudill Dennison, "Babies for Suffrage," *Woman's Art Journal* (Fall 2003/Winter 2004): 27.

CHAPTER SIX

115 *They are to be numbered:* Margherita Arlinna Hamm, "New York Newspaper Women," *Peterson Magazine,* April 1895, 403.

The federal census: Maurine H. Beasley and Sheila J. Gibbons, *Taking Their Place: A Documentary History of Women and Journalism* (Washington, D.C.: American University Press, 1993), 10. Many female journalists worked part time, so estimates are difficult.

117 *Moreover, a quick look:* No single resource exists identifying female journalists for this period. The following resources are among those identifying women journalists of the day: Margherita Arlinna Hamm, "Some Women Editors," *Peterson Magazine,* June 1896, 609–21; Frank Luther Mott, *A History of American Magazines, 1865–1885,* vol. 3 (Cambridge, Mass.: Belknap Press of Harvard University Press, 1938); Ishbel Ross, *Ladies of the Press* (1936; repr. New York: Arno Press, 1974); "Notes on Some Magazine Editors," *The Bookman: A Review of Books and Life,* December 1900, 367–68; "Chronicle and Comment," *The Bookman,* September 1896, 17. *See also,* Maurine H. Beasley and Sheila Gibbons, *Taking Their Place: A Documentary History of Women in Journalism* (Lanham, Md.: University Press of America, 1993); Linda Steiner, "Gender at Work: Early Accounts by Women Journalists," *Journalism History* 23, no. 1 (Spring

1997): 2–11; Elizabeth V. Burt, *Women's Press Organizations, 1881–1999* (Westport, Conn.: Greenwood Press, 2000); autobiographies of individual women in the bibliography; and sources noted below.

117   *Florence Finch Kelly:* Florence Finch Kelly, *A Flowing Stream* (New York: E. P. Dutton, 1939), 242.

Victoria Earle: Flora McDonald, "Some Female Writers of the Negro Race," quoted in Beasley and Gibbons, *Taking Their Place,* 39–44.

118   *A correspondent:* Dinah Sturgis, "Newspaper Women," *New York Times,* November 12, 1898, RBA757.

James Gordon Bennett: Quoted in Ross, 23.

119   *The surge of activity:* Elizabeth V. Burt, ed., *Women's Press Organizations;* Elizabeth V. Burt, "A Bid for Legitimacy The Woman's Press Club Movement, 1881–1900," *Journalism History* (Summer 1997): 72–84; Agnes Hooper Gottlieb, "Networking in the Nineteenth Century: Founding of the Woman's Press Club of New York City," *Journalism History* 21, no. 4 (Winter 1995): 154–63; Maurine H. Beasley, "The Women's National Press Club: Case Study of Professional Aspirations," *Journalism History* (Winter 1988): 112–21; Fannie Palmer Tinker, "The Woman's Press Club of New York," *Chautauquan,* November 1892, 209–10; "Women in Journalism," *New York Times,* May 25, 1893, 1.

The popular belief: Ann Colbert, "Philanthropy in the Newsroom: Women's Editions of Newspapers, 1894–1896," *Journalism History* 22, no. 3 (Autumn 1996): 91–99; "Women Edit an Orange Paper," *New York Times,* April 6, 1895, 91.

Ours is another: Margaret Sangster, "Editorship as a Profession for Women," *Forum,* December 1895, 446.

Women are: "Newspaper Women," *New York Times,* July 11, 1897, 18.

The question was: "Women in Newspaper Work," *New York Times,* September 6, 1894, 9.

The latch-string: Foster Coates, "Women's Chances As Journalists," *Ladies' Home Journal,* September 1890: 13.

121 *Hundreds of them:* Ross, *Ladies of the Press,* 24.

122 *The reporters:* Ross, *Ladies of the Press,* 25.

Sinclair was appalled: Upton Sinclair, *The Brass Check: A Study of American Journalism* (Pasadena, Calif.: Pub. by author, 1920), 78.

123 *I am not:* Quoted in Faye B. Zuckerman, "Winifred Black (Annie Laurie)," *American Newspaper Journalists, 1901– 1925,* Perry J. Ashley, ed., *Dictionary of Literary Biography,* vol. 25 (Detroit, Mich.: Gale Research, 1985).

124 *He gave:* Elizabeth Bisland, *In Seven Stages: A Flying Trip Around the World* (New York: Harper and Brothers, 1891), 2.

It was an odd match: Brooke Kroeger, *Nellie Bly: Daredevil, Reporter, Feminist* (New York: Random House, 1994).

Her obituary: "Mrs. E. B. Wetmore, Author, Dies in South," *New York Times,* January 9, 1929, 29.

125 *Florence Finch Kelly:* Kelly, *A Flowing Stream,* 458.

It is a peculiarity: Elizabeth G. Jordan, "The Newspaper Woman's Story," *Lippincott's Monthly Magazine,* March 1893, 341–347.

126 *Haryot Holt Cahoon.* Haryot Holt Cahoon, "Women in Gutter Journalism," *The Arena,* March 1897, 568.

She is in the swim: Quoted Beasley and Gibbons, *Taking Their Place,* 45.

Physical demands: Margaret Sanger, "Editorship as a Profession for Women," *Forum,* December 1895, 445–55.

127 *Rheta Childe Dorr:* Rheta Childe Dorr, "A Convert from Socialism," *North American Review,* November 1927, 498.

Their abilities: S. D. Fry, "Newspaper Women," *Philadelphia Herald,* n.d., quoted in "Newspaper Women," *Journalist,* November 1882, 10.

If the front-page: Ross, *Ladies of the Press,* 13.

She must expect: Edward Bok, "Is the Newspaper Office the Place for a Girl?" *Ladies' Home Journal,* February 1901, 18.

128 *Gilder did a survey of:* Jeannette L. Gilder, "Does It Pay to Be a Literary Woman?" *Leslie's Monthly Magazine,* May 1905, 3–10.

128 *Sangster, a proponent:* Sangster, "Editorship as a Profession for Women," 455.

As modern research: Mary Ellen Waller-Zuckerman, "'Old Homes, in a City of Perpetual Change': Women's Magazines, 1890–1916," *Business History Review* 63, no. 4 (Winter 1989): 715–56.

Writing in: Eleanor Hoyt, "The Newspaper Girl," *Current Literature,* March 1903, 291.

In her first: Quoted in Linda Steiner, "Gender at Work, Early Accounts by Women Journalists," *Journalism History* 23, no. 1 (Spring 1997): 8.

Elizabeth Banks: Elizabeth Banks, *The Autobiography of a Newspaper Girl* (New York: Dodd, Mead, 1902), 212.

Ross thought: Ross, *Ladies of the Press,* 311.

129 *It is telling:* Margherita Arlinna Hamm, "Some Women Editors," *Peterson Magazine,* June 1896, 16.

131 *As Linda Steiner:* Linda Steiner, "Gender at Work," 2–5.

As Ross described: Ross, *Ladies of the Press,* 39.

At a time: "Work of Journalists," *New York Times,* December 4, 1889, 8.

133 *You're a tough guy:* Quoted by Linda J. Lumsden, "'You're a Tough Guy, Mary—and a First-Rate Newspaperman': Gender and Women Journalists in the 1920s and 1930s," *Journalism and Mass Communication Quarterly* 72, no. 4 (Winter 1995): 913–21.

Although the popular: "A Woman's Experience," *New York Times,* May 10, 1891, 6.

At the New York Times: Ross, *Ladies of the Press,* 145–49.

134 *Amouretta Beecher:* Quoted in Gottlieb, "Networking in the Nineteenth Century," 159, 160, 162.

135 *Women's opportunity:* Frances E. Willard, "Women in Journalism," *Chautauquan,* July 1886, 577.

138 *Women have a:* "A Ballad about Women," *New York Times,* February 3, 1894, 11.

139 *One such woman:* Marie Manning, *Ladies Now and Then* (New York: E. P. Dutton, 1944), 155, 158.

141 *When it appeared:* Ross, *Ladies of the Press,* 123.

142 *An estimated 400,000:* "400,000 Cheer Suffrage March." *New York Times,* 10 November 1912: 8–9.

  In 1911: "In the World of Fashion," *New York Times,* May 14, 1911, X6.

  At that time: Quoted in Mary Ellen Zuckerman, "Pathway to Success: Gertrude Battles Lane and the *Woman's Home Companion,*" *Journalism History* 16, no. 3–4 (Autumn/Winter 1989): 60, 67.

144 *But despite:* Susan Henry, "Reporting 'Deeply and at First Hand': Helen Campbell in the Nineteenth-Century Slums," *Journalism History* 11, no. 1–2 (Spring/Summer 1984): 18–25.

145 *But in 1912:* Kathleen Brady, *Ida Tarbell: Portrait of a Muckraker* (Pittsburgh: University of Pittsburgh Press, 1989), 202.

146 *I have always known:* Ibid., 242.

  As far as I could see: Rheta Childe Dorr, *A Woman of Fifty* (1910; repr. New York: Kraus Reprint, 1971), 50.

147 *Dorr's first book:* Quoted in Agnes Hooper Gottlieb, "The Reform Years at *Hampton's:* The Magazine Journalism of Rheta Childe Dorr, 1909–1912" (paper presented at the annual meeting of the Association for Education in Journalism and Mass Communication, August 1993).

  I think: Dorr, *A Woman of Fifty,* 296.

148 *Through it all:* "How to be Beautiful," *Current Literature,* August 1889, 122; "Distinguished American Women," *Ladies' Home Journal,* March 1888, 3; Lydia Hoyt Farmer, *What America Owes to Women* (Buffalo, N.Y.: Charles Wells Moulton, 1893); Mrs. Frank Leslie, "Are Our Girls Too Independent?" *Ladies' Home Journal,* March 1892: 6; Mrs. Frank Leslie, *Are Men Gay Deceivers?* (New York: F. Tennyson Neely, 1895); Mrs. Frank Leslie, "Women in Business Life," *Ladies' Home Journal,* May 1890, 3; "Our Editor," *Frank Leslie's Popular Monthly,* November 1898, n.p.

  At the time of her death: Eleanor Flexner, *A Century of Struggle: The Woman's Rights Movement in the United States* (1959;

repr. Cambridge, Mass.: Belknap Press of Harvard University Press, 1975), 74.

CHAPTER SEVEN

149 *Probably public sympathy:* Constance D. Leupp, "The Shirt Makers' Strike," *Survey* 18, December 1909. *See also,* Mary Van Kleeck, "The Shirtwaist Strike and Its Significance" (unpublished lecture, 1910); Mary Van Kleeck Papers, Box 29, Sophia Smith Collection, Smith College, Northampton, Mass.; Alexander Street Press and Center for the Historical Study of Women and Gender, State University of New York at Binghamton, Women and Social Movements in the United States, 1600–2000 Document Project, http://www.alexanderstreet6.com/wasm/wasrestricted/shirt/doc.23.htm.

150 *The* New York Times: "Calls Waist Strike Anarchy," *New York Times,* January 20, 1910, 18.

Inez Haynes Irwin recalled the years between: Quoted in Margaret C. Jones, *Heretics and Hellraisers: Women Contributors to* The Masses, *1911–1917* (Austin: University of Texas Press, 1999), 2.

151 *Clara Bewick Colby:* Carol S. Lomicky, "Frontier Feminism and the *Woman's Tribune,*" *Journalism History* 28, no. 3 (Fall 2002): 102–10.

Temperance supporters: Amy R. Slagell, "The Rhetorical Structure of France E. Willard's Campaign for Women's Suffrage, 1876–1896," *Rhetoric and Public Affairs* 4, no. 1 (2001): 1–23.

Carrie Chapman Catt: Carrie Chapman Catt and Nellie Shuler, *Woman Suffrage and Politics: The Inner Story of the Suffrage Movement* (New York: Charles Scribner's Sons, 1923), 279.

Abigail Duniway: Ruth Barnes Moynihan, *Rebel for Rights: Abigail Scott Duniway* (New Haven, Conn.: Yale University Press, 1983), 146.

151 *Willard complied:* Linda Clare Steiner, "The Woman's Suffrage Press, 1850–1900: A Cultural Analysis" (Ph.D. diss. University of Illinois, Urbana, 1979), 262.

152 *The second problem:* Amy R. Slagell, "The Rhetorical Structure," 2.

154 *The report made by:* Address by Anna Howard Shaw, "History of Women's Suffrage," in Elizabeth Cady Stanton, Susan B. Anthony, Matilda Joslyn Gage, eds., *History of Woman Suffrage,* 6 vols. (1881–1922, repr. New York: Arno Press, 1969), 5:25.v.

155 *In California:* Rudolph M. Lapp, "Mabel Craft Deering: A Young Woman of Advanced Ideas," *California History* 66 (1987): 168.

    By 1913: A. Elizabeth Taylor, "The Last Phase of the Woman Suffrage Movement in Georgia," *Georgia Historical Quarterly* 43 (1959):11.

156 *Like Dorr:* Aileen S. Kraditor, *The Ideas of the Woman Suffrage Movement* (New York: Columbia University Press, 1965), 294; "Suffragists See Wilson," *New York Times,* March 18, 1913, 2; Ida Husted Harper, "Suffragist Expect Nation-Wide Victory," *New York Times,* February 3, 1918, 41; Ida Husted Harper, "Women Away from Home," *New York Times,* October 16, 1910; "Mrs. Ida H. Harper, Author, Dead at 79," *New York Times,* March 13, 1931, 29; *History of Woman Suffrage,* 6 vols., Elizabeth Cady Stanton, Susan B. Anthony, and Matilda Joselyn Gage, eds. (1892; repr. New York: Arno Press, 1969), 5:528–30.

157 *Rheta Childe Dorr's:* Rheta Childe Dorr, *A Woman of Fifty* (New York: Funk and Wagnalls, 1924), 285.

158 *The whole suffrage:* Ibid., 283.

    It was symbolic: Ibid., 287.

160 *Five thousand:* Quoted in Linda J. Lumsden, "Beauty and the Beasts: Significance of Press Coverage of the 1913 National Suffrage Parade," *Journalism and Mass Communication Quarterly* 77, no. 3 (Autumn 2000), 595.

160 *Less noticed:* Ibid., 599.

161 *In 1888:* Marsha L. Vanderford, "The *Woman's Column,* 1888–1904: Extending the Suffrage Community," in Solomon, ed., *A Voice of Their Own,* 129–52.

Although The Revolution: Steiner, *The Woman's Suffrage Press,* 262; Frank Luther Mott, *A History of American Magazines, 1885–1905,* vol. 4 (Cambridge, Mass.: Belknap Press of Harvard University Press, 1938), 4:346; Sherilyn Cox-Bennion, "*The New Northwest* and *Woman's Exponent:* Early Voices for Suffrage," *Journalism Quarterly* 54 (Summer 1977): 286–292; "*The Pioneer:* The First Voice of Women's Suffrage in the West," *Pacific Historian* 25 (Winter 1981): 15–21; "*The Woman's Exponent:* Forty-Two Years of Speaking for Women," *Utah Historical Quarterly* 44 (Summer 1976): 222–39; "Women Suffrage Papers of the West, 1869–1914," *American Journalism* 3 (1986): 124–41.

Barbara Reed: Barbara Strauss Reed, "Rosa Sonneschein and *The American Jewess," Journalism History* 7, no. 4 (Autumn/Winter 1990/1991): 54–63.

162 *The Woman's Era:* Nora Hall, "Josephine St. Pierre Ruffin," *American Magazine Journalists, 1850–1900,* Sam G. Riley, ed., *Dictionary of Literary Biography,* vol. 79 (Detroit, Mich.: Gale Research, 1989), 79:265–68.

Alice Paul: Dorr, *A Woman of Fifty,* 290.

The paper had: Alice Shepperd, *Cartooning for Suffrage* (Albuquerque: University of New Mexico Press, 1994).

164 *The ensuing hunger:* Linda Lumsden, "Suffragist: The Making of a Militant," *Journalism and Mass Communication Quarterly* 72, no. 3 (Autumn 1995), 529.

165 *Gilder, whose argument:* Jeannette L. Gilder, "Why I Am Opposed to Woman Suffrage," *Harper's Bazar* May 19, 1894, 24; "Miss Gilder Helps Campaign of Antis," *New York Times,* August 24, 1915, 11.

Manuela Thurner: Manuela Thurner, "'Better Citizens without the Ballot': American Antisuffrage Women and Their Rationale During the Progressive Era," *Journal of Women's History* 5, no. 1 (Spring 1993): 44.

165 *In her examination:* Elizabeth V. Burt, "The Ideology, Rhetoric, and Organizational Structure of a Countermovement Publication: *The Remonstrance, 1880–1920,*" *Journalism and Mass Communication Quarterly* 75, no. 1 (Spring 1998): 69–82.

As The Anti-Suffragist: "Realities and Ideals," *The Anti-Suffragist,* December 1908, 7.

166 *But Miss Pankhurst: Woman's Protest,* May 1912, 10.

The Protest: "Suffragist Leader Endorses Free Love," *The Woman's Protest against Woman Suffrage,* May 1912, 91.

In her 1901 report: Shaw, *History of Women's Suffrage.*

167 *While suffrage proponents:* Alice Stone Blackwell, "A Contrast," *New York Times,* March 20, 1919, 8.

168 *Boston's North American:* Frank Luther Mott, *A History of American Magazines,* vol. 3 (Cambridge, Mass.: Belknap Press of Harvard University Press, 1938), 3:90.

In 1892, another: Marion Harland, "Women as Human Beings," *North American Review,* June 1892, 759.

At Stanton's death: Susan B. Anthony, "Women's Half-Century of Evolution," *North American Review,* December 1902, 800–11.

Later it published: Ida Husted Harper, "Suffrage—A Right," *North American Review,* September 1906, 484–99.

Shortly thereafter: "The Editor's Diary: The Necessity of Woman Suffrage," *North American Review,* October 1906, 689–91.

Benjamin Flowers: Frank Luther Mott, *A History of American Magazines,* vol. 4 (Cambridge, Mass.: Belknap Press of Harvard University Press, 1938), 4:405.

169 *The* American Magazine: "Editorial Note," *American Magazine,* July 1906, 285.

And other monthlies: Mary Johnston, "The Woman's War," *Atlantic Monthly,* April 1910, 18; Annie R. Ramsey, "Woman Suffrage in America," *Lippincott's Monthly Magazine,* July

1908, 101–05; Ouida, "The Woman Problem: Shall Women Vote?" *Lippincott's Monthly Magazine,* May 1909, 497–502; M. Grier Kidder, "Woman Suffrage," *Overland Monthly and Out West Magazine,* January 1909, 0–5; Lurana Sheldon, "The 'Bad Woman's' Vote," *Overland Monthly,* February 1913, 165–70.

169 *In 1912:* "The Spokesman for Suffrage in America," *McClure's,* July 1912, 1.

Puck may: "Shall Women Vote?" *Puck,* March 31, 1909, 65–66; "Madame Anti Makes Her Annual Report," *Puck,* February 20, 1915, 6; Vera Boarman Whitehouse, "We Want to Vote," *Puck,* October 30, 1915, 7.

170 *In the first decade:* Jane Addams, "Why Women Should Vote," *Ladies' Home Journal,* January 1911, 21; Lyman Abbot, "Why the Vote Would be Injurious to Women," *Ladies' Home Journal,* February 1910, 21–22; Grover Cleveland, "Would Woman Suffrage be Unwise?" *Ladies' Home Journal,* October 1905, 7.

Bok published: Margaret Deland, "The Third Way in Women Suffrage: A Plan for Possible Solution of a Vexing Problem," *Ladies' Home Journal,* January 1913, 11–12.

171 *At the* Woman's Home Companion: Anna Steese Richardson, "The Work of the Antis," *Woman's Home Companion,* March 1911, 15–16; Dorothy Dix, "Mirandy on Why Women Can't Vote," *Good Housekeeping,* February 1912, 285–87; Dorothy Dix, "The Girl of Today," *Good Housekeeping,* March 1916, 291; Mrs. O. H. P. Belmont, "The Story of the Women's War," *Good Housekeeping,* November 1913, 57; Rose Young, "The Women Who Get Together," *Good Housekeeping,* December 1913, 742–50.

172 *By the end of the:* Mary Ellen Zuckerman, *A History of Popular Women's Magazines in the United States, 1792–1995* (Westport, Conn.: Greenwood Press, 1998), 90.

173 *A lecturer who:* "New-York Girls Giddy Butterflies," *New York Times,* March 19, 1895, 5; "About Women in Business," *New York Times,* August 20, 1893, 11.

173   *When Brooklyn antisuffragists organized:* "Planning Their Campaign: Anti-Suffragists Need More Room and More Help," *New York Times,* April 28, 1895, 9; "Is Not for Woman's Suffrage," *New York Times,* April 21, 1894, 3; "Not as a Counterfeit Man," *New York Times,* May 4, 1894, 18; "Arguments for Women's Suffrage," *New York Times,* January 25, 1894, 12; "Arguments for Woman's Suffrage," *New York Times,* January 25, 1894, 12.

   There is absolutely: Harriot Stanton Blatch, "The *Times's* Suffrage News," *New York Times,* February 19, 1915, 8.

174   *The* Times *published:* "Bad Reports on Cities Where Women Vote," *New York Times,* October 10, 1910, 6.

   Carrie Chapman Catt: "Mrs. Catt Answers Barry: Never Said Women's Votes Would Eliminate Social Evil," *New York Times,* November 3, 1910, 3.

   The reporter: "Mr. Barry Answers Mrs. Catt," *New York Times,* November 5, 1910, 6; "Not without Protest," *New York Times,* November 12, 1910.

   Nor was the paper: "Woman's Sense of Humor: It Is Frequently Alleged That She Does Not Possess Any," *New York Times,* April 1895, 25.

   In this frame: "Suffrage Appeals to Lawless and Hysterical Women," *New York Times,* March 30, 1913, 8.

175   *It was a magazine:* Quoted in Jones, *Heretics and Hellraisers,* 4.

176   *Votes for women:* Ibid., 2.

   Yet, even The Masses: Carolyn Kitch, "Sexual Saints and Suffering Sinners: The Uneasy Feminism of *The Masses,* 1911–1917" (paper presented at the annual meeting of the Association for Education in Journalism and Mass Communication, August 1998).

177   *As Paula Baker writes:* "The Domestication of Politics: Women and American Political Society, 1780–1920," *American Historical Review* 89, no. 3 (June 1984): 638.

   In response: Kay Sloan, "Sexual Warfare in the Silent Cinema: Comedies and Melodramas of Woman Suffragism," *American Quarterly* 33, no. 4 (Autumn 1981): 412–36. See, for example, "Harvey Scoffs at Anti-Suffragists," *New York Times,* March 25, 1910, 5.

178 *Anti-suffragists have:* "Force Bills and Race Prejudice," *Woman Patriot,* July 10, 1920, 3.

It is said that: "South Fears Loss in Congress Seats," *Woman Patriot,* June 14, 1919, 3.

The newspaper noted: "Mississippi Will Reject," *Woman Patriot,* December 20, 1920, 8.

Under the standing head: "Votes for Colored Women!" *Woman Patriot,* September 26, 1920, 3.

Go ask the farmer's wife: James Callaway, "The White Woman's Problem," *Woman Patriot,* June 26, 1920, 8.

180 *The elective franchise is withheld from one half of its citizens:* Mary Terrell, *Washington Post,* February 10, 1900, 8. Mary Church Terrell Papers, Library of Congress, Washington, D.C.; Alexander Street Press and Center for the Historical Study of Women and Gender, State University of New York at Binghamton, Women and Social Movements in the United States, 1600–2000 Document Project, http://www .alexanderstreet6.com/.

181 *In 1910:* "Women Join in Suffrage Fight," *New York Times,* February 7, 1910, 4.

As the ratification process: "The Alabama Campaign," *Suffragist,* July 26, 1919, 5.

In National Suffrage: "National Suffrage and the Race Problem," *Suffragist,* November 13, 1915, 3.

Media of the time: "Race Issues Hit Feminist Party," *World,* August 17–18, 1924.

182 *It is surely:* Mary Ovington to Alice Paul, January 4, 1921, Mary Church Terrell Papers, Library of Congress, Washington, D.C.; Alexander Street Press and Center for the Historical Study of Women and Gender, State University of New York at Binghamton, Women and Social Movements in the United States, 1600–2000 Document Project, http://www .alexanderstreet6.com/.

CHAPTER EIGHT

183 *She did receive:* Wilda M. Smith and Eleanor A. Bogart, *The Wars of Peggy Hull: The Life and Times of a War Correspondent* (El Paso: Texas Western Press, 1991).

184 *Hull was the:* Linda J. Lumsden, "'No Woman's Land': Challenges and Themes Among the 20th Century's First Women War Reporters," paper presented at the annual meeting of the Association for Education in Journalism and Mass Communication, Toronto, Ont., August 2005; Madeleine Zabriskie Doty Papers, 1880–1984, Sophia Smith Collection, Smith College, Northampton, Mass.

Woman's place: Sarah Addington, "The Newspaper Woman, Who Is She, What Is She?" *New York Tribune,* August 8, 1915, Part 4, 13.

Despite all the: Rose Young, "Your Daughter's Career," *Good Housekeeping,* September 15, 1916, 314. Young also mentions several prominent journalists of the day.

A successful newspaper: Ethel Maude Colson, *Writing and Editing for Women: A Bird's Eye View of the Widening Opportunities for Women in Newspaper, Magazine and Other Writing Work* (New York: Funk and Wagnalls, 1927), 7.

186 *As the Associated Press:* "Ruth Cowan Nash," interview by M. H. Knight, Washington Press Foundation Women in Journalism Oral History project, September 26, 1987, http://npc.press.org/wpforal/rcn1.htm. Cowan Nash's papers can be found at the Arthur and Elizabeth Schlesinger Library on the History of Women in America, Harvard University, Cambridge, Mass.

I am not a feminist: Agness Underwood, *Newspaperwoman* (New York: Harper and Brothers, 1949), 1.

Flora Lewis: Penny Bender Fuchs, "Women in Journalism Oral History Collection of the Washington Press Club Foundation," *Journalism History* 28, no. 4 (Winter 2003): 191–97.

189 *Mildred Gilman:* Ishbel Ross, *Ladies of the Press* (1936; repr. New York: Arno, 1974), 248; Jean E. Collins, *She Was There:*

Stories of Pioneering Women Journalists (New York: Julian Messner, 1980), 247.

190 *Florabel Muir:* Florabel Muir, *Headline Happy* (New York: Henry Holt, 1950), 53–55.

Kathleen McLaughlin: Collins, *She Was There,* 27–33.

Adela Rogers St. Johns: Adela Rogers St. Johns, *The Honeycomb* (Garden City, N.J.: Doubleday, 1969).

The Herald Tribune: Barbara Belford, *Brilliant Bylines, A Biographical Anthology of Notable Newspaper Women in America* (New York: Columbia University Press, 1986), 231–42.

Lorena Hickok: Ross, *Ladies of the Press,* 203–15.

When it came: The winner in 1936 was Lauren D. Lyman "for his exclusive story revealing that the Charles Lindbergh family was leaving the United States to live in England" (The Pulitzer Prizes, History, http://www.pulitzer.org).

Genevieve Forbes Herrick: Linda Steiner and Susanne Gray, "Genevieve Forbes Herrick: A Front Page Report 'Pleased to Write about Women,'" *Journalism History* 12, no. 1 (Spring 1985): 8–16.

Mildred Seydell: "Mildred Seydell Honored," *Equal Rights* 20, no. 19 (June 9, 1934), 152.

Dorothy Ducas: Ross, *Ladies of the Press,* 210.

191 *Bess Furman:* Liz Watt, "Bess Furman: Front Page Girl of the 1920s," *Journalism History* 26, no. 1 (Spring 2000): 23–31; Bess Furman, *Washington By-Line: The Personal History of a Newspaperwoman* (New York: Alfred A. Knopf, 1949).

Winifred Mallon: Ross, *Ladies of the Press,* 342–45.

Ruby Black: Ibid., 347–49.

Hickok, on her own: Doris Faber, *The Life of Lorena Hickok, E. R.'s Friend* (New York: William Morrow, 1980).

Inez Robb: Alfred E. Clark, "Inez Robb, an Ex-Columnist Dies; Was a World War II Correspondent," *New York Times,* April 6, 1979, D13.

Emma Bugbee: "Emma Bugbee, 93; Reporter 55 Years," *New York Times,* October 10, 1981, 17.

191 *Florence Finch Kelly:* Florence Finch Kelly, *A Flowing Stream: The Story of Fifty Years in American Newspaper Life.* (New York: E. P. Dutton, 1939).

Irita Van Doren: "Irita Van Doren, Editor of Books, *Herald Tribune Review,* Is Dead," *New York Times,* December 19, 1966, 37.

Cora Rigby: Ross, *Ladies of the Press,* 332–34.

Anna Steese Richardson: Frank Luther Mott, *A History of American Magazines 1885–1905,* vol. 4 (Cambridge, Mass.: Belknap Press of Harvard University Press, 1957), 4:604, 769.

192 *Vera Connolly:* Mary Ellen Zuckerman, "Vera Connolly: Progressive Journalist," *Journalism History* 15, no. 2–3 (Summer/Autumn 1988): 80–87.

Carolyn Trowbridge-Radnor: Norman Lewis, *How to Become an Advertising Man* (New York: Ronald Press, 1927), 104.

Ellen Tarry: Ellen Tarry, *The Third Door: The Autobiography of an American Negro Woman* (New York: David McKay, 1955), 79.

One early exception: Rodger Streitmatter, *Raising Her Voice: African-American Women Journalists Who Changed History* (Lexington: University Press of Kentucky, 1994), 73–83.

193 *Alice Allison Dunnigan:* Ibid., 107–17.

Charlotta A. Bass: Ibid., 95–106.

Marvel Jackson Cooke: Kay Mills, *A Place in the News: From the Women's Pages to the Front Page* (New York: Columbia University Press, 1988), 176–78.

194 *Hazel Garland:* Collins, *She Was There,* 103–18.

I think you were ignored: "Ethel Payne," interview by Kathleen Currie, *Washington Press Club Foundation Women in Journalism Oral History Project,* September 28, 1987, http://npc.press.org/wpforal/payn1.htm.

195 *Anne O'Hare McCormick:* Nan Robertson, *The Girls in the Balcony: Women, Men, and the New York Times* (New York: Random House, 1992), 19, 24.

In 1927: Ross, *Ladies of the Press,* 342–45.

196 *By the 1930s:* Collins, *She Was There*, 27–33.

Dorothy Thompson: Peter Kurth, *American Cassandra: The Life of Dorothy Thompson* (Boston: Little, Brown, 1990); Lynn D. Gordon, "Why Dorothy Thompson Lost Her Job: Political Columnists and the Press Wars of the 1930s and 1940s," *History of Education Quarterly* 34, no. 3 (Autumn 1994): 281–303; "Lewis Is Repudiated by 24 of News Guild," *New York Times,* November 2, 1940, 13.

Margaret Bourke-White: Vicki Goldberg, *Margaret Bourke-White* (New York: Harper and Row, 1986).

197 *Adela Rogers St. Johns:* St. Johns, *The Honeycomb,* 27.

In her 1937 column: Kurth, *American Cassandra,* 239–40.

Irene Kuhn: Quoted in Linda J. Lumsden, "'You're a Tough Guy, Mary—and a First-Rate Newspaperman:' Gender and Women Journalists in the 1920s and 1930s," *Journalism and Mass Communication Quarterly,* 72, no. 4 (Winter 1995): 916.

If I were asked: Underwood, *Newspaperwoman,* 1.

Florabel Muir: Muir, *Headline Happy,* 3.

Underwood said: Underwood, *Newspaperwoman,* 1.

198 *For Carolyn Anspacher:* Collins, *She Was There,* 103–18.

Muir briefly: Muir, *Headline Happy,* 113.

For St. Johns: St. Johns, *The Honeycomb,* 32, 35.

I hurry back: Kathleen Ann Smallzreid, *Press Pass: A Woman Reporter's Story* (New York: E. P. Dutton, 1940), 80–81.

199 *In 1934:* Susan Ware, *It's One O'Clock, and Here's Mary Margaret McBride: A Radio Biography* (New York: New York University Press, 2004).

But the need: Donna L. Halper, *Invisible Stars: A Social History of Women in American Broadcasting* (Armonk, N.Y.: M. E. Sharpe, 2001), 24.

Lisa Sergio: "Miss Sergio with 'Fluent Phonetics' Points Way for Women Announcers," *New York Times,* July 18, 1937, X10.

Finally, women: Quoted in Susan Henry, "'There Is Nothing in This Profession . . . That a Woman Cannot Do': Doris E. Fleischman and the Beginnings of Public Relations," *American Journalism* 16, no. 2 (Spring 1999): 100.

200 *In a 1927:* Lewis, *How to Become an Advertising Man,* 105.

Judith Cary Waller: Mary E. Williamson, "Judith Cary Waller: Chicago Broadcasting Pioneer," *Journalism History* 3 (Winter 1976–1977): 111–15.

In the late 1920s: Ruth Cowan Nash interview, Washington Press Club Foundation, September 26, 1987.

201 *Cowan found:* Ibid.

No one was exempt: Barbara Sicherman and Carol Hurd Green, eds. *Notable American Women: The Modern Period, A–Z,* vol. 4 (Cambridge: Belknap Press of Harvard University Press, 1980), 4:439.

202 *Lumsden wonders:* Lumsden, "'You're a Tough Guy, Mary,'" 918.

The messages certainly: Linda Steiner, "Stories of Quitting: Why Did Women Journalists Leave the Newsrooms?" *American Journalism* 15, no. 3 (Summer 1998): 89–116.

No sadder case: Robert Jones and Louis K. Falk, "Caro Brown and the Dukes of Duval: The Story of the First Woman to Win the Pulitzer Prize for Reporting," *American Journalism* 14, no. 1 (Winter 1997): 40–53.

203 *In 1886:* James S. Bradshaw, "Mrs. Rayne's School of Journalism," *Journalism and Mass Communication Quarterly* 60, no. 3 (Fall 1983): 513–17.

Despite Pulitzer's: Albert Alton Sutton, *Education for Journalism in the United States from Its Beginning to 1940* (Evanston, Ill.: Northwestern University Press, 1945), 39.

204 *As the University of Missouri:* Sara Lockwood Williams, *Twenty Years of Education for Journalism: A History of the School of Journalism of the University of Missouri* (Columbia, Mo.: E. W. Stephens Publishing, 1929), 53.

In 1920: Ibid.

The template: Sutton, *Education for Journalism,* 106–24.

206 *According to:* Williams, *Twenty Years of Education,* 161.

207 *Lucile Bluford:* "Lucile Bluford," Washington Press Club Foundation Women in Journalism Oral History Project, May 13, 1989, http://npc.press.org/wpforal/int1.htm.

207 *That position:* James Boylan, *Pulitzer's School: Columbia University's School of Journalism, 1903–2003* (New York: Columbia University Press, 2003), 28.

Grudgingly opening: C. W. Steffler, *Columbia Journalism Graduates: A Study of Their Employment and Earnings* (New York: Columbia University Press, 1926), 41–44.

208 *Five of the:* Ibid., 43.

Reporting and copyediting: "Reporting Called Young Man's Job," *New York Times,* December 5, 1930.

I think the school: Boylan, *Pulitzer's School,* 68.

The underlying assumption: Ibid., 79–80.

209 *Maureen O'Neill:* Betsy Wade, "In Memoriam: A Trail Blazer," *Columbia University Graduate School of Journalism* (Spring 2002), 81, www.jrn.columbia.edu.

Phyllis T. Garland was hired: Boylan, *Pulitzer's School,* 149, 195–96; author correspondence with Phyllis T. Garland, May 20, 2005.

We don't hire: Quoted in Steiner, "Stories of Quitting," 105.

210 *Elizabeth McLaughlin:* Collins, *She Was There,* 30.

McCormick told: "Sees More Libel Risks from Women Writers," *New York Times,* April 18, 1935, 13.

211 *In 1939:* Quoted in Ramona R. Rush, Carol Oukrop, and Pamela J. Creedon, *Seeking Equity for Women in Journalism and Mass Communication Education: A 30-Year Update* (Mahwah, N.J.: Lawrence Erlbaum Associates, 2004), 36.

While editors: "In the Classroom and on the Campus: Journalism Schools Report Scarcity of Capable Men for Jobs Offered: Girl Student a Problem," *New York Times,* May 2, 1937, N6.

212 *Ruby Black:* Ruby Black, "Equal Rights for Women Journalists," *Equal Rights,* December 6, 1924, 341.

214 *Jane Cunningham Croly:* Elizabeth V. Burt, ed., *Women's Press Organizations, 1898–1999.* Westport, Conn.: Greenwood Press, 2000).

I don't think you do it: "Beth Campbell Short," interview by Margot Knight, Washington Press Club Foundation

Women in Journalism Oral History Project, April 23, 1987, http://npc.press.org/wpforal/bcs1.htm.

215 *Roosevelt recalled:* Quoted by Maurine H. Beasley, *Eleanor Roosevelt and the Media: A Public Quest for Self-Fulfillment* (Urbana: University of Illinois Press, 1987), 39.

216 *Beginning on:* "The Eleanor Roosevelt Press Conferences," videotape interview by Kathleen Currie, Washington Press Club Foundation Women in Journalism Oral History Project, May 22, 1989.

217 *She is also credited:* Ralph G. Martin, *Cissy: The Extraordinary Life of Eleanor Medill Patterson* (New York: Simon and Schuster, 1979), 279.

   In Richard Kluger's assessment: Richard Kluger, *The Paper: The Life and Death of the* New York Herald Tribune (New York: Random House, 1989), 286.

   Elizabeth V. Burt: Elizabeth V. Burt, "Helen Rogers Reid," in Nancy Signorielli, ed., *Women in Communication: A Biographical Sourcebook* (Westport, Conn: Greenwood Press, 1996), 312–20.

219 *Reid learned:* Richard Kluger, *The Paper,* 289, 293, 385, 439, 441.

   Gruber was a: Beverly Merrick, "Ruth Gruber: Arctic Journalism Carves a Northwest Passage Through the Ice Age of the Red Scare" (paper presented at the annual meeting of the Association for Education in Journalism and Mass Communication, New Orleans, La., August 1999).

220 *In the 1940s:* Joyce Antler, *The Journey Home: Jewish Women and the American Century* (London: Free Press, 1997).

   When she died: "Mrs. Reid of *The Tribune,*" *New York Times,* July 29, 1970, 38.

221 *Thanks to the work:* Nancy Caldwell Sorel, *The Women Who Wrote the War* (New York: Arcade Publishing, 1999); Julia Edwards, *Women of the World: The Great Foreign Correspondents* (Harper and Row, 1988); David H. Hosley, *As Good as Any: Foreign Correspondents on American Radio, 1930–40* (Westport, Conn.: Greenwood Press, 1984); "Women Go to the Front: Journalists, Photographers, and Broadcasters During World War II," Library of Congress exhibition, www.loc.gov./exhibits/wcf.

221 *Agnes Smedley, who:* Ruth Price, *The Lives of Agnes Smedley* (Oxford, UK: Oxford University Press, 2004).

CHAPTER NINE

223 *When Helen Rogers Reid:* "Mrs. Reid of *The Tribune,*" *New York Times,* July 29, 1970, 38.

224 *As Joanne Meyerowitz:* Joanne Meyerowitz, "Beyond *The Feminine Mystique:* A Reassessment of Postwar Mass Culture 1946–1958," in Joanne Meyerowitz, ed., *Not June Cleaver: Women and Gender in Postwar America, 1945–1960* (Philadelphia: Temple University Press, 1994), 229–72.

225 *By 1943, women:* Kathleen Weigand, *Red Feminism: American Communism and the Making of Women's Liberation* (Baltimore, Md.: Johns Hopkins University Press, 2001).

Although Friedan would: David Horowitz, "Rethinking Betty Friedan and *The Feminine Mystique:* Labor Union Radicalism and Feminism in Cold War America," *American Quarterly* 48, no. 1 (March 1996): 1–42.

As documented: Judith Adler Hennessee, *Betty Friedan: Her Life* (New York: Random House, 1999).

226 *During her:* Betty Friedan, "UE Fights for Women Workers" (United Electrical Workers, 1952); Horowitz, Daniel, *Betty Friedan and the Making of "The Feminine Mystique"* (Amherst: University of Massachusetts Press, 1998), 92; Hennessee, *Betty Friedan,* 35.

Even without intention: Patricia Bradley, *Mass Media and the Shaping of American Feminism, 1963–1975* (Jackson: University of Mississippi Press, 2004), 19.

228 *As women took to heart:* Quoted in Alice Echols, *Daring to Be Bad: Radical Feminism in America 1967–1975* (Minneapolis: University of Minnesota Press, 1989), 42.

229 *The press flocked:* Lindsy Van Gelder, "The Truth about Bra-Burners," *Ms.,* December 1978, 80–81.

232 *For some time:* Quoted in Bradley, *Mass Media,* 33–34, 35.

233 *Like many of the:* Ibid., 35–37.

Her report noted: Toni Carabillo, Judith Meuli, and June Budy Csida, eds., *Feminist Chronicles* (Los Angeles, Calif.: Women's Graphics, 1992), http://www.feminist.org/research/ chron icles/chronicl.html.

Stress the black: Quoted in Bradley, *Mass Media,* 41.

235 *The African American:* Ibid., 73.

236 *That mixture of philosophies:* Ibid., 71.

When Carter was: Lenore Hershey, *Between the Covers: The Lady's Own Journal* (New York: Coward-McCann, 1983), 91.

237 *ABC anchor:* Marlene Sanders and Marcia Rock, *Waiting for Prime Time: The Women on Television News* (Urbana: University of Illinois Press, 1988).

238 *Barbara Walters:* Barbara Walters, narrator, "New York Illustrated: Equal Rights Anyone?" (New York: WNBC-TV, November 1, 1975).

Liz Trotta: Liz Trotta, *Fighting for Air: In the Trenches with Television News* (Columbia: University of Missouri Press, 1994), 58.

Lesley Stahl: Lesley Stahl, *Reporting Live* (New York: Simon and Schuster, 1999), 237.

240 *As Castleberry has described it:* Quoted by Rodger Streitmatter, "Transforming the Women's Pages: Strategies That Worked," *Journalism History* 24, no. 2 (Summer 1998): 73.

241 *Susan Brownmiller:* Susan Brownmiller, "Sisterhood Is Powerful: A Member of the Women's Liberation Movement Explains What It's All About," *New York Times Magazine,* March 11, 1970, 26–27, 127–30, 132, 134–36, 140.

242 *You could have heard:* "Carole Simpson," interview by Donita Moorhus, Washington Press Club Foundation Women in Journalism Oral History Project, September 8, 1993, http://npc.press.org/wpforal/sim5.htm.

243 *Anne Koedt's:* "Can This Marriage Be Saved?" *Ladies' Home Journal,* August 1971, 52.

244 *As St. Johns recalled:* Adela Rogers St. Johns, *The Honeycomb* (Garden City, N.J.: Doubleday, 1969), 29.

246 *Eventually:* Gloria Steinem, "Sex, Lies and Advertising," *Ms.,* July/August 1990, 18–28; reprinted in Gail Dines and Jean M. Humez, eds., *Gender, Race, and Class in Media: A Text-Reader* (Thousand Oaks, Calif.: Sage, 1995), 112–20. *See also,* Bradley, *Mass Media,* 186–87.

247 *Indeed, Griffiths:* Bradley, *Mass Media,* 108–09.

248 *Jacqui Ceballos:* Jacqui Ceballos, "The Turning Point—The Strike That Made Us a Movement," *Veteran Feminists of America* 3, no. 1 (Spring 1996): 3–4.

Friedan remembers: Betty Friedan, *Life So Far: A Memoir* (New York: Simon and Schuster, 2000), 241.

The march prompted: "The Revolution That Will Affect Everybody," *Life,* September 4, 1970, 1–2.

249 *Marches in cities:* Bradley, *Mass Media,* 116–17.

Meanwhile, we goody: Quoted in Bradley, *Mass Media,* 261.

250 *Even the men:* Quoted in Rush et al., *Seeking Equity for Women,* 10.

251 *Hazel Dicken-Garcia:* Ibid., 16–17.

Does history have: Marie Manning [Beatrice Fairfax], *Ladies Now and Then* (New York: E. P. Dutton, 1944), 155.

CHAPTER TEN

253 *When Terry Gross:* Quoted in Robert L. Hilliard and Michael C. Keith, eds., *The Broadcast Century: A Biography of American Broadcasting* (Boston: Focal Press, 1997), 226.

254 *Research that has:* Meenakshi Gigi Durham, "Girls, Media, and the Negotiation of Sexuality: A Study of Race, Class and Gender in Adolescent Peer Groups," *Journalism and Mass Communication Quarterly* 76, no. 2 (Summer 1999): 210.

Her strongly worded: Myrna Blyth, "Girls Just Wanna Have Pundits," National Review Online, March 24, 2005, 1, http://www.nationalreview.com/blyth/blyth200503240755.asp.

255 *For Lakshmi Chaudhry:* "Women without a Clue," AlterNet, March 17, 2005, http://www.alternet.org/story.

255 *Underneath the political:* Anne Applebaum, "Writing Women Into a Corner," *Washington Post,* March 16, 2005, A23.

The experienced foreign: Georgie Anne Geyer, "Women Columnists? We're Right Here," *WomenMagazine,* March 23, 2005, 2, http://womenmagazine.com/ManageArticle .asp?c=930&a=1974.

Chaudhry represents: Chaudhry, "Women without a Clue."

256 *Despite the dismal:* Project for Excellence in Journalism and Rick Edmonds of the Poynter Institute, "Newspaper Newsroom Work Force, The State of the New Media: An Annual Report on American Journalism," 2004, http:// www.stateofthemedia.org.

However, the Annenberg: "Women Fail to Crack the Glass Ceiling in Communications Companies" (Washington, D.C.: The Annenberg Public Policy Center), April 27, 2002, www.appcpenn.org.

Moreover: "Who's Missing from the News?" (Minneapolis, Minn.: Minnesota Women's Press, Inc, April 6, 2005), http: //www.womenspress.com/newspaper/2005/2101news .html; Media Report to Women, for example (http://www .mediareporttowomen.com) has tracked women in journalism since its founding in 1972.

257 *One examination:* Lee Joliffe and Terri Catlett, "Women Editors at the 'Seven Sisters' Magazines, 1965–1985: Did They Make a Difference?" *Journalism and Mass Communication Quarterly* 71, no. 4 (Winter 1994): 800–08.

A 1999 study: Julie L. Andsager and Angela Powers, "Social or Economic Concerns: How News and Women's Magazines Framed Breast Cancer in the 1990s," *Journalism and Mass Communication Quarterly* 76, no. 3 (Autumn 1999): 531–50.

Other health care scholars: Sheryl B. Ruzek, Virginia L. Oleson, and Adele E. Clark, *Women's Health: Complexities and Difficulties* (Columbus: Ohio State University Press, 1997).

Barbara Seaman: Barbara Seaman, "The Media and the Menopause Industry: Advertising Muted Dangers of Estrogen Therapy," *Extra!* March/April 1997, 2.

257 *At one time:* Dustin Harp, "Newspapers Transition from Women's to Style Pages: What Were They Thinking?" (paper presented at the annual meeting of the Association for Education in Journalism and Mass Communication, Kansas City, Mo., August 2003).

258 *In 1991:* Therese L. Lueck, "'Her Say' in the Media Mainstream: A Cultural Feminist Manifesto," *Journalism and Communication Monographs* 6, no. 2 (Summer 2004): 64.

As Alice Echols describes: Alice Echols, *Daring to Be Bad: Radical Feminism in America 1967–1975* (Minneapolis: University of Minnesota Press, 1982), 244.

These ideas: Gloria Steinem, "Why We Need a Woman President in 1976," *Look,* January 13, 1970, 50; Gloria Steinem, "What It Would Be Like If Women Win," *Time,* August 31, 1970, 22.

259 *The March for:* Julie Hollar, "Muting the Women's March: Media Lose Focus When Women Protest in Washington," *Extra!* 1–8; Fairness and Accuracy in Reporting, http://www.fair.org/extra/0407/womens-march.htlm.

262 Time *magazine's:* Richard Lacayd, "The Sensuous Intellectual," *Time,* January 10, 2005, 72; Carolyn Kitch, "Reporting on the Birth and Death of Feminism: Three Decades of Mixed Messages in *Time* Magazine" (paper presented at the annual meeting of the Association for Education in Journalism and Mass Communication, Washington, D.C., August 1999.

263 *In the United States:* Naomi Wolf, *The Beauty Myth: How Images of Beauty Are Used against Women* (New York: William Morrow, 1991).

264 *The first extended:* Jennifer Baumgardner and Amy Richards, *Manifesta: Young Women, Feminism and the Future* (New York: Farrar, Straus and Giroux, 2000), 134, 136.

To quote: Ibid., 141.

265 *Third Wave approaches:* Rosalind C. Barnett and Caryl Rivers, *Same Difference: How Gender Myths Are Hurting Our Rela-*

tionships, Our Children, and Our Jobs (New York: Basic Books, 2004).

265 *That statement:* James Traub, "Lawrence Summers, Provocateur," *New York Times,* January 23, 2005, 4.

267 *Journalist Zoe Heller:* Quoted in Deborah Chambers, Linda Steiner, and Carole Fleming, *Women and Journalism* (London: Routledge, 2004), 227.

Observing this: Ibid., 9.

We might note: Julia B. Corbett and Motomi Mori, "Medicine, Media, and Celebrities: News Coverage of Breast Cancer, 1960–1995," *Journalism and Mass Communication Quarterly* 76, no. 2 (Summer 1996): 229–49.

268 *The British journalist:* "Sisters just ain't doing it for themselves," January 30, 2005, Guardian Unlimited. http://observer .guardian.co.uk/business/story/O,,1401609,00.html [sic].

But as Heller: Chambers et al., *Women and Journalism,* 218.

BIBLIOGRAPHY

Abramson, Phylllis. *Sob Sister Journalism*. Westport, Conn.: Greenwood Press, 1990.

Andsager, Julie L., and Angela Powers. "Social or Economic Concerns: How News and Women's Magazines Framed Breast Cancer in the 1990s." *Journalism and Mass Communication Quarterly* 76, no. 3 (Autumn 1999): 531–50.

Antler, Joyce. *The Journey Home: Jewish Women and the American Century*. London: Free Press, 1997.

Baker, Paula. "The Domestication of Politics: Women and American Political Society, 1780–1920." *American Historical Review* 89, no. 3 (June 1984): 620–47.

Banks, Elizabeth. *The Autobiography of a "Newspaper Girl."* New York: Dodd, Mead, 1902.

Barnet, Rosalind C., and Caryl Rivers. *Same Difference: How Gender Myths Are Hurting Our Relationships, Our Children and Our Jobs*. New York: Basic Books, 2004.

Baumgardner, Jennifer, and Amy Richards. *Manifesta: Young Women, Feminism and the Future*. New York: Farrar, Straus and Giroux, 2000.

Beasley, Maurine H. "Women and Journalism in World War II: Discrimination and Progress." *American Journalism* 2, no. 3 (Summer 1995): 321–33.

———. "The Women's National Press Club: Case Study of Professional Aspirations." *Journalism History* 15, no. 4 (Winter 1988): 112–21.

———. *Eleanor Roosevelt and the Media: A Public Quest for Self-Fulfillment*. Urbana: University of Illinois Press, 1987.

———. "Pens and Petticoats: Early Women Washington Correspondents." *Journalism History* 1, no. 4 (1974): 112–15.

Beasley, Maurine H., and Sheila J. Gibbons. *Taking Their Place: A Documentary History of Women and Journalism.* Washington, D.C.: American University, 1993.

Beasley, Maurine H., and Kathryn T. Theus. *The New Majority: A Look at What the Preponderance of Women in Journalism Educations Means to the Schools and to the Professions.* New York: University Press of America, 1988.

Belford, Barbara. *Brilliant Bylines: A Biographical Anthology of Notable Newspaperwomen in America.* New York: Columbia University Press, 1986.

Bennett, Milly. *On Her Own: Journalistic Adventures from San Francisco to the Chinese Revolution 1917–1927.* Armonk, N.Y.: M. E. Sharpe, 1993.

Bennion, Sherilyn Cox. "The New Northwest and Woman's Exponent: Early Voice for Suffrage." *Journalism Quarterly* 54 (Summer 1977): 186–292.

———. "The Woman's Exponent: Forty-Two Years of Speaking for Women." *Utah Historical Quarterly* 44 (Summer 1976): 222–39.

Bennion (Cox-Bennon), Sherilyn Cox. "*The Pioneer*: The First Voice of Women's Suffrage in the West." *Pacific Historian* 25 (Winter 1981): 15–21.

Blanchard, Paula. *Margaret Fuller From Transcendentalism to Revolution.* New York: Dell, 1978.

Blyth, Myrna. *Spin Sisters: How the Women of the Media Sell Unhappiness—and Liberalism—to the Women of America.* New York: St. Martin's Press, 2004.

Bok, Edward. *The Americanization of Edward Bok, the Autobiography of a Dutch Boy Fifty Years After.* New York: Charles Scribner's Sons, 1921.

Born, Donna. "Sara Jane Clarke Lippincott (Grace Greenwood)." *Dictionary of Literary Biography.* Vol. 43, *American Newspaper Journalists, 1690–1872.* Edited by Perry J. Ashley. Detroit, Mich.: Gale Research, 1985: 303–09.

Boylan, James. *Pulitzer's School: Columbia University's School of Journalism, 1903–2003.* New York: Columbia University Press, 2003.

Bradley, Patricia. *Mass Media and the Shaping of American Feminism, 1963–1975.* Jackson: University Press of Mississippi, 2004.

———. *Slavery, Propaganda and the American Revolution,.* Jackson: University Press of Mississippi, 1998.

———. "John Wanamaker's 'Temple of Patriotism' Defines Early 20th Century Advertising and Brochures." *American Journalism* 15, no. 2 (Spring 1998): 15–38.

———. "Media Leaders and Personal Ideology: Margaret Cousins and the Women's Service Magazines." *Journalism History* 21, no. 2 (September 1995): 79–87.

Brady, Kathleen. *Ida Tarbell: Portrait of a Muckraker.* Pittsburgh, Pa.: University of Pittsburgh Press, 1989.

Broussard, Jinx Coleman. *Giving a Voice to the Voiceless: Four Pioneering Black Women Journalists.* New York: Routledge, 2004.

Brown, Charles Brockden. *Alcuin: A Dialogue.* New York: Grossman Publishers, 1971. First published 1798.

Brown, Charles. "A Woman's Odyssey: The War Correspondence of Anna Benjamin." *Journalism Quarterly* 46 (1969).

Brown, Herbert Ross. *The Sentimental Novel in America 1778–1860.* Durham, N.C.: Duke University Press, 1940.

Brownmiller, Susan. "Sisterhood Is Powerful: A Member of the Women's Liberation Movement Explains What It's All About." *New York Times Magazine* (11 March 1970): 27, 127–30, 132, 134–36, 140.

Burt, Elizabeth V., ed. *Women's Press Organizations, 1881–1999.* Westport, Conn.: Greenwood Press, 2000.

———. "Pioneering for Women Journalists: Sallie Joy White, 1870–1909." Paper presented at annual meeting of the Association for Education in Journalism and Mass Communication, Baltimore, Md., 1998.

———. "The Ideology, Rhetoric, and Organizational Structure of a Countermovement Publication: *The Remonstrance,* 1980–1920." *Journalism and Mass Communication Quarterly* 75, no. 1 (Spring 1998): 69–83.

———. "The Wisconsin Press and Woman Suffrage, 1911–1919: An Analysis of Facts Affecting Coverage in Ten Diverse

Newspapers." *Journalism and Mass Communication Quarterly* 73, no. 3 (Autumn 1996): 620–34.

Catt, Carrie Chapman, and Nellie Shuler. *Woman Suffrage and Politics: The Inner Story of the Suffrage Movement.* New York: Charles Scribner's Sons, 1923.

Chambers, Deborah, Linda Steiner, and Carole Fleming. *Women and Journalism.* London and New York: Routledge, 2004.

Clapp, Elizabeth J. "'A Virago-Errant in Enchanted Armor?' Anne Royall's 1829 Trial as a Common Scold." *Journal of the Early Republic* 23 (Summer 2003): 207–32.

Colbert, Ann. "Philanthropy in the Newsroom: Women's Editions of Newspapers, 1894–1996." *Journalism History* 22, no. 3 (Autumn 1996): 91–99.

Collins, Jean E. *She Was There: Stories of Pioneering Women Journalists.* New York: Julian Messner, 1980.

Corbett, Julia B., and Montomi Mori. "Medicine, Media and Celebrities: News Coverage of Breast Cancer, 1960–1995." *Journalism and Mass Communication Quarterly* 76, no. 2: 229–49.

Cott, Nancy F. *No Small Courage A History of Women in the United States.* New York: Oxford University Press, 2000.

Craft, Christine. *Too Old, Too Ugly, and Not Deferential to Men: An Anchorwoman's Courageous Battle Against Sex Discrimination.* (Rocklin, Calif.: Prima Publications and Communications, 1988).

Dennison, Mariea Caudill. "Babies for Suffrage: The Exhibition of Painting and Sculpture by Women Artists for the 'Benefit of the Woman Suffrage Campaign.'" *Woman's Art Journal,* Fall 2003/Winter 2004: 23–30.

Dobson, Joanne. "The Hidden Hand: Subversion of Cultural Ideology in Three Mid-Nineteenth-Century American Women's Novels." *American Quarterly* 38, no. 2 (Summer 1986): 223–42.

Dorr, Rheta Childe. *A Woman of Fifty.* New York: Kraus Reprint, 1971. First published 1910.

DuBois, Ellen Carol. *Elizabeth Cady Stanton Susan B. Anthony Correspondence, Writing Speeches.* New York: Schocken Books, 1981.

Dunnigan, Alice Allison. *A Black Woman's Experience—from Schoolhouse to White House.* Philadelphia: Dorrance, 1974.

Durham, Meenakshi Gigi. "Girls, Media, and the Negotiation of Sexuality: A Study of Race, Class and Gender in Adolescent Peer Groups." *Journalism and Mass Communication Quarterly* 7, no. 2 (Summer 1999): 193–216.

Echols, Alice. *Daring to Be Bad: Radical Feminism in America, 1967–1975.* Minneapolis: University of Minnesota Press, 1989.

Edwards, Julia. *Women of the World: The Great Foreign Correspondents.* New York: Harper and Row, 1988.

Ehrenreich, Barbara, and Deirdre English. *For Her Own Good: 150 Years of the Experts' Advice to Women.* Garden City, N.J.: Anchor Press/Doubleday, 1978.

Endres, Kathleen. "Jane Grey Swisshelm." *Dictionary of Literary Biography.* Vol. 43, *American Newspaper Journalists, 1690–1872.* Perry J. Ashley, ed. Detroit, Mich.: Gale Research, 1985: 430–35.

———. "Jane Grey Swisshelm: Nineteenth Century Journalist and Feminist." *Journalism History* 2, no. 4 (Winter 1975–1976): 128–31.

Engstrom, E., and A. J. Ferri. "From Barriers to Challenges: Career Perceptions on Women TV News Anchors." *Journalism and Mass Communication Quarterly* 75, no. 4 (Winter 1998): 794.

Evans, Sara M. *Born for Liberty: A History of Women in America.* New York: Free Press, 1989.

Faludi, Susan. *Backlash: The War Against Women.* New York: Crown, 1991.

Flanders, Laura. *Real Majority, Media Minority: The Cost of Sidelining Women in Reporting.* Monroe, Me., Common Courage Press, 1997.

Fleener, Nickiann. "Anne Royall." *Dictionary of Literary Biography.* Vol. 43, *American Newspaper Journalists, 1690–1872.* Perry J. Ashley, ed. Detroit, Mich.: Gale Research, 1985: 402–08.

Farrell, Amy Erdman. *Yours in Sisterhood: Ms. Magazine and the Promise of Popular Feminism*. Chapel Hill: University of North Carolina Press, 1998.

Furman, Bess. *Washington By-Line: A Personal History of a Newspaperwoman*. New York: Knopf, 1949.

Garvey, Ellen Gruber. *The Adman in the Parlor Magazines and the Gendering of Consumer Culture*. New York: Oxford University Press, 1996.

Gastel, Ada Van. "Caroline M. Kirkland." *Dictionary of Literary Biography*. Vol. 73, *American Magazine Journalists, 1741–1850*. Sam G. Riley, ed. Detroit, Mich.: Gale Research, 1988: 207–16.

Gere, Anne Ruggles. *Intimate Practices. Literary and Cultural Work in U.S. Women's Clubs, 1880–1920*. Urbana: University of Illinois Press, 1997.

Gottlieb, Agnes Hooper. "Networking in the Nineteenth Century: Founding of the Woman's Press Club of New York City." *Journalism History* 21, no. 4 (Winter 1995): 154–63.

———. "The Reform Years at *Hampton's:* The Magazine Journalism of Rheta Childe Dorr, 1909–1912." Paper presented at annual meeting of the Association for Education in Journalism and Mass Communication, Atlanta, Ga., August 1994.

———. *Women Journalists and the Municipal Housekeeping Movement, 1868–1914*. Lewiston, N.Y.: Edwin Mellon Press, 2001.

Gower, Karla A. "Agnes Smedley: A Radical Journalist in Search of a Cause." *American Journalism* 13, no. 4 (Fall 1996): 416–39.

Greenwald, Marilyn S. *A Woman of the Times: Journalism, Feminism, and the Career of Charlotte Curtis*. Athens: Ohio University Press, 1999.

———. "The Portrayal of Women in Newspapers: A MetaAnalysis." Paper presented at annual meeting of the Association for Education in Journalism and Mass Communication, Washington, D.C., August 1989.

Gurko, Miriam. *The Ladies of Seneca Falls: The Birth of the Woman's Rights Movement*. New York: Schocken Books, 1976.

Gustafson, Sandra M. "Choosing a Medium: Margaret Fuller and the Forms of Sentiment." *American Quarterly* 47, no. 1 (March 1995): 34–65.

Halper, Donna L. *Invisible Stars: A Social History of Women in American Broadcasting.* Armonk, N.Y.: M. E. Sharpe, 2001.

Harris, Corra. *My Book and Heart.* Boston: Houghton-Mifflin, 1924.

Harris, Sharon M., ed. *American Women Writers to 1800.* New York: Oxford University Press, 1996.

Harp, Dustin. "Newspapers Transition From Women's to Style Pages: What Were They Thinking?" Paper presented at annual meeting of the Association for Education in Journalism and Mass Communication, Kansas City, Mo., August 2003.

Hedrick, Joan D. *Harriet Beecher Stowe: A Life.* New York: Oxford University Press, 1994.

———, ed. *The Oxford Harriet Beecher Stowe Reader.* New York: Oxford, 1991.

Hennessee, Judith Adler. *Betty Friedan: Her Life.* New York: Random House, 1999.

Henry, Susan. "Gambling on a Magazine and a Marriage: Jane Grant, Harold Ross, and *The New Yorker.*" *Journalism History* 30, no. 2 (2004): 54–65.

———. "'There Is Nothing in This Profession . . . That a Woman Cannot Do': Doris E. Fleischman and the Beginnings of Public Relations." *American Journalism* 16, no. 2 (Spring 1999): 85–111.

———. "Reporting 'Deeply and at First Hand': Helen Campbell in the 19th-Century Slums." *Journalism History* 11, no. 1–2 (Spring–Summer 1984): 18–25.

Hershey, Lenore. *Between the Covers: The Lady's Own Journal.* New York: Coward-McCann, 1983.

Hine, Thomas. *The Total Package: The Evolution and Secret Meanings of Boxes, Bottles, Cans, and Tubes.* Boston: Little, Brown, 1996.

Hoganson, Kristin. "Garrisonian Abolitionists and the Rhetoric of Gender, 1850–1860." *American Quarterly* 45, no. 4 (December 1993): 588–95.

Horowitz, David. "Rethinking Betty Friedan and *The Feminine Mystique:* Labor Union Radicalism and Feminism in Cold War America." *American Quarterly* 48, no. 1 (March 1996): 1–42.

Hosley. David H. *As Good as Any. Foreign Correspondents on American Radio, 1930–40.* Westport, Conn.: Greenwood Press, 1984.

Hyatt May P. *Style and the "Scribbling Women": An Empirical Analysis of Nineteenth-Century American Fiction.* Westport, Conn.: Greenwood Press, 1993.

John, Arthur. *The Best Years of the Century: Richard Watson Gilder, Scribner's Monthly, and Century Magazine, 1870–1909.* Urbana: University of Illinois Press, 1981.

Joliffe, Lee, and Terri Catlett. "Women Editors at the 'Seven Sisters' Magazines, 1965–1985: Did They Make a Difference?" *Journalism and Mass Communication Quarterly* 71, no. 4 (Winter 1994): 800–08.

Jones, Margaret C. *Heretics and Hellraisers: Women Contributors to "The Masses," 1911–1917.* Austin: University of Texas Press, 1999.

Jones, Robert, and Louis K. Falk. "Carol Brown and the Duke of Duval: The Story of the First Woman to Win the Pulitzer Prize for Reporting." *American Journalism* 14, no. 1 (Winter 1997): 40–53.

Jordan, Elizabeth. *Three Rousing Cheers.* New York: D. Appleton-Century, 1938.

Kelly, Florence Finch. *Flowing Stream.* New York: E. P. Dutton, 1939.

Kelley, Mary. *Private Woman, Public State: Literary Domesticity in Nineteenth-Century America.* New York: Oxford University Press, 1984.

Kerber, Linda K. *Toward an Intellectual History of Women.* Chapel Hill: University of North Carolina Press, 1997.

———. "Separate Spheres, Female Worlds, Woman's Place: The Rhetoric of Women's History." *Journal of American History* 75, no. 1 (June 1988): 9–39.

———. *Women of the Republic: Intellect and Ideology in Revolutionary America*. Chapel Hill: University of North Carolina Press, 1980.

Kern, Donna Rose Casella. "Sentimental Short Fiction by Women Writers in Leslie's Popular Monthly." *Journal of American Culture* 3, no. 1 (Spring 1980): 113–22.

Kitch, Carolyn. "The American Woman Series: Gender and Class in the *Ladies' Home Journal, 1897.*" *Journalism and Mass Communication Quarterly* 75, no. 2 (Summer 1998): 243–62.

———. "'The Courage to Call Things by Their Right Names': Fanny Fern, Feminine Sympathy, and Feminist Issues in the Nineteenth-Century American Journalism." *Journalism History* 13, no. 3 (Summer 1996): 286–303.

———. "Destructive Women and Little Men: Masculinity, the New Woman, and Powers in 1910s Popular Media." *Journal of Magazine and New Media Research* 1, no. 1 (Spring 1999): 1–16, http://aejmcmagaxine.bsu.edu.

———. *The Girl on the Magazine Cover: The Origins of Visual Stereotypes in American Mass Media*. Chapel Hill. University of North Carolina Press, 2001.

———. "The Work That Came Before Art: Willa Cather's Journalism, 1883–1912." Paper presented at annual meeting of the American Journalism Historians Association, London, Ont., October 1996.

Kluge, Richard. *The Paper: The Life and Death of the New York Herald Tribune*. New York: Random House, 1989.

Knight, Mary. *On My Own*. New York: MacMillan, 1938.

Kroeger, Brooke. *Nellie Bly: Daredevil, Reporter, Feminist*. New York: Random House, 1994.

Kuhn, Irene. *Assigned to Adventure*. Philadelphia: Lippincott, 1938.

Kurth, Peter. *American Cassandra: The Life of Dorothy Thompson*. Boston: Little, Brown, 1990.

Lemons, J. Stanley. *The Woman Citizen: Social Feminism in the 1920s*. Charlottesville: University Press of Virginia, 1973.

Lewis, Norman. *How to Become an Advertising Man*. New York: Ronald Press, 1927.

Lomicky, Carol S. "Frontier Feminism and the *Woman's Tribune*: The Journalism of Clara Bewick Colby." *Journalism History* 18, no. 3 (Fall 2002): 102–10.

Lueck, Therese L. "'Her Say' in the Media Mainstream: A Cultural Feminist Manifesto." *Journalism and Mass Communication Monographs* 6, no.2 (Summer 2004).

———. "Women's Moral Reform Periodicals of the 19th Century: A Cultural Feminist Analysis of *The Advocate*." *American Journalism* 16, no. 3 (Summer 1999): 37–52.

Lumsden, Linda. "Beauty and the Beasts: Significance of Press Coverage of the 1913 National Suffrage Parade." *Journalism and Mass Communication Quarterly* 77, no. 3 (Autumn 2000): 591–611.

———. *Inez: The Life and Times of Inez Milholland*. Bloomington: Indiana University Press, 2004.

———. "'No Woman's Land': Challenges and Themes Among the 20th Century's First Women War Reporters." Paper presented at annual meeting of the Association for Education in Journalism and Mass Communication, Toronto, Ont., August 2004.

———. "Suffragist. The Making of a Militant." *Journalism and Mass Communication Quarterly* 72, no. 2 (Autumn 1995): 525–38.

———. "The 'Woman's Angle' in War: World War II Reporter Ruth Cowan Nash Tightrope Act Across Separate Spheres." Paper presented at annual conference of the Association of Education in Journalism and Mass Communication, Toronto, Ont., 2004.

———. "'You're a Tough Guy, Mary—and a First-Rate Newspaperman': Gender and Women Journalists in the 1920s and 1930s." *Journalism and Mass Communication Quarterly* 72, no. 4 (Winter 1995): 913–21.

Manning, Marie [Beatrice Fairfax]. *Ladies Now and Then*. New York: E. P. Dutton, 1944.

Marsh, Margaret, and Wanda Ronner. *The Empty Cradle: Infertility in America From Colonial Times to the Present*. Baltimore, Md.: Johns Hopkins, 1996.

Martin Ralph G. *Cissy: The Extraordinary Life of Eleanor Medill Pat-terson.* New York: Simon and Schuster, 1979.

Marzolf, Marion. *Up From the Footnote: A History of Women Journal-ists.* New York: Hastings House, 1977.

Masel-Walters, Lynn. "A Burning Cloud by Day: The History and Content of the 'Woman's Journal.'" *Journalism History* 3, no. 4 (Winter 1976–77): 103–10.

———. "For the 'Poor Mute Mothers': Margaret Sanger and The Woman Rebel." *Journalism History* 11, nos. 1–2 (Spring–Summer): 3–10.

———. "Their Rights and Nothing More: A History of the Rev-olution, 1968–1870." *Journalism Quarterly* 53, no. 2 (Summer 1976): 242–51.

———. "To Hustle With the Rowdies: The Organization and Functions of the American Woman Suffrage Press." *Journal of American Culture* 3, no. 1 (Spring 1980): 167–83.

McDannell, Colleen. *The Christian Home in Victorian America, 1840–1900.* Bloomington: University of Indiana Press, 1986.

Merrick, Beverly G. "Ruth Gruber: Arctic Journalism Carves a Northwest Passage Through the Ice Age of the Red Scare." Paper presented at annual conference of the Association for Education in Journalism and Mass Communication, New Orleans, La., August 1999.

———. "Ishbel Ross, From Bonar Bridge to Manhattan: The Gaelic Beginnings of an American Reporter." *American Jour-nalism* 13, no. 4 (Fall 1996): 440–53.

Meyerowitz, Joanne, ed. *Not June Cleaver: Women and Gender in Post-war America, 1945–1960.* Philadelphia: Temple University Press, 1994.

Miller, Kristie. *Ruth Anna McCormick: A Life in Politics.* Albu-querque: University of New Mexico Press, 1992.

Mills, Kay. *A Place in the News: From the Women's Pages to the Front Page.* New York: Columbia University Press, 1988.

Mott, Frank Luther. *American Journalism: A History, 1690–1960.* 3rd ed. New York: MacMillan, 1962.

————. *A History of American Magazines*. 5 vols. Cambridge, Mass.: Belknap Press of Harvard University Press, 1938–1968.

Moynihan, Ruth Barnes. *Rebel for Rights: Abigail Scott Duniway*. New Haven, Conn.: Yale University Press, 1983.

Muir, Florabel. *Headline Happy*. New York: Henry Holt, 1950.

Murray, Judith Sargent [Constantia]. *The Gleaner: A Miscellaneous Production*. Schenectady, N.Y.: Union College Press, 1992. First published 1798.

Okker, Patricia. *Our Sister Editors: Sarah J. Hale and the Tradition of Nineteenth-Century American Women Editors*. Athens: University of Georgia Press, 1995.

Pattee, Fred Lewis. *The Development of the American Short Story*. New York: Harper, 1923.

Ponce De Leon, Charles. *Self-Exposure: Human Interest Journalism and the Emergence of Celebrity in America, 1890–1940*. Chapel Hill: University of North Carolina Press, 2002.

Price, Ruth. *The Lives of Agnes Smedley*. Oxford, UK: Oxford University Press, 2004.

Purvis, Jennifer. "Grrls and Women Together in the Third Wave: Embracing the Challenges of Intergenerational Feminism(s)." *NWSA Journal* 16, no. 3 (2004): 3–123.

Reed, Barbara Straus. "Rosa Sonneschein and *The American Jewess*." *Journalism History* 7, vol. 4 (Autumn/Winter 1990/1991): 54–63.

Riley, Sam G. "Ann Sophia Stephens." *Dictionary of Literary Biography*, Vol. 73, *American Magazine Journalists, 1741–1850*. Sam G. Riley, ed. Detroit, Mich.: Gale Research, 1988: 299–306.

Rinehart, Mary Roberts. *My Story*. New York: Rinehart, 1947.

Robertson, Nan. *The Girls in the Balcony: Women, Men, and the New York Times*. New York: Random House, 1992.

Ross, Ishbel. *Ladies of the Press: The Story of Women in Journalism by an Insider*. New York: Arno Reprint, 1974. First published 1936.

Rush, Ramona R., Carol Oukrop, and Pamela J. Creedon. *Seeking Equity for Women in Journalism and Mass Communication Edu-*

cation: A 30-Year Update. Mahwah, N.J.: Lawrence Erlbaum Associates, 2004.

Ruzek, Sheryl B., Virginia L. Oleson, and Adele E. Clark. *Women's Health: Complexities and Difficulties*. Columbus: Ohio State University Press, 1997.

Sachsman, David B., S. Kittrell Rushing, and Debra Redding van Tuyll, eds. *The Civil War and the Press*. New Brunswick, N.J.: Transaction Publisher, 2000.

Sanders, Marlene, and Marcia Rock. *Waiting for Prime Time: The Women of Television News*. Urbana: University of Illinois Press, 1988.

Satterwite, Joseph. "The Tremulous Formula: Form and Technique in *Godey's* Fiction." *American Quarterly* 8 (Summer 1956): 99–113.

Scanlon, Jennifer. *Inarticulate Longings: The Ladies' Home Journal, Gender and the Promises of Consumer Culture*. New York: Routledge, 1995.

Schechter, Patricia. *Ida B. Wells-Barnett and American Reform*. Chapel Hill. University of North Carolina Press, 2001.

Schneirov, Matthew. *The Dream of a New Social Order: Popular Magazines in America 1893–1914*. New York: Columbia University Press, 1994.

Shepperd, Alice. *Cartooning for Suffrage*. Albuquerque: University of New Mexico Press, 1994.

Signorielli, Nancy, ed. *Women in Communication: A Biographical Sourcebook*. Westport, Conn.: Greenwood Press, 1996.

Simpson, Carole. "Carole Simpson." Women in Journalism Oral History Project, Washington Press Club Foundation, Washington, D.C. 8 September 1993; online at http://npc.press.org.

Sinclair, Upton. *The Brass Check: A Study of American Journalism*. Pasadena, Calif.: Pub. by author, 1920.

Slagell, Amy R. "The Rhetorical Structure of Frances E. Willard's Campaign for Woman Suffrage, 1876–1896." *Rhetoric and Public Affairs* 4, no. 1 (2001): 1–23.

Sloan, Kay. "Sexual Warfare in the Silent Cinema: Comedies and Melodramas of Woman Suffragism." *American Quarterly* 33 (Autumn, 1981): 412–36.

Smallzreid, Kathleen Ann. *Press Pass: A Woman Reporter's Story.* New York: E. P. Dutton, 1940.

Smith, Henry Ladd. "The Beauteous Jennie June: Pioneer Woman Journalist." *Journalism Quarterly* 40, no. 1 (Spring 1963): 169–74.

Smith, Wilda, and Eleanor A. Bogart. *The Wars of Peggy Hull: The Life and Times of a War Correspondent.* El Paso: Texas Western Press, 1991.

Smith Rosenberg, Carroll. "Beauty, the Beast and the Militant Woman: A Case Study in Sex Roles and Social Stress in Jacksonian America." *American Quarterly* 23, no. 4 (October 1971): 562–84.

Smythe, Ted Curtis. *The Gilded Age Press, 1865–1900.* Westport, Conn.: Praeger, 2003.

Solomon, Martha M., ed. *A Voice of Their Own: The Woman Suffrage Press, 1840–1910.* Tuscaloosa: University of Alabama Press, 1991.

Sorel, Nancy Caldwell. *The Women Who Wrote the War.* New York: Arcade, 1999.

St. Johns, Adela Rogers. *The Honeycomb.* Garden City, N.J.: Doubleday, 1969.

Stahl, Lesley. *Reporting Live.* New York: Simon and Schuster, 1999.

Stearns, Bertha-Monica. "Reform Periodicals and Female Reformers, 1930–1860." *American Historical Review* 37, no. 4 (July 1932): 678–99.

Steffler, C. W. *Columbia Journalism Graduates: A Study of Their Employment and Earnings.* New York: Columbia University Press, 1926.

Steiner, Linda. "Construction of Gender in Newsreporting Textbooks, 1890–1990." *Journalism and Mass Communication Monographs* 135. Columbia, N.C.: Association for Education in Journalism and Mass Communication, 1992.

————. "Do You Belong in Journalism? Career Guidance Books, 1880–1990." *American Journalism* 11 (1994): 321–35.

————. "Finding Community in Nineteenth Century Suffrage Periodicals." *American Journalism* 1, no. 1 (Summer 1983): 1– 15.

————. "Gender at Work: Early Accounts by Women Journalists." *Journalism History* 23, no. 1 (Spring 1997): 2–11.

————. "Stories of Quitting: Why Did Women Journalists Leave the Newsrooms?" *American Journalism* 15, no. 3 (Summer 1998): 89–116.

————. "The Woman's Suffrage Press 1850–1900: A Cultural Analysis." Ph. D. diss. University of Illinois, 1979.

Steiner, Linda, comp. "Autobiographies by Women Journalists: An Annotated Bibliography." *Journalism History* 23 (Spring 1997): 13–15.

Steiner, Linda, and Susanne Gray. "Genevieve Forbes Herrick: A Front Page Report 'Pleased to Write About Women.'" *Journalism History* 12, no. 1 (Spring 1985): 8–16.

Streitmatter, Rodger. "Transforming the Women's Pages: Strategies that Worked." *Journalism History* 24, no. 2 (Summer 1998): 72–91.

————. *Raising Her Voice: African-American Women Journalists Who Changed History.* Lexington: University Press of Kentucky, 1994.

————. "Alice Allison Dunnigan: An African-American Woman Journalist Who Broke the Double Barrier." *Journalism History* 16, no. 3–4 (Autumn–Winter 1989): 87–97.

Sutton, Albert Alton. *Education for Journalism in the United States from Its Beginning to 1940.* Evanston, Ill.: Northwestern University Press, 1945.

Talmadge, John E. *Corra Harris: Lady of Purpose.* Athens: University of Georgia Press, 1968.

Tarry, Ellen. *The Third Door: The Autobiography of an American Negro Woman.* New York: David McKay, 1955.

Thurner, Manuela. "'Better Citizens Without the Ballot': American Antisuffrage Women and Their Rationale During the Progressive Era." *Journal of Women's History* 5, no. 1 (Spring 1993): 33–59.

Trotta, Liz. *Fighting for Air: In the Trenches with Television News.* 1991, repr. Columbia: University of Missouri Press, 1994.

Underhill, Louis Beachy. *The Woman Who Ran for President: The Many Lives of Victoria Woodhull.* New York: Penguin Books, 1996.

Underwood, Agness. *Newspaperwoman.* New York: Harper, 1949.

U.S. Library of Congress. Exhibition. September 28–November 18, 1995. *Women Come to the Front: Journalists, Photographers and Broadcasters During World War II.* http://www.loc.gov/exh/ wcf/wcf001.

Venet, Wendy Hamand. "The Emergence of a Suffragist: Mary Livermore, Civil War Activism, and the Moral Power of Women." *Civil War History* 48, no. 2 (2002): 143–64.

Wade, Mason. *Margaret Fuller: Whetstone of Genius.* New York: Viking, 1940.

Walker, Peter F. *Moral Choices.* Baton Rouge: Louisiana State University Press, 1978.

Waller-Zuckerman, Mary Ellen. "Old Homes, in a City of Perpetual Change: Women's Magazines, 1890–1916." *Business History Review* 63, no. 4 (Winter 1989): 715–56.

Ware, Susan. *It's One O'Clock, and Here's Mary Margaret McBride. A Radio Biography.* New York: New York University Press, 2004.

Watts, Liz. "Bess Furman: Front Page Girl of the 1920s." *Journalism History* 26, no. 1 (Spring 2000): 22–33.

Weigand, Kate. *Red Feminism: American Communism and the Making of Women's Liberation.* Baltimore, Md.: Johns Hopkins University Press, 2001.

Welter, Barbara. "The Cult of True Womanhood: 1920–1860." *American Quarterly* 18, no. 2, part I (Summer 1966): 151–74.

Williams, Sara Lockwood. *Twenty Years of Education for Journalism, A History of the School of Journalism of the University of Missouri.* Columbia, Mo.: E. W. Stephens, 1929.

Williamson, Mary E. "Judith Cary Waller: Chicago Broadcasting Pioneer." *Journalism History* 3 (Winter 1976–1977): 111–15.

Wilson, Forrest. *Crusader in Crinoline: The Life of Harriet Beecher Stowe.* Philadelphia: Lippincott, 1941.

Wood, Ann D. "The 'Scribbling Women' and Fanny Fern: Why Women Wrote." *American Quarterly* 23, no. 1 (Spring 1971): 3–24.

Zagarri, Rosemarie. "The Rights of Man and Woman in Post-Revolutionary America." *William and Mary Quarterly* 3rd ser., 55, no. 2 (April 1998): 203–30.

Zuckerman, Mary Ellen. *A History of Popular Women's Magazines in the United States, 1792–1995.* Westport, Conn.: Greenwood Press, 1998.

———. "Pathway to Success: Gertrude Battles Lane and the Woman's Home Companion." *Journalism History* 16, no. 3–4 (Autumn–Winter 1989): 64–75.

INDEX

researchers, xiv, 241
retail, 98–99
Revere, Paul, 7
The Revolution, 72, 74–75, 81,
  161
revolutionary era, 4–8
Richards, Amy, 263–264
Richards, William B., 37
Richardson, Anna Steese, 171,
  191
Ride, Sally, 245
Rigby, Cora, 191, 213
rights, 1–18
right to vote, 143
Rinehart, Mary Roberts, 183
Riot Grrls, 264
Rivers, Caryl, 265
Robb, Inez, 185, 191, 211, 221
Robert Merry's Museum, 26
Robertson, Nan, 195, 211
Rockefeller, John D., 145
Rohe, Alice, 183
Romanticism, 24
Roosevelt, Alice, 104
Roosevelt, Eleanor, xiii, 188,
  191, 215–216
Roosevelt, Franklin D., 191, 196,
  225
Roosevelt, Theodore, 104, 152
Rorer, Mrs. S.T., 116
Rose, Ernestine, 42–43
Rosenberg, Carroll Smith, 44
Ross, Ishbel, 121, 127–128, 131,
  190–191
Ross, Jewell P., 250
Rowson, Susanna, 20–21, 24
Royall, Anne, 60–62, 64
Ruffin, Josephine St. Pierre, 92,
  161–162, 179

Rush, Benjamin, 5
Rush, Ramona, 250
Russell, Annie, 105
Russian revolution, 184
Rutgers University, 203

salary discrimination, 126–127,
  143, 193, 241, 250
Sanders, Marlene, 237
San Francisco Chronicle, 117,
  197–198
San Francisco Examiner, 117,
  122–123, 249
Sanger, Margaret, xxi, 109, 187
Sangster, Margaret, 116, 119,
  128, 171
Sargent's, 37
Sartain's, 26, 33
satire, 121
Saturday Evening Post, 29, 31,
  183
Savitch, Jessica, 241
Schlafly, Phyllis, 249
Schultz, Sigrid, 221
Scribner's, 111, 184
Seaman, Barbara, 257
Seattle Times, 239
Second Wave, 40, 167, 221,
  223–251; consciousness rais-
  ing, 67; fiftieth anniversary
  march, 246–250; reform ac-
  tivism, 49, 59; strategies, xxi,
  136
Sedgewick, Catharine M., 23, 32
seduction, 196–199
selling brand-name products,
  98–99
Seneca Falls Convention, 54,
  55–58, 60